LABOR CAMP
SOCIALISM

The New Russian History

Series Editor: Donald J. Raleigh,
University of North Carolina, Chapel Hill

This series makes examples of the finest work of the most eminent historians in Russia today available to English-language readers. Each volume has been specially prepared with an international audience in mind, and each is introduced by an outstanding Western scholar in the same field.

THE REFORMS OF PETER THE GREAT
Progress Through Coercion in Russia
Evgenii V. Anisimov
Translated with an introduction by John T. Alexander

IN STALIN'S SHADOW
The Career of "Sergo" Ordzhonikidze
Oleg V. Khlevniuk
Translated by David Nordlander
Edited with an introduction by Donald J. Raleigh,
with the assistance of Kathy S. Transchel

THE EMPERORS AND EMPRESSES OF RUSSIA
Rediscovering the Romanovs
Edited by Donald J. Raleigh
Compiled by Akhmed A. Iskenderov

WOMAN IN RUSSIAN HISTORY
From the Tenth to the Twentieth Century
Natalia Pushkareva
Translated and edited by Eve Levin

THE RUSSIAN EMPIRE IN THE EIGHTEENTH CENTURY
Searching for a Place in the World
Aleksandr B. Kamenskii
Translated and edited by David Griffiths

RUSSIA AFTER THE WAR
Hopes, Illusions, and Disappointments, 1945–1957
Elena Zubkova
Translated and edited by Hugh Ragsdale

LABOR CAMP SOCIALISM
The Gulag in the Soviet Totalitarian System
Galina Mikhailovna Ivanova
Edited by Donald J. Raleigh
Translated by Carol Flath

LABOR CAMP SOCIALISM

THE GULAG IN THE SOVIET TOTALITARIAN SYSTEM

Galina Mikhailovna Ivanova

Edited by Donald J. Raleigh

Translated by Carol Flath

M.E. Sharpe
Armonk, New York
London, England

LIBRARY

English translation, editorial matter, introduction, and conclusion © 2000 by M.E. Sharpe, Inc. An earlier version of this work was published in Moscow in 1997 by the Moscow Fund for the Social Sciences under the title *GULAG v sisteme totalitarnogo gosudarstva*. Copyright © 1997 by G.M. Ivanova and MONF.

Library of Congress Cataloging-in-Publication Data

Ivanova, G.M. (Galina Mikhailovna), 1953–
 [Gulag v sisteme totalitarnogo gosudarstva. English]
 Labor camp socialism : the gulag in the Soviet totalitarian system / by Galina
Mikhailovna Ivanova ; translated by Carol Flath ; edited by Donald J. Raleigh.
 p. cm. — (The new Russian history)
 Includes bibliographical references (p.) and index.
 ISBN 0-7656-0426-4 (cloth: alk. paper)
 ISBN 0-7656-0427-2 (pbk.: alk. paper)
 1. Prisons—Russia—History. 2. Prisons—Soviet Union—History. 3. Forced labor—
Russia—History. 4. Forced labor—Soviet Union—History. 5. Russia—Politics and govern-
ment—1894–1917. 6. Soviet Union—Politics and government. I. Title: Gulag in the Soviet
totalitarian system. II. Flath, Carol A. (Carol Apollonio) III. Raleigh, Donald J. IV. Title. V.
Series.

HV9712.I9417 2000
365'.45'0947—dc21   99-087794

Printed in the United States of America

The paper used in this publication meets the minimum requirements of
American National Standard for Information Sciences
Permanence of Paper for Printed Library Materials,
ANSI Z 39.48-1984.

BM (c)   10   9   8   7   6   5   4   3   2   1
BM (p)   10   9   8   7   6   5   4   3   2   1

Dedicated to the memory of my grandfather,
Vladimir Afanasevich Tsarev

Contents

List of Abbreviations   ix

Editor's Introduction   *Donald J. Raleigh*   xiii

Author's Note to Readers of the English-Language Edition   xix

Preface   xxi

Introduction: Courts and Convicts in Tsarist Russia   3

Chapter 1.   Repression and Punishment   12

Chapter 2.   The Camp Economy   69

Chapter 3.   Gulag Personnel   127

Conclusion: What Was the Gulag?   185

Afterword   191

Notes   193

Index of Personal Names   203

Index of Camp Names   207

Photographs follow pages 68, 126, 184

List of Abbreviations

BAM	Baikal-Amur Mainline Railroad
BBK	White Sea–Baltic Complex
CCCP	Central Committee of the Communist Party
DTO	Roads and Transportation Department
GA RF	State Archive of the Russian Federation
glavmilitsiia	Chief Militia (Chief Administration of the Workers' and Peasants' Militia
GPU	State Political Administration
gubispolkom	Provincial Executive Committee
gubsovnarkhoz	Provincial Council of the Economy
GUGB	Chief Administration of State Security
GULAG	Chief Administration of Corrective-Labor Camps and Colonies
GULGMP	Chief Administration of Camps for the Mining and Metallurgy Industry
GULLP	Chief Administration of Camps for the Forestry Industry
GULZhDS	Chief Administration of Camps for Railroad Construction
GUMZ	Chief Administration for Places of Incarceration
GUPR	Chief Administration of Forced Labor
GUShOSDOR	Chief Administration of Highways
ITK	Corrective-Labor Colony
ITL	Corrective-Labor Camp
ITU	Corrective-Labor Facility
KGB	Committee for State Security
k-r	counterrevolutionary
kraiispolkom	Regional Executive Committee
KVO	Cultural and Educational Department
MGB	Ministry of State Security
MK	Moscow Party Committee

MVD	Ministry of Internal Affairs
NII	Scientific-Research Institute
NKGB	People's Commissariat of State Security
NKPS	People's Commissariat of Roads and Communication
NKIu (Narkomiust)	People's Commissariat of Justice
NKVD (Narkomvnudel)	People's Commissariat of Internal Affairs
obkom	oblast Party committee
oblispolkom	oblast Party executive committee
ODK	Children's Colonies Department
OGPU	Joint State Political Administration
OITK	Corrective-Labor Colonies Department
OKB	Special Construction Bureau
OLP	Individual Camp Facility
OSO	Special Board
PFL	Identification and Screening Camp
PRP	Polish Workers' Party (PPR in Polish)
RKKA	Workers' and Peasants' Red Army
RO MVD	District Section of the Ministry of Internal Affairs
RSFSR	Russian Socialist Federal Soviet Republic
SAZLAG	Central Asian Corrective-Labor Camp
ShIZO	solitary confinement cell
SLON	Solovetskii Special Designation Camp
Smersh	Death to spies (Soviet military counterintelligence)
SNK (Sovnarkom)	Council of People's Commissars
SRs	Socialist Revolutionaries
TsAODM	Central Archive of Social Movements of the City of Moscow
TsKhSD	Center for the Preservation of Contemporary Documents
TsK RKP(b)	Central Committee of the Russian Communist Party (Bolsheviks)
TsK VKP(b)	Central Committee of the All-Union Communist Party (Bolsheviks)
UB	Polish Security Service
UITLiK	Administration of Corrective-Labor Camps and Colonies
UMVD	Administration of the Ministry of Internal Affairs

UNKVD   Administration of the People's Commissariat
                           of Internal Affairs
USLAG   Administration of the Solovetskii Corrective-
                           Labor Camp
VChK   All-Russian Extraordinary Commission for
                           the Struggle against Counterrevolution,
                           Sabotage, and Work-Related Crime (Cheka)
VOKhR   Armed Guard Service
VSNKh   Supreme Economic Council
VSO   Armed Rifle Guards
VTsIK   All-Russian Central Executive Committee

Editor's Introduction

Donald J. Raleigh

Galina Mikhailovna Ivanova's unpretentious book on the role the Gulag played in the Soviet state is the best single-volume historical survey of the ill-famed Soviet labor camp archipelago to appear to date. Concise yet comprehensive, the volume covers the entire history of this unique social and economic phenomenon, from the emergence of the labor-camp system in the 1920s through its dismantling in the mid-1950s. In shifting attention away from the Great Terror of the 1930s, the author brings some sorely needed balance to the historical discussion of the prison camps and underscores the immense role they played in Soviet life before, during, and after World War II. By shooting her picture of the Gulag with a wide-angle lens, she is able to treat it as an integral part of Soviet society rather than as something apart. As she puts it: "The totalitarian regime involved a multitude of people in its crimes. It is not always possible, however, to draw a clear dividing line between executioners and victims. Soviet society and the Gulag are much more tightly interwoven than may appear at first glance."

There is an obvious need for such a book. The glasnost era inaugurated a flood of publications on the subject in Russia; most of them are memoirs, document collections, statistical studies on the number of camp inmates, or reference works issued by Memorial and other societies and agencies.[1] Practically no specifically historical studies have appeared,[2] and none of them has examined the Gulag over the whole period of its existence. Western historical writing on the camps has focused almost exclusively on the Great Terror of the 1930s; many of the defining works in this corpus of literature were published before pertinent Soviet archival sources became accessible.[3] More recently, Edwin Bacon has considered the forced labor system in light of the archives, yet his monograph treats only the war years and draws on a limited number of archival files.[4] Several works in progress dealing with specific Gulag sites tap heretofore elusive archival materials and take us inside the camps, thereby promising to offer invaluable insights into the functioning of the system and to answer essential questions about the camp experience.[5] But they will most likely complement Ivanova's monograph, which should remain the starting point for all serious studies on the Gulag for some time to come.

Although the work is based on a wide reading of recently opened archival files as well as memoirs and published literature, the author acknowledges that many of the documents crucial to a more complete history of the Gulag remain off limits to scholars. Nevertheless, she makes strategic use of the archival sources available, and of published work based on holdings she did not consult, in addressing the role the Gulag played in both supporting and undermining the Soviet socialist experiment. Ivanova conceptualizes the Gulag as a state within a state, "a colony with its own laws, customs, moral standards, and social groups." A symbiotic relationship and mutual dependency existed between the "separate country behind barbed wire" and the rest of the Soviet Union, between the "small zone" and the big one. The author concludes that "the country of colonies and camps owes its birth to the Bolshevik regime, which institutionalized violence as a universal means of attaining its goals." The phenomenon emerged under Stalinism, "but its historical roots can be traced to the ancient and enduring traditions of tyranny and authoritarianism of the Russian state, whose laws consistently defended and preserved the interests of the empire without guaranteeing the rights and freedoms of the individual." In illustrating this point, she places great importance on the sharp rise in forced labor and the use of the death sentence as punishments under the autocracy in the wake of the Revolution of 1905. Ivanova likewise highlights the emergence of labor camps under Lenin during the militant and vindictive atmosphere of the civil war years, when the idea emerged that the camps could serve a punitive and economic purpose. Stalin and the top Party leadership later put the innovation into practice not only to control society and to undermine opposition, but also to shore up the economy through the use of slave labor. Ivanova devotes little attention to Stalin and his chief associates; however, her citing of key documents, often beginning with the revealing address to Stalin, "in accordance with your instructions," speaks volumes.[6]

In chapter 1, Ivanova offers a summary of the state's punitive practices. She takes a broad view of the Gulag itself and of who constituted its victims, considering not only "political" prisoners (58ers) but also

those in special settlements, identification and screening camps, labor
armies, prisoner-of-war camps, educational labor colonies for juveniles,
and other facilities. The terror was both random, in that it could strike
anyone, and specific, in that it also targeted certain unfortunate groups
and peoples. On average, the annual Gulag population amounted to
2.5 million individuals ("innocent victims of class struggle, lawlessness,
tyranny, and terror"), and it reached its peak in the summer of 1950,
when it climbed to 2.8 million inmates. By this time typical Gulag inhabitants were farmers "who stole a sack of potatoes" or members of
one of the punished peoples deported during the war and subjected to
Soviet apartheid policies. All in all, the author maintains that approximately 20 million Soviet citizens revolved through the camps during
their existence, of whom one-third were political prisoners and 10–15
percent were criminal recidivists. In addition, millions of others were
subjected to forced labor and various discriminatory policies. The author, however, is reluctant to offer a figure for how many people died
in camps and colonies, emphasizing that the official data do not give
the total number of deaths among prisoners. The exception is for the
war years, when over 2 million people perished in camps between 1941
and 1944. During the same period roughly 1 million prisoners were
released early and sent to the front. But the need for forced labor remained great, and, as a result, 5 million citizens poured into the camps
during the war, when the percentage of women prisoners rose from 7
to 26 percent.

Chapter 2 offers a wide-ranging consideration of Gulag labor, which
supplied twenty key branches of Soviet industry. As the author makes
clear, economic needs of state determined the location of camps and
colonies. In a sense, the Gulag was everywhere, for there was a "small
zone" in every oblast in the country. The Gulag system comprised 476
camps, in addition to their many branches, and no less than two thousand colonies. In demonstrating the wasteful inefficiency of the Gulag
economic order, Ivanova shows how it became a constitutive, quintes-
sential element of the Stalinist system. On the whole unprofitable, the
predatory camp economy was roughly only half as productive as the
rest of the state economy.

In chapter 3 Ivanova presents a rich social and psychological por-
trait of those who ran the camps, considering the size and the ethnic
and social composition of the Gulag personnel, as well as their educational level and gender. Her longitudinal study of camp cadres deftly
delves into their mentality, suggesting how they became a "primary

social foundation of the regime." After all, during the period from the late 1920s to the mid-1950s roughly one million individuals staffed the Gulag. And they were not an isolated group of people. "They lived in society, brought up children, spent time with their loved ones and those close to them, transmitting to their families and society as a whole the subcultures of violence that had taken shape in the world of the camps."

Thus, as a state within a state, the Gulag was a government within a government, an economy within an economy, and a subculture of violence within an ideologically shaped value system.

The author insists that her book represents but a modest first step toward a multifaceted history of the Gulag. To be sure, readers will not encounter in it, among other topics, histories of specific campsites, information on foreigners in the Gulag, discussion of sexual victimization, which probably finds poor reflection in the documents, or analysis of the inmates' reabsorption into society. But the author admirably accomplishes what she sets out to do, and the book is more than a cautionary tale. I am certain that the reader of this English edition will agree.

I would like to take this opportunity to thank the author for her cooperation in bringing this project to fruition. A standing ovation goes to my colleague at Duke, Carol Flath, an accomplished translator who not only provided a fluent translation but also cheerfully adhered to all deadlines. It is a pleasure for me as well to thank Elena Zubkova, who called Galina Ivanova's work to my attention, David J. Nordlander, who commented on my draft introduction and Jon Wallace, who helped read proofs. Finally, I wish to express my sincere gratitude to Patricia A. Kolb and her staff at M.E. Sharpe, particularly Elizabeth Granda and Ana Erlic, for their unflagging support of the series and of this particular volume. Their sound professional advice has made this a better book.

Notes

1. A civic group created in 1987 to expose and remember the crimes of the Stalin years. For an example of the society's reference publications, see M.B. Smirnov, comp., *Sistema ispravitel'no-trudovykh lagerei v SSSR, 1923–1960: Spravochnik* (Moscow: Zven'ia, 1998).

2. An exception, but one that focuses on the Great Terror, is V.Z. Rogovin's *1937* (Moscow: [V. Rogovin], 1996). Mehring Books in Oak Park, Michigan, has recently put out an English-language edition under the title *1937: Stalin's Year of Terror.*

3. One exception is J. Arch Getty and Roberta Manning, eds., *Stalinist Terror: New Perspectives* (New York: Cambridge University Press, 1993).

4. Edwin Bacon, *The Gulag at War: Stalin's Forced Labour System in the Light of the Archives* (New York: New York University Press, 1994).

5. For example, David J. Nordlander, "Capital of the Gulag: Magadan in the Early Soviet Era, 1929–1941," 1997 Ph.D. dissertation, University of North Carolina at Chapel Hill.

6. As this book went to press, the latest volume in Yale University Press's Annals of Communism series appeared. In it, American editor J. Arch Getty confirms that Stalin's fingerprints can be found "all over the archives." See J. Arch Getty and Oleg V. Naumov, eds., *The Road to Terror: Stalin and the Self-Destruction of the Bolsheviks, 1932–1939* (New Haven and London: Yale University Press), xiii.

Author's Note to Readers of the English-Language Edition

Galina Mikhailovna Ivanova

The subject of the present study is not new to the American reader. But in the vast and varied literature on the history of the Gulag that has been published in the United States and Western Europe over the past half century, memoirs, journalism, and literary works predominate. There are far fewer specifically historical studies, and the scholarly integrity of these works has at times been called into question, particularly in the case of works with a socialist orientation, whose authors for many years denied the very existence of the Gulag. The criticism, mistrust, and controversy relating to these works on the history of forced labor is primarily due to the unrepresentative nature of the sources used. Until the end of the 1980s the available source base was limited to eyewitness accounts and memoirs and official Soviet documents on demographics and economics; Soviet archives that had anything to do with forced labor, even indirectly, were closed to Soviet scholars as well as to foreign researchers.

The new—though still extremely limited—access to essential archival materials at the end of the 1980s and the beginning of the 1990s enabled a qualitative shift in the scholarship. Public interest in the camps was particularly strong during this period and led to the publication in the Soviet Union of numerous works on the history of the Gulag. Still, memoirs and journalistic works continued to predominate. The scholarly publications of O. Khlevniuk, V. Zemskov, and other scholars, which presented abundant new factual material on the history of the Gulag and the People's Commissariat of Internal Affairs (NKVD), addressed only some of the issues associated with the Soviet system of repression. To a large extent, readers turned to literature in translation by such authors as Robert Conquest, Stephen Cohen, and others, which were well known to the American reader.

I began my own book on the Gulag in the mid-1990s, after the initial

wave of interest had peaked; by then the topic seemed to have been
thoroughly "worked over" and had lost its headline appeal. This was a
time of disillusionment in Russia, with a deepening rift between cherished expectations and real possibilities. There was a tendency, if not
to justify the Gulag, then to present it as merely a system of corrective
institutions that held primarily criminal offenders. Renewed attempts
were made to explain the need for the Gulag, citing external political
circumstances, and of course to distance the Gulag itself from the Communist regime as a whole. The only way to respond to this tendency
was through authentic scholarship.

My primary purpose was to research the Gulag as a social and economic phenomenon of the Soviet state and to trace the economic and
social interconnections between the Gulag and the totalitarian state.
My research focused on three issues: the repressive system and punitive policy, the camp economy, and the Gulag personnel. This approach
has allowed me to provide a comprehensive picture of the place and
role of the Gulag in Soviet society as a whole.

The issues of "administrative mass murder" and forced labor are
somewhat abstract for the American reader, who has never suffered
under totalitarianism and whose scholars are free from immediate
political pressures. In Russia the situation is different: not only those
who "served time" in the camps but those who put them there are still
alive; their children are alive, as are, most importantly, their beliefs.
New generations of young people come of age, many of them clearly
enamored of totalitarian ideologies. For these reasons the topic of the
Gulag, whether we like it or not, remains politically and socially relevant. The history of the camps must not be allowed to sink into
oblivion. Disseminating knowledge about the Gulag is truly a matter of
international importance.

I am pleased that my book is being published in the United States
for a readership that, with its education in democratic traditions and
respect for human rights and liberties, can fully appreciate the author's
conclusions and their social relevance. I hope that my book will provide a deeper understanding of important issues in the social and political history of the twentieth century.

This work was carried out at the Institute of Russian History of the
Russian Academy of Sciences under the auspices of the Moscow Fund
for the Social Sciences program "The Russian Social Sciences: A New
Perspective," sponsored by the Ford Foundation. Photographs are cour-
tesy of the Central Moscow Archive for Documents on Special Media
and the Russian State Archive of Documentary Films and Photographs.

Preface

Totalitarianism shattered the lives of hundreds of millions of people and left an indelible mark on the history of the twentieth century. Concentration camps have served as an integral part of all totalitarian regimes. In terms of longevity, sheer scale, and number of victims, the notorious Gulag of the USSR claims sad priority of place.

The concept of the "Gulag," which A.I. Solzhenitsyn introduced into the study of world history, is by no means limited to the system of Soviet forced-labor camps that existed from the 1930s to the 1950s. The Gulag as a unique socioeconomic phenomenon emerged under Stalinism, but its historical roots can be traced to the ancient and enduring traditions of tyranny and authoritarianism of the Russian state, whose laws consistently defended and preserved the interests of the empire without guaranteeing the rights and freedoms of the individual.

The Chief Administration of Corrective-Labor Camps and Colonies (GULAG) of the People's Commissariat of Internal Affairs (NKVD) and the Ministry of Internal Affairs (MVD) of the USSR was a typical bureaucratic institution in form, but in essence it was a state within the state, a veritable colonial country of labor camps with its own laws, customs, moral standards, and social groups. One of these groups was the people employed in the camp system. Their professional activity, which earned them salaries, housing, prizes, and government awards, revolved around the arrest and incarceration of millions of their fellow citizens and the daily exploitation of their slave labor. One of the goals of the present study has been to explore the numerical, ethnic, and social composition of the personnel of the Gulag, to provide a social profile of Gulag workers, and to examine their mentality, psychology, and moral character. This task is of key importance for understanding the totalitarian regime, for in effect these people served as its primary social foundation. Our study of large-scale surveys and the latest documents that have become available makes it clear that the real tragedy of the country was not simply that a part of the population "served time" but that the Gulag, existing as it did under cover of strict secrecy, divided society, set important segments of the population in opposition to each other, and spread terror and lawlessness. Writer Oleg Volkov observes: "We were constantly aware of the gaping jaws of the Gulag threatening to devour us. The slogan they came up with to justify their existence, 'Reform through Labor,' elevated hard labor to the status of an institution of cultural education."[1]

Even today, the Gulag continues to be characterized in some quarters as a corrective-labor institution that worked to educate and rehabilitate hardened criminals (unjustly convicted innocent prisoners were indeed incarcerated together with murderers, thieves, and gangsters—and this only exacerbated the plight of the former). The legal scholar Professor S.I. Kuzmin views the Gulag as an integral part of a crime-fighting mechanism that "developed and became more sophisticated in response to the increasing complexity of the tasks of socioeconomic construction and the political circumstances." True to the traditions of a trench-war mentality that sees struggle and military threats everywhere, Kuzmin identifies the hostility of our neighbors, which he believes increased in response to the political and economic successes of the "Stalinist" state, as one of the main reasons for the expansion of the Gulag. "Under these conditions," writes Kuzmin, "the Gulag was a logical and necessary response to numerous domestic and international circumstances." Claiming that his manuscript, "which is based on an objective analysis of archival documents," represents a monopoly on the truth, Kuzmin dismisses those authors, and in particular Solzhenitsyn, who "failed to provide an objective assessment of the system of corrective-labor institutions in our country—and in fact did not set out to do so." Kuzmin views his task to be not simply the defense of his "professional honor," as it may appear at first glance. He has a far more ambitious goal: to represent the institutions of the Gulag and its treatment of prisoners in such a way as to teach his readers—he has in mind the staff of corrective-labor institutions—"a great deal that is interesting and instructive and that can and ought to be used in their professional activity" in the Russian state at its current stage of development.[2] The Gulag as a model for emulation! This is indeed an idea worth pondering.

The personal opinions of a single author would not have been worth quoting at such length if they in fact had remained private. But our study of the history of Soviet society from the 1960s through the 1990s has convinced us that the Gulag not only left deep scars on the mentality of the people who were its prisoners but had a significant effect on the psychology, behavior, way of life, and thinking of the general population as well. We must study and analyze the Gulag and its metastases seriously; their effects continue to be felt today.

The first attempts to understand and make sense of the camp system were made by people who had come to know the Gulag "from inside," whose historical sources were primarily their own personal experience, impressions, and observations. These works constitute an extensive body of literature about the Gulag in which elements of direct observation and memoir are interwoven with intellectual analysis. The works of Solzhenitsyn, E. Ginzburg, A. Antonov-Ovseenko, V. Shalamov, O. Volkov, J. Rossi, and many other former prisoners of Soviet concentration camps in turn have become a documentary source for subsequent, primarily foreign, research.

Serious study of the Gulag did not begin in our country until the end of the 1980s and beginning of the 1990s, when the relevant archival materials became available (though under severely restricted conditions) and glasnost became a reality. The works of V. Zemskov, A. Dugin, M. Detkov, and others that were published during this time are primarily statistical and documentary in nature. The literature to date contains practically no specifically historical studies on the subject. The present work is also unique in its representation of the Gulag in, as it were, two dimensions, "from inside" as well as "from outside," for the Gulag and the totalitarian state existed in a symbiotic system of mutual economic and social dependence. We have devoted a significant amount of attention to an in-depth analysis of the camps as an economic system built on the use of various kinds of forced labor.

The study is based primarily on unpublished materials. Archival research conducted by the author in former Communist Party archives and the State Archive of the Russian Federation (GA RF) uncovered a set of unique documents reflecting the activity of Party, Komsomol, and trade-union organizations in the Gulag. These documents, which are being presented in a scholarly analysis for the first time, include shorthand reports of closed NKVD and Gulag conferences, official records of Party and Komsomol meetings in individual camps and colonies, accounts, summaries, reports from political departments, resolutions made at trade-union meetings of Gulag personnel, and many others. Unfortunately, access to certain archival documents concerning Party activities continues to be restricted; for that reason the author has not always been able to quote the specific source. This set of materials is particularly valuable because of the dominant role that Party organizations and political agencies played in the life of the Gulag.

The sources used in this monograph also include published and unpublished legislation, materials from administrative and law-enforcement agencies, documents of the Central Committee of the Communist Party

(VKP[b]), the Presidium of the Supreme Soviet of the USSR, the Ministry of Internal Affairs, and a number of other governmental and Party institutions. The author also drew from memoirs, journalistic sources, and published statistics, as well as from numerous published documents on the history of the repressions.

Chronologically, the study is not limited to the period of the Gulag's official existence, that is, from the end of the 1920s to the mid-1950s, since by the first decade of Soviet power an extensive network of various kinds of isolation facilities and concentration camps was already operating on the territory of the country; in other words, the Gulag did not arise out of nowhere, but was built on patterns of terror and restrictions on free thought that had taken root during the preceding years. As part of the correctional system, the Gulag took over all the penitentiary institutions of the Russian empire and absorbed its rich experience in the practice of repression. To be sure, the punitive policies of any state are determined by its political traditions, its economic capabilities, and the intellectual and psychological level of the population. Therefore, the author has begun with a short introduction illuminating the basic lines of development of the Russian law-enforcement system, showing who was convicted and punished in tsarist Russia, for what, and in what manner. Even a superficial awareness of the punitive policies of the autocracy makes it clear that the scope of repressions under tsarism does not come close, by any measure, to the massive scale of the terror of the Soviet years. But in any case, can it really be simply a question of degree?

The lack of political freedoms and guarantees of the inviolability of the individual, the routine practice of repressions imposed without judicial process, the devaluation of human life through mass executions for political crimes, the punitive practices of military field justice and the extraordinary courts, and so forth, taken against the background of the traditions of a despotic form of state administration and the general lack of human rights in Russia—these were the factors at work in the growth of totalitarianism in our country and of its most representative institution—the Gulag.

Notes

1. V.T. Shalamov, *Vishera: Antiroman*, predislovie Olega Volkova (Moscow, 1989), 3–4.

2. See S.I. Kuz'min, "ITU: istoriia i sovremennost'," *Chelovek: prestuplenie i nakazanie. Vestnik Riazanskoi vysshei shkoly MVD RF*, no. 2 (1995): 46–58.

Labor Camp
Socialism

Introduction

Courts and Convicts in Tsarist Russia

Russia entered the twentieth century with a well-developed repressive judicial apparatus that was neither excessively cruel nor particularly humane. There were two court systems, justice of the peace courts (*mirovaia sistema*) and general courts (*obshchaia sistema*), not counting the numerous special courts—military, ecclesiastical, commercial, rural (*volostnye*), and so forth. The justice of the peace courts decided misdemeanors and civil cases. The system of general courts, which included district (*okruzhnye*) courts, regional appellate courts (*sudebnye palaty*), and the Governing Senate (*pravitel'stvuiushchii Senat*), considered all criminal and civil cases. The State Council excluded political cases and cases involving work-related crimes from the jurisdiction of the district courts, which seated, in addition to the three permanent members, twelve jurors. Such cases were turned over to the appellate courts, which were the courts of first instance and included representatives of various segments of society with expertise on business, governmental, religious, and political matters. The district and appellate courts were staffed by investigators, bailiffs, and prosecutors, as well as a council of barristers.

At the beginning of the twentieth century there were 105 district courts and 14 regional appellate courts operating in Russia. In 1903 they were staffed by 3,159 people in the European part of Russia.[1] The supreme court of appeal of the empire and the highest supervisory body was the Governing Senate, which consisted of two departments— criminal and civil. The overall judicial system in Russia was administered by the Ministry of Justice.

Before the Revolution of 1905, "not-guilty" verdicts were quite common in Russian judicial practice. According to E.N. Tarnovskii, the eminent Russian specialist in criminal statistics, approximately half of the cases involving state crimes were dismissed on various grounds before coming to trial; of the remainder, one-third resulted in acquittal, and only one-third of all people placed under investigation were ultimately convicted.[2]

The punitive policy of the Russian state was unique in that, in addition to investigations and trials carried out by the courts, the authorities engaged in widespread extrajudicial reprisals as well. The legal basis for these reprisals was the Statute on Measures for Maintaining Law and Order and Public Tranquility, which was adopted on August 14, 1881, following the assassination of Alexander II, and remained in effect until February 1917. According to this document, the declaration of an area as being "in a state of heightened or emergency security" granted civil and military authorities, local police chiefs, and gendarmes practically unlimited powers to administer punitive measures. The statute also established procedures for turning over cases to district military courts, whose essential function was to simplify and expedite the process of investigation and trial and to increase the degree of punishment, up to and including the death penalty.

The tsarist government made no secret of its crime statistics. Collections of criminal statistics, covering forty-three types of crimes, were published annually. By the end of the nineteenth century, however, the growth of the revolutionary movement had resulted in the removal of political cases from the overall statistical count, and their numbers were no longer made public. According to Tarnovskii, who considers the revolutionary movement to be an "important but tragic phenomenon of Russian life," "the policy of suppressing and hiding the dark and ominous sides of our reality led to great misery and misfortune."[3] Statistics on state crimes began to be published again only in 1904, after the adoption of a new Criminal Code.

In his analysis of statistics on state crimes, Tarnovskii observed a constant and steady growth in the number of people convicted of political crimes, while general criminal convictions remained at practically the same level over a period of twenty years.

Under Russian law, state, that is, political, crimes included the following: (1) insurrection against the supreme authorities and crimes against the person of the emperor and members of the imperial family; (2) treason against the state; (3) sedition; (4) participation in illegal societies; and (5) crimes violating customary law. It is perfectly natural that trials of such cases should have reached their peak during the first years after the Revolution of 1905. Between 1906 and 1912, a total of 35,353 people were tried for state crimes. Of these, 10,006 were acquitted in district and appellate courts, 70 were amnestied under the Imperial Manifestos, and 25,277 were convicted.[4]

The most common crimes were insurrection, which often took the form of insults or threats made against the tsar in private company, "uttered in folly, ignorance, or in a state of intoxication," and sedition. Given the nature of such crimes, the most common punishment was simple detention. Of the total 25,277 people convicted, 10,312 (40.8 percent) were sentenced to detention, 8,752 (34.6 percent) were incarcerated in a fortress without deprivation of property rights, 2,342 (9.3 percent) were exiled, 1,774 (7 percent) were imprisoned without deprivation of property rights, 1,138 (4.5 percent) were exiled to hard labor, 453 (1.8 percent) were sent to reformatories, 259 (1 percent) received punishment appropriate for juveniles under the age of seventeen, and 247 (1 percent) were sentenced to other forms of punishment. It should be noted that the punishments for general criminal acts were much more severe: from 30 percent to 60 percent of those convicted were sent to hard labor, depending on the gravity of their crime. Between 1906 and 1912 no death sentences were imposed, and only two convicts were sentenced to life at hard labor.[5] All these cases of state crimes were considered by "general judicial institutions," that is to say, district and appellate courts.

The punitive policy of the state, however, was by no means limited to the activity of these courts. More severe repressions were imposed by military district courts, which considered both political and criminal cases. Data from the Ministry of War show that, during the period from 1902 to 1909, 8,974 people were brought before military courts for state crimes; of these, 2,968 were acquitted, 4,367 were exiled to hard labor, and 208 were sentenced to death.[6]

In addition to the military district courts, military field courts operated in Russia between August 19, 1906, and April 19, 1907. Their jurisdiction primarily covered civil and military personnel caught engaging in political agitation among the troops. Military field justice made a significant contribution to the statistics of repression: 1,102 death sentences in eight months.[7]

What was the public reaction in Russia to the increase in death sentences, which had previously been so rare? "In the conscience and consciousness of the overwhelming majority of Russian legal professionals, thoughts and feelings about capital punishment evolved through three phases," wrote the St. Petersburg lawyer O.O. Gruzenberg in 1910:

> First it was considered a senseless and abominable punishment, but a punishment all the same. Later, when it began to be applied without the elementary legal proceedings and protections that are the only thing distinguishing a court of law from a mechanism for meting out punish-

ment, it ceased to be a punishment and became a crime itself. More time passed, and capital punishment became commonplace, as V.G. Korolenko put it, a "phenomenon of everyday life," just something to get used to.[8]

Could this terrible devaluation of human life be the source of the Russian tragedy to come? Capital punishment cannot and must not be a "phenomenon of everyday life" under any political system. This was well understood by many contemporaries—legal scholars, writers, academics, and journalists—who tried to attract public attention to each individual death sentence. When Professor M.N. Gernet began working on his book *Capital Punishment* and was unable to find the necessary statistical data, he "began compiling a list of individuals who had been sentenced to death."[9] Similar lists, some of them quite comprehensive, were compiled by other researchers as well.

According to Gruzenberg's data, which is drawn from the annual reports of the Chief Military Judicial Administration, 2,678 people were executed by order of military district courts during the period from 1875 through 1908; of these, 280 were executed for purely political crimes, that is, crimes that posed no threat to human life or property. A disproportionately large number of these death sentences were carried out during the last four years of this thirty-four-year period. Between 1905 and 1908, 2,215 people were executed by order of military courts, 195 of them for state crimes.[10] Gruzenberg calls these numbers, which "breathe death," monstrous, and it is difficult to disagree with him.

What was the reason for such a sharp increase in the repressions? What crimes earned the death penalty? Statistics show that the majority of death sentences were imposed for premeditated murder and robbery. An attempt to explain the cruelty of the government, and perhaps even partially to justify it, was made by M. Borovitinov, assistant head of the Chief Prison Administration: "The remnants of the revolutionary forces continued their destructive activity," he wrote in his report to the Eighth International Congress on Prisons in Washington in 1910. "Open struggle degenerated into pillage. The so-called revolutionaries, whose ranks were made up primarily of 'savages,' set about expropriating citizens, accompanying pillage with violence and murder."[11] Borovitinov quoted the following figures: Between 1906 and 1909 the "so-called revolutionaries" committed 28,443 terrorist acts and robberies, during which 7,293 people were killed and 8,061 were wounded; the murder victims included 2,640 officials and 4,653 civilians. For these crimes, 2,825 people were sentenced to death.[12]

The Russian population as a whole did not support capital punishment. When the mass executions began, many towns could not find someone who would agree to act as executioner (the law provided that execution was to be carried out by hanging). Even felons who had committed grave criminal offenses refused to perform executions in spite of the incentives that were offered, including monetary compensation and even official pardons. The newspapers of the time recorded many cases in which convicted criminals would attack a fellow prisoner who had agreed to serve as executioner. After a year or so, however, the situation changed markedly. According to the observations of a contemporary, the St. Petersburg lawyer E. Kulisher, "The daily executions have already led to a significant coarsening in people's sensibilities. . . . The feelings of revulsion for the executioner have dulled somewhat as well. . . . The price for a hanging has gone down, and it has became easier to find people willing to serve as executioners.[13]

Still, public opinion remained opposed to capital punishment. Hundreds of protest resolutions were signed at rallies, petitions addressed to the monarch and the State Duma were circulated, and newspapers printed protests against individual executions. One newspaper gathered over 23,000 signatures protesting the execution of Lieutenant P.P. Shmidt.* "Although mass executions have become more common and no longer attract attention," wrote criminal law professor P. Liublinskii in 1910, "Russian public opinion can be characterized as nearly unanimously critical of capital punishment."[14]

Russia had its own unique version of the death penalty as a form of criminal punishment. "This punishment," noted Liublinskii, "is applied not so much for general crimes as for political ones; it is applied not so much by courts as by discretion of local authorities; trials follow not routine procedures but exceptional ones; executions are not an isolated, but a mass phenomenon; public opinion is completely ignored."[15]

The most severe criminal punishments in Russia were hard labor and exile. Contemporaries noted with concern "the terrible increase in the number of convicts sentenced to hard labor" in the postrevolutionary years. As of January 1, 1906, there were 5,748 convicts exiled to hard labor; a year later this number had increased to 7,779. There were 12,591 in 1908, and by January 1, 1909, the number reached 20,936. The hard-labor prisons of Siberia, which were intended for a few thousand people, could not accommodate the huge (for that

---

*P.P. Shmidt was the leader of the first mutiny organized by an officer in the Russian navy during the Revolution of 1905.—Ed.

time) number of prisoners, and consequently a significant proportion of convicts served their time under house arrest where they were legally registered. Of the total 20,936 convicts, 6,143 were held in Siberian prisons, about 4,000 were held in specially organized "temporary" hard-labor prisons, and the remainder were incarcerated elsewhere, including in district prisons in the provinces.[16]

Government officials who traveled on inspection tours to camps in Siberia at various times repeatedly noted the terrible conditions in hard-labor prisons. For example, of the seven hard-labor prisons in the Nerchinsk region, only three were judged acceptable for housing prisoners; the others were in such a dilapidated state that they were deemed beyond repair.

One of the most difficult problems faced by the tsarist government during the establishment of Siberian penal servitude was the task of organizing the labor of prisoners. "In hard-labor prisons in remote locations in Siberia," we read in the report of the Chief Prison Administration for the year 1908,

> given the limited demand among the local population and the lack of any market for goods that could be produced in prison workshops, it is extremely difficult to arrange any kind of work for the prisoners. A large number of the prisoners being held in hard-labor prisons in Siberia remain completely idle out of necessity and in the best cases are kept occupied with routine chores such as carrying water, chopping firewood, and so forth. This is also partly due to the severe climate of Siberia, which has an adverse effect on one's health and, consequently, on the able-bodiedness of those prisoners who lived in a milder climate before their conviction.[17]

Keeping prisoners in far-away Siberia caused a significant drain on the state treasury. If the average annual cost of holding a prisoner in imperial prisons in 1910 was around 167 rubles, the maintenance of a single hard-labor prisoner in Irkutsk Province amounted to 197 rubles per year, while in Nerchinsk it cost up to 287 rubles.* [18]

What was the government's rationale for insisting on retaining Siberian penal servitude? A bill on reforming the penal-servitude system, approved at the end of 1909 by the Council of Ministers, argued, among other things, for "the potential for expansion in the near future of the outdoor work projects that are currently in operation in Siberia, and the potential for using prison labor in constructing the Amur Railroad and the second line of the Trans-Siberian."[19] Apparently this was one of the deciding factors in getting the bill passed.

---

*For comparison we note that in 1910 a Moscow textile worker on average earned 194 rubles per year.

Penal servitude in Russia was unique in that as a rule the work was done in closed prison workshops. Deprived of fresh air, prisoners, especially those serving long sentences, were frequently ill. All progressive specialists in the area of penitentiary policy supported the establishment of work projects outdoors in the fresh air. This policy was endorsed in 1905 by the International Prison Congress in Budapest. In Russia the question of outdoor work projects was first raised in 1902 at the Congress of Prison Workers. Because of limited economic resources, however, the prison agency was unable to organize such work projects on a large scale. Between May 1910 and January 1916, 2,500 to 3,000 prisoners worked on the construction of the Amur Railroad.[20] A number of privileges were established for them: their sentences were reduced by one-third; enhanced food rations were provided to prisoners who worked well; and they were paid for their work, with extra pay for overtime. The length of the workday depended on the time of year and the category of prisoner (there were three categories: probationary, corrective, and privileged) and lasted ten to twelve hours. These hours included time set aside for meals and for classes in school. It is doubtful that the state of affairs in the organization of railroad construction was as good as that described by government bureaucrats. We have no doubt as to the miserable conditions endured by prisoners in the majority of Russian hard-labor prisons. In a letter that was made public during that time, prisoners reported on conditions in the Pskov Hard-Labor Prison, where the rampant tuberculosis amounted to a death sentence for those suffering from it. The prisoners wrote that they "dreamed of being sent to work building the Amur Railroad, but, it turns out, they don't accept political prisoners, people from the Caucasus region, or Jews."[21]

Once he had completed his term at hard labor, a convict was sent to a settlement. There he faced a hungry life, completely deprived of legal rights, which may have served some purpose but did not contribute to his rehabilitation. Proposals were repeatedly made in government circles to abolish the exile system, but they were never passed.

The system of places of incarceration, which included hard-labor prisons, corrective-labor facilities, and provincial, regional, and district prisons, fell under the Chief Prison Administration, which was part of the Ministry of Justice. In addition, Russia maintained a broad network of houses of arrest, transport stages and half-stages, military prisons and disciplinary units, monastery prisons, institutions for juveniles, and so forth, which reported to various agencies.

At the beginning of 1917, the overall number of people held in places of incarceration amounted to 155,134; of them, 51,714 were under investigation and 87,492 had been sentenced to various forms of punishment, including 36,337 to penal servitude.[22]

The February Revolution introduced substantial changes into the state's punitive policy. Order No. 1 of March 8, 1917, issued by A.A. Zhizhilenko, a law professor who had been appointed director of the Chief Prison Administration by A.F. Kerenskii, emphasized that the primary purpose of punishment was the reeducation of a person who "had had the misfortune of descending into crime due to specific character traits or to an unfavorable set of external circumstances," and that "the most important prerequisite for achieving this task is to treat prisoners humanely."[23]

The Provisional Government's policy of liberalization and humanization of the repressive system was reflected in a series of prison reforms. An amnesty was declared on March 17, resulting in the release of 88,097 prisoners, including 5,737 political prisoners and 67,824 criminals; 14,536 prisoners were released without the corresponding order from the "appropriate authorities." As of April 1, 1917, 41,509 prisoners remained incarcerated.[24] The process of releasing prisoners, both "from above" and "from below" (massive escapes of prisoners were an everyday phenomenon during that period) continued approximately until the fall of 1917, when circumstances forced the Chief Prison Administration to tighten the regimen and conditions of imprisonment.

On April 26, 1917, the Provisional Government abolished exile as a punishment, as well as exile subsequent to terms of penal servitude. Released prisoners were granted the right to choose their place of residence, with the exception of a few specified locations.

Not having the economic means to organize convict labor and at the same time wanting to prevent idleness in prisons, the prison authorities abolished all previous restrictions on reading and worked at developing library facilities.

The reorganization of the prison system was signaled by a change of the name Chief Prison Administration to Chief Administration for Places of Incarceration (*Glavnoe upravlenie po delam mest zakliucheniia*: GUMZ) and an administrative restructuring aimed at achieving its stated social goals. The personnel list of the GUMZ contained a total of 89 positions.

The sharp decrease in the number of prisoners, along with a wave of prison pogroms that spread through a number of provinces at the end of February and the beginning of March, led to the closing of a number of prison facilities. As of September 1, 1917, 712 places of incarceration were operating in Russia, with a total of 36,468 prisoners. The state spent a considerable amount of money maintaining the prison system. The 1917 budget provided for monetary appropriations totaling over 19 million rubles, of which almost 16 million rubles had been spent by autumn.[25]

The evolutionary path of reform in the Russian punitive system was interrupted by the October Revolution, which dismantled the old state apparatus, including the system of places of incarceration that had been one of its components.

Chapter 1

Repression and Punishment

The Soviet repressive system originated in the chaos of revolution and was several years in the making. Forced-labor camps, previously unknown in Russia, began to appear after the October Revolution, taking their places alongside traditional places of incarceration. These new camps were to become the primary channel for enforcing the Soviet state's punitive policies.

The first camps appeared on Soviet territory during the summer of 1918. On August 9, Lenin, in his capacity as chairman of the Council of People's Commissars (*Sovnarkom*, SNK), instructed the Penza Provincial Executive Committee to "conduct a merciless campaign of mass terror against kulaks, priests, and White Guardists; suspicious persons are to be incarcerated in a concentration camp outside city limits."[1] The new punitive facilities were authorized by a Sovnarkom Decree of September 5, 1918, entitled "On the Red Terror." This document prescribed execution by shooting for persons "implicated in White Guard organizations, plots, and rebellions" and imprisonment in concentration camps for "class enemies."[2] Casting aside all generally accepted procedural norms and legal guarantees, the Bolsheviks launched a systematic program of extermination of real and potential opponents. Hostage taking, a new measure that had not been applied in Russia before the revolution, was introduced to suppress opposition among various groups of the population.

In their struggle for survival, the Bolsheviks aimed, if not to annihilate all their enemies physically, at least to isolate them and break down their spirit and morale by placing them under guard and forcing them to work for them. The various camps—concentration, forced-labor, special designation, corrective-labor, and so on, whose names had no real significance in distinguishing their nature and functions—were perfectly suited for this purpose and were relatively simple and inexpensive to establish.

Legal regulation of camp operations began with the decree of the All-Russian Central Executive Committee (VTsIK) "On Forced-Labor

Camps," published in *Izvestiia* on April 15, 1919. The initial organization and management of forced-labor camps was entrusted to provincial extraordinary commissions. The administration of the NKVD camps was turned over to the Central Camp Administration, created by agreement with the All-Russian Extraordinary Commission for the Struggle against Counterrevolution, Sabotage, and Work-Related Crime (VChK or *Cheka*). On May 17, 1919, the VTsIK issued a resolution "On Forced-Labor Camps," pursuant to the April 15 decree, setting forth detailed procedures and conditions for organizing the camps. It recommended that the initial planning should take into account local conditions, "both within city limits and on the estates, in the monasteries, at the country homes, and so on, located nearby." The decree required the establishment within stipulated time limits of camps with a capacity of at least 300 prisoners each in all the provincial capitals. The overall administration of all the camps on the territory of the RSFSR was entrusted to the NKVD's Department of Forced Labor. It was assumed that the costs of running the camps would be covered by the labor of the prisoners (only people capable of physical labor were sent to camps). Attempts to escape were punished severely: for the first attempt, the prisoner's sentence was increased tenfold; for the second, he could be sentenced by a revolutionary tribunal to be shot.[3] These documents in effect legalized the activity of the camps, which had emerged during a period of political terror, extrajudicial reprisals, and civil war.

The number of camps grew quickly: at the end of 1919 there were a total of 21 in the RSFSR; in the summer of 1920, the number had grown to 49; by November there were 84; in January 1921, the number had reached 107; and by November 1921 there were 122 camps in all.[4] In 1921 there were fifty-two provinces and regions in the Russian Federation, which meant an average of two camps for each province. In reality, these hastily established facilities were distributed unequally. Moscow and Moscow Province, for example, had a total of eight concentration camps.

The NKVD report for 1920 recorded four types of forced-labor camps under its authority: "(1) 'special designation'—the Andronev and Ivanov camps in Moscow for foreigners and other prominent prisoners, persons convicted before the end of the Civil War, and those serving long terms; (2) regular concentration camps; (3) prisoner-of-war camps; (4) one screening facility, Novopeskovskii in Moscow, which temporarily held prisoners before they were sent on to other camps."[5] In the relevant documents the terms "concentration camps" and "forced-labor camps" tend to be used synonymously to refer to the same facilities; these documents also contain the terms "forced-labor concentration camps" and "special designation concentration camps." Occasionally the term "concentration camps" refers to places of incarceration for a particular category of prisoners, hostages and captives, or to camps under the jurisdiction of the Cheka, which for the most part held citizens who had been arrested administratively, without judicial procedure, "just in case."

We do not have reliable information as to the total number of people imprisoned during the civil war years in Cheka–NKVD camps. The fragmentary data available show that in September 1921, 60,457 prisoners were held in 117 NKVD camps. Of these, 44.1 percent had been sentenced by the Cheka, 7.9 percent by other administrative agencies, 24.5 percent by people's courts, 8.7 percent by revolutionary tribunals, 11.6 percent by revolutionary military tribunals, and 3.2 percent by other courts (regimental or comrades' courts). According to the official statistics of the repressive bodies themselves, approximately 17 percent of prisoners served time for counterrevolutionary crimes. The largest group (30.3 percent) was made up of prisoners serving terms of up to five years; the others were serving from three months to three years.[6] In 1921 there were almost 50,000 prisoners in Cheka camps.[7]

As the camp system developed, the administrative structures became more refined. The NKVD Department of Forced Labor was reorganized in 1921 into the Chief Administration of Forced-Labor Camps, which had two sections—one for administrative affairs and the other for economic management. The overall number of central administrative personnel was forty-seven.

In 1922 three agencies were responsible for punitive policy in the Soviet state: (1) the People's Commissariat of Justice (NKIu), specifically its Central Department of Corrective Labor; (2) the State Political Administration (GPU), which had its own camps and prisons; (3) the People's Commissariat of Internal Affairs (NKVD), where this sphere of activity was managed by the Chief Administration of Forced Labor and the Chief Militia (*Glavmilitsiia*), which administered houses of arrest. It is interesting to note that these governmental structures viewed punitive policy not as a part of overall state policy but as one of their own internal functions. For example, the Statute on General Places of Incarceration in the RSFSR of November 15, 1920, developed by the People's Commissariat of Justice, explicitly specified that local punitive departments were responsible for "carrying out the principles underlying the punitive policy of the People's Commissariat of Justice."[8]

The places of incarceration under the People's Commissariat of Justice included prisons, which numbered 251 at the end of 1920; agricultural colonies and farms, whose number was increasing rapidly (in 1922 there were 32 colonies and 28 farms); as well as corrective institutions for juveniles and the chronically ill.[9] The People's Commissariat of Justice understandably wanted to retain the right to conduct its "own" punitive policy and considered it necessary to concentrate all penitentiary institutions under its administration. The NKIu maintained a very cautious attitude toward the camps. One of the draft resolutions of the Sovnarkom, proposed by the Commissariat of Justice, reads: "Incarceration in forced-labor camps is to be abolished as a form of punishment. All persons sentenced to deprivation of liberty by judicial institutions are to be kept in general and special places of incarceration under the jurisdiction of the NKIu."[10] Another document drafted at the beginning of 1922 by a special Central Executive Committee commission created to reexamine the institutions of the RSFSR stated: "The People's Commissariat of Internal Affairs (NKVD) is required immediately to begin turning over all its concentration camps to the People's Commissariat of Justice. . . . The People's Commissariat of Justice is instructed to integrate the camps into the overall system of places of incarceration for housing prisoners serving light sentences."[11]

But the camps were here to stay. The Fifth All-Russian Congress of Directors of Administrative Departments of Provincial Executive Committees in 1922 came out in favor of retaining and expanding them. In its discussion on long-term planning in the area of punitive policy, the congress approved of the policy of "basing punitive policy on forced-labor camps; the NKVD has a more powerful administrative system than the NKIu."[12]

In justifying their point of view, NKVD representatives gave the following argument:

> Over the past four years, the NKIu has not only been unable to improve the prison system that was in fairly good shape when it was turned over to them, but it has in fact seriously neglected it; for example, the district prisons have been practically completely dismantled.* Meanwhile, in less than three years the Chief Administration of Forced Labor has created a strong system of camps literally out of thin air, thereby freeing themselves from state support.[13]

The congress weighed the arguments of the NKVD representatives and came out in favor of transferring all places of deprivation of liberty to the People's Commissariat of Internal Affairs.

---

*In 1918, 115 small prisons were closed for economic reasons.

In our view, the differences in opinion between the two competing agencies—the Commissariats of Justice and Internal Affairs—in the area of punitive policy can be explained by the fact that at that time there were a significant number of so-called "bourgeois experts" in the NKIu, major specialists in the law, legal practitioners and scholars who, although they did adapt and adjust their views, nevertheless could not reconcile themselves to the illegal actions of the Bolshevik authorities. Meanwhile, many of the officials of the NKVD were professional revolutionaries for whom the elevation of terror to the level of official policy was a matter of principle.

On July 25, 1922, the Sovnarkom passed a resolution concentrating all places of incarceration under the sole administration of the NKVD. On October 12 of the same year, the NKVD and the NKIu worked out a joint agreement reorganizing and dividing their authorities. The NKVD Chief Administration of Forced Labor and the Central Department of Corrective Labor were disbanded, and their functions and subsidiary agencies were turned over to the new Chief Administration of Places of Incarceration under the NKVD. The NKIu retained the rights of prosecutorial oversight.[14]

The desperate state of the economy and the overall devastation and famine in the country made life in the camps unbearable. Physically healthy people became disabled within very short periods of time. At the end of 1921, NKVD officials noted "desperate conditions in the camps due to severe reductions in rations and increased mortality from emaciation and the epidemic diseases that have emerged under these conditions."[15]

The critical situation in the concentration camps was exacerbated by a lack of budgetary allocations for their support. Unable to run the camps, many provinces proposed closing them. One of the reasons for the crisis was the transfer of fiscal responsibility for their maintenance to local budgets in August 1922. The state budget continued to fund only fifteen places of incarceration that were considered to be of national importance. These included the largest isolation prisons, workhouses for juveniles, and prisons for people convicted of political crimes. Unwilling to overburden their already meager budgets, local authorities rejected all requests for material support from places of incarceration. In some cases, provincial executive committees passed resolutions refusing to accept prisoners from outside their borders.[16]

Unable to cope with the critical situation on its own, the NKVD applied to the Sovnarkom for assistance. "The entire network of places of incarceration," states a February 19, 1925, memorandum by A.G. Beloborodov, people's commissar of internal affairs, which was designed for approximately 73,000 prisoners, at present holds 100,924. Everyone's rations have to be cut in order to feed those 30,000 prisoners not accounted for in the supply plan. . . . As a result, thousands of prisoners are starving; unsanitary conditions in the camps have brought on the threat of epidemics, and escapes from places of incarceration cannot be prevented, because of the lack of personnel. The People's Commissariat of Internal Affairs of the RSFSR for the Chief Administration of Places of Incarceration considers the situation critical and requests that the central authorities provide immediate aid to local budgets to cover the needs of places of incarceration.[17]

During the first half of the 1920s, Soviet authorities issued various early-release orders and amnesties freeing thousands of prisoners from prisons and camps. In our view these "outbursts of humanitarianism" can be explained by the critical material conditions in the camps. In any case, this policy of "airing out the cells," as it was called by prison staff, was ineffective, since within a few days the prisons would fill up again with a new supply of prisoners.

NKVD places of incarceration were regulated by the Corrective-Labor Code of the RSFSR of October 16, 1924. Interestingly, camps are not included among the institutions listed in the code "for implementing social defense measures of a correctional nature."[18] The report of the Chief Administration of Places of Incarceration of the Republic, presented at the Eleventh Congress of Soviets, claims that by 1923 concentration camps had been completely eliminated or converted into general-profile places of incarceration.[19] But that is not quite accurate, for in fact two punitive systems continued to function in the country. Now, however, they were no longer under the authority of the NKIu and the NKVD, but had become a part of the NKVD and the State Political Administration and Combined State Political Administration (GPU–OGPU).

The GPU, which replaced the Cheka within the NKVD in February 1922, was transferred from the People's Commissariat of Internal Affairs in 1923 to the Sovnarkom. The GPU took with it the special, separate system of repression, which included GPU facilities such as internal prisons, isolation facilities, and special-designation concentration camps, such as the Solovki Island complex, which was established by a resolution of the Sovnarkom of the RSFSR on October 2, 1923.[20] This system was regulated by intra-agency acts; its activities were not subject to general legislation and were kept secret from the public. The Chief Censorship Administration issued a number of secret circulars, "On the Solovki Concentration Camps," "On Information Concerning the Work and Structure of the OGPU," and others, which banned the publication of information on the activities of the Political Administration. Thus "the castigating sword of the revolution" disappeared from the view of the public, both domestically and abroad. The absence of glasnost, on the one hand, allowed the GPU to decide human fates unilaterally and with impunity and, on the other, shielded the consciences of those who sang, with sincere enthusiasm:

> Darling, grieve no more
> that we are hungry.
> We were slaves before,
> But now we are free.

It was this very freedom of individual citizens who, for whatever reason, had earned the displeasure of the Party, the government, the regional Party secretary, or the chairman of the rural soviet that brought them to the attention of the GPU, which had been endowed with "the right of extrajudiciary reprisal, up to and including execution by shooting."

On August 10, 1922, the Central Executive Committee issued a decree granting a special commission under the NKVD the right to exile "persons implicated in counterrevolutionary actions" either abroad or to specified locations in the RSFSR for purposes of isolation, administratively, without arrest, for a term of up to three years. Administrative exiles were deprived of suffrage rights for the duration of their term and were kept under the supervision of local GPU officials.[21] On October 16 of the same year, a new VTsIK decree was added to this order, granting the additional right to the special NKVD commission on exile to imprison persons deemed to be a threat to society in forced-labor camps for terms of up to three years. This was to apply to recidivists and people active in anti-Soviet political parties.[22] On March 28, 1924, the Central Executive Committee approved the "Statute on the Rights of the OGPU Relating to Administrative Exile, Internal Exile, and Imprisonment in Concentration Camps." Such decisions were approved by a special three-person board of the OGPU. The collegium of the OGPU continued to conduct its own extrajudiciary activities parallel to the work of the Special Board.[23]

Practically anyone could fall under the millstones of this extrajudiciary repressive agency, and anyone who had served time "there" remained forever in the field of vision of the "all-seeing eye." "The conditions of political exile," reads a 1925 report by P.A. Krasikov, the prosecutor of the Supreme Court of the USSR,

> causes exiles to band tightly together; as a result, young people return to society more embittered and politically indoctrinated and thus better

prepared to oppose us. Therefore camp and exile have the effect of training and disciplining our enemies. The Special Board has to devote enormous amounts of time to so-called "reevaluation" cases involving "politicals" (i.e., political prisoners) whose terms have expired and who need to have new restrictions imposed on them. This is done to protect society, not because these people have committed any new crimes, but because their nature makes them likely to do so in the future. Thus, a special category of persons is emerging perfectly naturally, before the very eyes of the OGPU.

In spite of all the efforts of the Soviet authorities to treat political and criminal prisoners equally, at the beginning of the 1920s "politicals" still differed markedly in status from criminal convicts. The politicals formed collectives and staged long hunger strikes and suicides to defend their rights as political prisoners. One typical case was the campaign to close down the cruel camps in Kholmogory and Pertominsk, located on the shores of the Northern Dvina and the White Sea. Malaria was rampant in these camps, and there was no room for the anarchists and moderate socialists who had been brought there in 1922. The struggle to maintain human dignity and to ensure tolerable subsistence conditions continued in Solovki as well, where political prisoners began to arrive in the summer of 1923.

On December 19, 1923, one confrontation between prisoners and the camp administration ended in tragedy, with six political prisoners buried in a communal grave. Rumors of the Solovki shootings reached the world community and sparked mass protests among workers' organizations in a number of countries. In general, the Bolshevik authorities were not sensitive to public opinion at home or abroad, but this time they backed down. On June 10, 1925, the Sovnarkom of the USSR resolved "to discontinue incarceration of members of anti-Soviet parties (Right SRs, Left SRs, Mensheviks, and anarchists) in the Solovki Special Designation Concentration Camp."[24] The prisoners were transferred to OGPU facilities on the continent. The Soviet press hastened to publicize the closing of Solovki abroad, although in fact the concentration camp remained open. This incident gave the authorities a perfect pretext to make public statements proclaiming an improvement in law and order and an end to the reign of terror, and in general to expound the humanitarianism of the Bolshevik regime. M. Tomskii, the trade-union leader, even gave a public report to this effect to a workers' delegation from France and Belgium.

The political prisoners who had been transferred from Solovki to the mainland composed a special "Address" to the world proletariat, telling the truth about this "humane act." The fact was, only some of the political prisoners had been transferred, just three hundred who had been specifically recognized as "politicals" by the OGPU. The other prisoners, including workers who had been arrested for striking, members of workers' movements and organizations, peasants who had been involved in rebellions, religious believers, and others who did not have the status of political prisoners, remained in the camp under the same regimen as the criminal element. The prisoners who were transferred were given two hours to get their things together and then were forced to run all the way to the pier. No special consideration was given to the women and sick people among them. The ship's hold, packed to overflowing with people, the crowded train cars, the lack of sufficient water and food, the overwhelming stuffiness, the coarseness of the convoy guards—such were the conditions of the nine-day journey of the "politicals." And what was the end result? Some 100 people were taken to the Tobolsk hard-labor prison. Another group of about 200 prisoners was sent to Verkhne-Uralsk. This was essentially a new, far more cruel punishment. Conditions in Solovki, with its hard-won privileges, seemed almost like heaven to the moderate socialists by comparison with what the OGPU had prepared for them on the mainland.

Soviet hard-labor prisons differed from those of tsarist times in their specially selected administrative and supervisory staff, whose chief attribute was a feeling of visceral hatred toward the "Menshevik swine" and the "peddlers of Christ." It was as though the Red Army soldiers and the supervisors had been lying in wait for the right opportunity to inflict bloody reprisals. There could be no talk of privileges here.

The reasons socialists ended up in Bolshevik torture chambers and the paths that led them there are worth mentioning. Of the 126 political prisoners in the Tobolsk hard-labor prison, only 21 had been sentenced by a court. Only 1 of the 200 political prisoners in the Verkhne-Uralsk prison had been tried in court; the rest had been imprisoned by a GPU order not for any specific crimes or for armed struggle against Soviet authority, but simply because they had belonged, in some cases only in the past, and only passively, to socialist and anarchist parties. This earned them sentences in prisons and concentration camps and in four cases to execution, commuted to ten years in prison. Of the 126, 29 were sentenced in 1922, 53 in 1923, and the rest in 1924 and 1925, after the end of the Civil War.

The purpose of the Bolshevik policy of terror was to destroy any possibility of political opposition and intercept any attempts at dissidence. The leaders of the Communist Party, Tomskii in particular, were often heard to say, "Under the dictatorship of the proletariat, there can be two, three, or four parties, but only under the condition that one party will be in power and all others in prison."[25]

The "prison motif" was a prominent theme as well at the Fifteenth Congress of the Bolshevik Party (1927). A.I. Rykov, the head of the government, declared, "It is impossible to guarantee that the population of the prisons will not have to be increased somewhat in the near future."[26] Against whom were these threats directed? The Mensheviks and SRs were no longer a force to be reckoned with; there was no apparent threat to Bolshevik power, so who was to account for the increase in the prison population? This left members of the Bolshevik Party itself, comrades-in-arms in the recent revolutionary struggles and extrajudiciary reprisals. Imaginary and actual opposition was crushed with the enthusiasm and relentlessness inherent to the Bolsheviks. Arrest, prison, exile, and concentration camps were to become the primary arguments in political disputes.

In the fall of 1927, members of the United Opposition* circulated a leaflet to rank-and-file members of the Party that ended with the words: "Down with executions, down with the GPU, long live workers' democracy, long live freedom of speech, the press and assembly!"[27] But it was too late. The pattern of wanton repressions and denunciations had become an organic part not only of the Party but of the country as a whole.

Many Communists accepted the repressions as "completely justified revolutionary reprisals" conducted for the sake of the bright future. Dreams of this "bright future" became for the majority of citizens of Soviet Russia a kind of narcotic that helped them survive from day to day. There were always people in Russia, however, who wanted a better life now, without putting it off for later. A group of workers from the Putilov Plant in Leningrad issued a unanimous declaration at a conference on cooperatives on September 6, 1927: "What we need is butter, not socialism." Of the 411 workers present, only 135 were not Party members. The Leningrad branch of the OGPU reported that the workers were so infuriated by the poor supplies that, based on the harshness of the speeches and the unrestrained nature and number of riotous outbursts, the conference could easily be characterized as a phenomenon of an "exceptional nature."[28]

Economic conditions in the country deteriorated from one day to the next. The workers joked grimly: "They say that the letter 'm' has been abolished: there's no meat, no margarine, no manufactured goods,

---

*The United Opposition was formed in the summer of 1926 by G.E. Zinoviev and Leon Trotsky. It brought together several factions within the Party that opposed the Stalinist course the Party was taking. The United Opposition went down in defeat at the end of 1927.—Ed.

no milk, and there's no point in keeping the letter 'm' just for the sake of a single name: Mikoyan."* The slogan "to catch up and surpass" for many had long ago mutated into "to revive and survive."** Workers punned both openly and in spiteful whispers about what the revolution had brought: "To the worker—lectures; to the chief administration—salary; to the bosses' wives—treasure; to the peasants—HELL."† This innocent play on words retained its relevance in later years as well, with the last phrase—"Revolution gave the peasants HELL"— sounding particularly apt.

A contemporary, the trade-union activist B.G. Kozelev, wrote in his diary during the summer of 1928:

> The situation in the country is tense. Panic has set in a number of areas; people are hoarding bread and other provisions, even soap and sugar. In the villages there are open expressions of discontent, even unrest. Red Army soldiers are sending bread back to the countryside. Workers, back from leave in the countryside, are restless and complain openly about the tyranny of the authorities. In Nikolaev some peasants brought a petition to the Marti Plant and were arrested. There wasn't a single kulak among those arrested. The policy of "war communism"‡ in our time will lead to no good. . . .
>
> In Kabarda the peasants revolted and marched over to the executive committee. They were shot at and returned fire, and six peasants were killed. In Rostov a number of individual Red Army unit commanders— most of them peasants—were disarmed and arrested.
>
> Peasants write letters from the countryside to Red Army soldiers in the cities, complaining about confiscations and oppression. "Take up your rifle, son, and go forth to defend your father and mother." Fifty percent of such letters are intercepted.[29]

---

*"*Miasa net, masla net, manufaktury net, myla net*": no meat, no butter, no manufactured goods, no soap.—Trans. (From 1926 through 1938 Mikoyan occupied, one after the other, the posts of People's Commissar of Foreign and Domestic Trade, People's Commissar of Supplies, and People's Commissar of the Food Industry.—G.I.)

**"*Dognat' i peregnat'*": to catch up and overtake; "*dozhit' i perezhit'*": to live through it and survive.

† "*Rabochemu dala DOKLAD, glavkam dala OKLAD, a zhenam ikh dala KLAD, a krest'ianstvu dala AD.*"

‡War Communism was a term used to define the Soviet state's economic program during the Civil War, roughly from mid-1918 to March 1921. Requisitioning of the peasantry's farm products, a ban on free trade, nationalization of most industrial establishments, and Party–state control over the production and distribution of goods characterized the increasingly unpopular policy. Many historians stress the similarities between War Communism and the Stalin Revolution launched in 1928.—Ed.

So began a new phase of civil war, a protracted, undeclared war of the Party and state against their own civilian population. The dead in this war were buried secretly, and their loved ones were not permitted to mourn them. The prisoners of war were sent to the Gulag.

On March 26, 1928, the All-Russian Central Executive Committee and the Sovnarkom of the RSFSR adopted a resolution, "On Punitive Policy and the State of Places of Incarceration." The document noted a number of problems and serious errors in the activity of the courts and in the orientation of the punitive system. In particular it noted that "privileges granted to class aliens and socially dangerous elements are insufficiently justified." The response of the government of the Russian Republic was to demand "severe measures of repression exclusively against class enemies and déclassé professional criminals."[30]

On November 6, 1929, the Central Executive Committee and Sovnarkom of the USSR amended the "Basic Principles of Criminal Legislation of the Union of SSR and the Union Republics" adopted in 1924. Article 13 of this document reads, in part: "Social protection measures of a judicial-correctional nature are: . . . (b) deprivation of liberty in corrective-labor camps in remote locations in the USSR"; and Article 18 added, "for a term of three to ten years."[31] This was the first mention in Soviet legislation of the term "corrective-labor camp" (*ispravitel'no-trudovoi lager'*: ITL), referring to a new type of criminal punishment, which was to change the lives of millions of completely innocent Soviet citizens.

Corrective-labor camps grew and became more powerful, but there was no official document regulating their activity until April 7, 1930, when the Sovnarkom of the USSR adopted the "Statute on Corrective-Labor Camps."[32] This document opened one of the most tragic pages in the history of the penitentiary policy of the Russian state. The authorities were presented with a "legal" instrument for exercising political and economic coercion against society—the Gulag.

People sentenced by courts to deprivation of freedom for terms of no less than three years, as well as those convicted by the collegium or the Special Commission of the OGPU, were sent to corrective-labor camps. The camps were under the administration of the OGPU, which managed their operation on the basis of intra-agency regulations. The OGPU was granted unlimited power over the fates of prisoners, who, once they entered its sphere of activity, were in effect excluded from the country's legal system as a whole.

The punitive system of the NKVD continued to operate alongside the OGPU camps. This system included the so-called "general places of incarceration"—prisons, corrective-labor colonies, transit points, and so forth. After the abolition, on December 15, 1930, of the People's Commissariats of Internal Affairs of the Union Republics, these places of incarceration were turned over to the People's Commissariats of Justice of the Union Republics. The People's Commissariat of Justice was granted authority "for the overall administration of corrective-labor policy and enforcement of corrective-labor legislation."[33] What legislation does this refer to? The "Statute on Corrective-Labor Camps"? No, these camps existed for "internal use." They had absolutely nothing to do with the proclaimed principles of legality and humanism. These principles are demonstrated by a different document—the Corrective-Labor Code of 1924. But it, too, was outdated. The policy of intensified class struggle was reflected in the new Corrective-Labor Code of the RSFSR, approved on August 1, 1933. The primary objective of the criminal policy of the proletariat [not the state—G.I.] during the transition from capitalism to communism was defined by the code as "the defense of the dictatorship of the proletariat and socialist construction from threats by alien class elements and offenses committed both by déclassé elements and unstable elements among the workers."[34] This document contained no mention of camps, ten-year prison sentences, or special powers granted to the OGPU. Its primary concerns were workers' colonies and prison sentences of under three years.

The Corrective-Labor Code was adopted during a period when the repressions eased slightly. Historians attribute this to a secret instruction, signed on May 8, 1933, by Stalin and Viacheslav Molotov. This circular, entitled "Instruction to All Soviet and Party Workers and to All Organs of the OGPU, the Court, and Prosecutors," stated,

> The Central Committee and the Sovnarkom believe that, at this time, given our successes in the countryside, there is no longer a need for mass repressions, which affect, as we all know, not only kulaks but also individual peasant farmers and some kolkhoz members as well.
> It is true that a number of oblasts continue to demand mass evacuations from the countryside and severe forms of repression. The Central Committee and the Sovnarkom have received requests for the immediate evacuation of about one hundred thousand families from regions and oblasts. The Central Committee and the Sovnarkom have information clearly showing that our workers continue to conduct unwarranted mass arrests in the countryside. Arrests are carried out by chairmen and members of the boards of collective farms, by chairmen of village soviets and secretaries of party cells, by district and regional representatives. Everyone who feels like it, including people who, strictly speaking, have no right to do so, is out arresting people. So it is not surprising that, given

this uncontrolled wave of arrests by members of the OGPU, especially the militia, people tend to lose their sense of measure and make arrests that are completely unjustified, following a rule of "arrest first, and then figure it out, then worry about the details."[35]

Stalin's criticism of "completely unjustified arrests" temporarily eased the wave of repressions, and the number of prisoners decreased sharply, but only for a very brief time.

On July 10, 1934, the Central Executive Committee passed a resolution creating an All-Union People's Commissariat of Internal Affairs (NKVD). The OGPU became part of the new commissariat at the level of a Chief Administration. The NKVD also included the Chief Administration of State Security (GUGB), the Chief Administration of the Workers' and Peasants' Militia, the Chief Administration of Border and Internal Guards, the Chief Administration of Corrective-Labor Camps and Labor Colonies, the Chief Administration of Fire Protection, the Department of Acts of Civil Status, and the Office of Administrative and Economic Management. Similar people's commissariats of internal affairs were created in the union republics and NKVD administrations in the autonomous republics and oblasts. The RSFSR had an authorized institution of the NKVD.[36] On September 17, the convoy guard troops were transferred to the authority of the NKVD; on October 27, corrective-labor facilities, which had earlier been a part of the NKIu system, also came under the NKVD. A Department of Places of Incarceration was created to manage them; this department was part of the Chief Administration of Corrective-Labor Camps, Labor Colonies, and Places of Incarceration under the NKVD of the USSR. Although the name of this central branch administration underwent numerous changes, it always retained its initial acronym: GULAG. These five letters were to become an ominous symbol of life on the brink of death, a symbol of lawlessness, convict labor, and human helplessness against tyranny. They gave a name to an entire country of camps and colonies populated by millions of Soviet people living and working there against their will.

Many of these people ended up in the Gulag by decision of the Special Board. This extrajudicial body was formed in the NKVD by order of the TsIK and the Sovnarkom of the USSR on November 5, 1934, and operated until September 1953. A report sent at the end of 1953 to N.S. Khrushchev, secretary of the Central Committee of the Communist Party of the Soviet Union, and signed by Minister of Internal Affairs S.N. Kruglov and General Prosecutor R.A. Rudenko, states that during the years of its existence the Special Board convicted 442,531 people, sentencing 10,101 of them to death; 360,921 to deprivation of liberty; 67,539 to exile and expulsion; and 3,970 to other forms of punishment (time spent under guard, exile abroad, forced medical treatment). The document also provided a detailed breakdown of the numbers of convictions by year.[37] Although these numbers were later to appear repeatedly in other official documents and at the end of the 1980s and the beginning of the 1990s were partially published and released for scholarly use,[38] there are grounds for doubting their reliability. Reference to other sources supports the conclusion that these figures are seriously underestimated. For example, the report states that in 1944 the Special Board convicted 10,611 people. But an analysis of forty-six memoranda sent by Lavrentii Beria to Stalin in 1944 reporting the dates of the meetings of the Special Board, the number of cases considered, and the overall number of persons convicted, including how many were sentenced to execution by shooting and how many to various terms of imprisonment, indicates that in 1944 the Special Board convicted not 10,611 people but 27,456.[39] And this information may itself be incomplete. Analysis of data from other years gives a similar picture. This disparity shows that the various official totals and MVD reports must be approached critically and, when possible, carefully cross-referenced against different kinds of sources. It should also be kept in mind that, after the division of the people's commissariats in 1943, an independent Special Board was formed under the People's Commissariat of State Security (NKGB), which acted independently from the NKVD Special Board (OSO).

The Special Board was chaired by the people's commissar himself, and its members were his closest aides and deputies. The prosecutor was not a member, but his presence at meetings was considered obligatory. Occasionally he even tried to intervene in the work of this extrajudiciary body. For example, on June 10, 1939, A. Vyshinskii felt it necessary to send a note to Comrade Stalin at the Central Committee of the Communist Party and Comrade Molotov at the Sovnarkom, reporting: "Recently the Special Board under the People's Commissariat of Internal Affairs of the USSR has been considering a large number of cases—between 200 and 300 at each meeting. Under these conditions it is possible that some verdicts may be erroneous." The prosecutor proposed "establishing a more frequent meeting schedule for the Special Board, allowing it to consider fewer cases at each meeting."[40] The head of the government, Molotov, had an interesting reaction to this note; he asked the all-powerful people's commis-

sar for advice: "Com. Beria. What do you recommend?"[41] It turned
out that 200 to 300 people was by no means the upper limit; in later
years the Special Board managed to convict 789, 872, even 980 people
at a single meeting.[42]

Initially the power of the Special Board was somewhat limited: it
had the right administratively, that is, without a court or an investigation, to exile and expel and to impose sentences in corrective-labor
camps of up to five years.[43] Gradually the restrictions were removed,
and by the beginning of the 1940s the Special Board had the right not
only to impose sentences of twenty-five years in prison but also to sentence people to be shot.

The widespread practice of political repression gave rise to three-
person and two-person bodies known as "troikas" and "dvoikas." Their
official mandate was the May 27, 1935, order of G.G. Iagoda, People's
Commissar of Internal Affairs, along with a series of NKVD orders issued by N.I. Ezhov on July 30, August 11, and September 20, 1937.
Some of these intra-agency normative acts had the written sanction of
Stalin, Molotov, L.M. Kaganovich, and S.V. Kosior.[44] At the beginning
of August 1937, a telegram signed by Stalin arrived in local state security offices, reporting that "special troikas are being established in the
oblast branches of the NKVD for deciding cases against Trotskyites,
spies, saboteurs, and major criminal offenders."[45]

Whereas the authorities of the "troikas" of 1935 were limited to the
right to impose exile and imprisonment in camps for terms of under
five years, the "special troikas" of 1937 were granted the right to decide
cases of category 1, that is, those subject to the death penalty, and category 2, that is, those warranting ten-year prison or camp sentences.
The "troikas" consisted of a chairman (the head of the region or oblast
NKVD administration) and two members. At the oblast level the "troika"
included the first secretary of the oblast Party committee and the chairman of the oblast executive committee. This composition of the
extrajudiciary bodies ensured full compliance at the local level with
orders from higher officials. By a special order from A. Vyshinskii, prosecutors were not involved in the "troikas." The former Chekist M.P.
Shreider, who occupied leadership positions in the NKVD system
through 1938, recalls the procedures followed in the "troikas": an
agenda book, or so-called "album," was compiled, with each page listing the given name, patronymic, family name, and date of birth of a
defendant, along with the "crime" he committed. Then the head of
the oblast administration of the NKVD would write a large letter "R,"
which meant "execution by shooting" (*rasstrel*), in red pencil on each

page and sign it. The sentence was carried out that same evening or night. The pages of the album were usually signed on the next day by the first secretary of the oblast Party committee and the chairman of the oblast executive committee.[46] This procedure, called "conviction by album," was widespread in Chekist practice during 1937–38. Another common practice was "conviction by list," which further streamlined the repression process. Beginning approximately in the middle of 1937, the oblast and regional NKVD administrative offices began to receive official quotas for a specific number of people to be arrested and shot. In the fall of 1937, for example, Ivanovo Oblast received a quota of 1,500. This meant that the local "troika"—though actually this would be the head of the oblast NKVD administration—was given the right to shoot 1,500 people at his own discretion, without trial or investigation. Furthermore, local offices were encouraged by the central Party organs to overfulfill their plans for neutralizing enemies of the people.

The Chekists had learned already in 1936 that the number of arrests and executions could be established in advance; this became clear when Ezhov, at one of his first meetings with leaders of local NKVD offices, began giving approximate numbers of the presumed enemies of the people for each individual region and oblast who were to be arrested and destroyed. At the time this approach genuinely shocked the officials present. E.P. Salyn, chief of the NKVD administration for Omsk Oblast, tried to raise an objection to the people's commissar, who seemed to have lost his senses: "I declare with full accountability," Salyn uttered calmly and confidently, "that there are not that many enemies of the people and Trotskyites in Omsk Oblast. And in general I consider it outrageous to establish in advance the number of people to be arrested and shot." The aging Chekist was not allowed to finish his speech. "Here he is, right here in this room, the first enemy!" cried Ezhov and then and there, in front of everyone, ordered the commandant to arrest Salyn.[47] It is not surprising that no one else attempted to raise any objections to the people's commissar. The participants at the meeting returned to their own regions completely at a loss. But the situation changed rapidly, the terror expanded, and before long nothing surprised people, not quotas issued from above for death sentences, or the torture of people under arrest, or the suicides of Party comrades. State security officials quickly figured out how to seek out and neutralize "enemies of the people," even where they had never existed. If there were not enough Trotskyites, spies, and saboteurs, then aged priests and widowed mothers with large families would serve their purpose. The systematic mass destruction and terrorization of particular groups and segments of the population deemed unsuitable was striking in its simplicity and even in its primitive nature, especially in the provinces.

For example, the campaign to destroy the clergy can be retraced by examining the materials of one typical case among the many thousand that were investigated.[48] During the second half of September 1937, officials of the Belkov district branch of the NKVD administration for Riazan Oblast arrested fifteen rural priests. There was no pretext and no formal grounds for the arrest beyond their identity as members of the clergy. The investigation was conducted by the branch chief himself, Second Lieutenant of State Security V. Chuev. Evidently he was still fairly inexperienced; the protocols of the interrogations of the priests are all exactly alike, like peas in a pod. Each one contains the very same questions and practically the same answers:

> *Question:* "You are accused of being an active member of a counterrevolutionary terrorist-insurgent organization. Do you admit your guilt?"
> *Answer:* "No, I do not."
>
> *Question:* "The inquest has precise and irrefutable evidence proving that you have been an active member of a counterrevolutionary terrorist-insurgent organization. Why are you telling lies and concealing this from the inquest?"
> *Answer:* "I have not been a member of any counterrevolutionary organization, and I have been telling nothing but the truth," and so forth in the same spirit.

In spite of the efforts of the investigators, the evidence and testimony from witnesses was clearly insufficient to justify a conviction. After all, when the local Chekists dreamed up this organization to please the higher authorities, they claimed that its goal was to "overthrow Soviet power by means of armed insurrection." Then, in order to lend substance and weight to the mythical organization, while at the same time eradicating religion once and for all from Riazan, they arrested twelve more people, among them the seventy-one-year-old A.A. Pravdoliubov, a much-esteemed Orthodox priest in Kasimovo, and five women, active defenders of the Orthodox faith. Not surprisingly, the arrest took place on November 6, on the eve of the twentieth anniversary of the October Revolution.

The new arrests were also of no use to the investigators, since all the defendants categorically denied their guilt. The young security officer V. Chuev had to build the guilty verdict—verdict number 896—solely out of his own imagination, patching together bits of vague testimony by witnesses. The evidence cited in the case against the priests included the following facts:

> On July 20 of this year, Pravdoliubov A.A., in a conversation with Dinariev, said, referring to counterrevolutionary activities:
> "I have reason to oppose Soviet power; that reason has to do with my children.* If my health permits, I will establish the groundwork for the future struggle against Soviet power among the citizens of Kasimovo by organizing cadres from among former tradespeople, craftsmen, and so on. I will use my connections in the clergy to recruit young people to the cause, and with these cadres we can expect action."

Here is another example of an "incriminating fact":

> In March of this year, V.F. Krupin, in his home, in the presence of A.A. Kudriavtsev and F.P. Volkov, expressed dissatisfaction with Soviet power, saying: "Look where Soviet power has brought us; we're walking around without boots; they're not even giving us enough bread any more. But soon our sufferings will come to an end. Spring will come and along with it a change in power. Then we will show these Communists a thing or two."

On the basis of these and other similar "facts," Second Lieutenant of State Security V. Chuev concluded, "Participants in the counterrevolutionary organization planted defeatist sentiments among the population, spread all kinds of rumors, and expressed terrorist views." During the investigation, which was marked by the most flagrant violations of all procedural norms and constitutional guarantees, five of the twenty-seven defendants confessed, while the others stood firm, categorically denying their guilt, which, by the way, did not prevent Chuev from considering them to be "completely incriminated." At the end of his passionate concluding speech the investigator was forced to add a postscript: "There is no material proof in this case." But none was needed. On December 6, 1937, the Riazan Oblast NKVD administration "troika" found all the citizens listed in the indictment guilty. Four women among the defendants, whose names had hardly even been mentioned, were sentenced to ten years in the camps, while the rest received the "supreme measure": execution by shooting. The Riazan priests were shot on December 23, 1937.

---

*Three of A.A. Pravdoliubov's sons had been convicted of counterrevolutionary activity and were in exile; the Pravdoliubov family had twelve children in all, three of whom had died in childhood.

Case No. 896 found its way into the hands of the public prosecutor nearly twenty years later. On March 15, 1956, having heard the appeal of the widow of the executed priest A.M. Tuberovskii, Colonel of Justice Kucheriavyi arrived at an unambiguous conclusion:

> This case contains no objective data indicating the existence of an anti-Soviet insurgency organization on the territory of Belkov District in 1937 or implicating the persons brought to trial in this case in any such organization or in any anti-Soviet activity. The confessions of four of the accused, in themselves completely vague and not supported by any objective data, clearly cannot serve as a basis for convicting twenty-seven people of counterrevolutionary activity.[49]

Bloody extrajudiciary reprisals, like the one in that out-of-the way corner of Prioksk Region, were taking place throughout the whole country. The criminal activity of the "dvoikas" and "troikas" continued for over a year. On November 26, 1938, Beria, the new chief of the NKVD, on instructions from the higher Party leadership, signed an order abolishing them.

Under the state's harsh policies against its own people, even the courts were conducting reprisals rather than judicial proceedings. The Military Collegium of the Supreme Court of the USSR, consisting of three brigade military lawyers (the regular members Dmitriev and Marchenko and the chairman Romanychev), managed to decide in the course of a single day, October 17, 1938, eleven cases against leading officials of Mtsensk District of Orlov Oblast. Each case took fifteen minutes, and all eleven officials were shot that same day. From the point of view of criminal law, the cases were groundless. They were thrown together based on excerpts and copies of investigation protocols, in many instances not witnessed or countersigned, and many of the signatures were forged. All the defendants retracted their testimony, and there were no cross-examinations, although protocols of such confrontations were appended.

In each of these cases, instead of the acquittal that was warranted, the Military Collegium sentenced the defendant to be shot. Those executed included First District Party Secretary Litvishkov; District Executive Committee Chairman Shumskii; Agarkov, the director of the industrial complex; Zorin, the director of a confectionery factory; and two more members of the district soviet, two members of the district Party committee, and other "leading" figures of Mtsensk, a place forsaken by God but not by the NKVD.

The courts decided other "cases" as well. On January 28, 1938, D.A.

Bulatov, secretary of the Omsk Oblast Party Committee, was arrested without the sanction of the prosecutor's office. The preliminary investigation lasted three years, during which he steadfastly and categorically denied his guilt. On June 17, 1940, Bulatov's case was sent back by the Military Collegium of the Supreme Court for further investigation. In spite of the fact that no new materials relevant to the case came to light during the investigation, a guilty verdict was reached and approved by B. Kobulov, and on October 17, 1941, Bulatov was shot. At the end of the war the NKVD gave his widow, A.I. Bulatova, an official document stating that her husband had been sent to the Khabarovsk region to serve a sentence of ten years without right of correspondence and had died there of a heart attack on April 13, 1944. Any number of similar examples could be quoted, and they all confirm the accuracy of Solzhenitsyn's remark that "violence does not and cannot survive in isolation: it is invariably interwoven with lies."[50]

In 1954, analyzing the repressive practices of those years, the military prosecutor of the Moscow military district, Colonel of Justice Ryzhikov, wrote:

> A significant share of the responsibility or outright complicity in creating the antagonistic and careerist atmosphere among individual officials in the branches of the Ministry of Internal Affairs belongs to officials of the chief military prosecutor's office and the Military Collegium. Military prosecutors would sign off on any falsification or arbitrary decision. They participated in investigations, sanctioned arrests, and backed up the prosecution in trials. Often, knowing full well that they were trying people either without the slightest evidence or based on obviously dubious testimony given by planted witnesses, they covered up for tyranny and lawlessness anyway, enabling it to flourish.

It is no secret today who was behind the mass repressions. There were plenty of people to carry them out; periodically they were replaced, with yesterday's executioners becoming today's victims, and the victims becoming executioners. The only one who remained at his post for the duration, the one at the center of it all, was Stalin. The changes in the tone of Stalin's directives as his own personal power increased make for interesting reading. Here are a few encoded telegrams from the Archive of the President of the Russian Federation, all of them signed by Stalin himself (frequently with two letters, "St"). One of them was sent to S.V. Kosior and V.Ia. Chubar in Kharkov on January 2, 1930:

> When is the trial for Efremov and the others scheduled? We believe that the trial should address not only the inflammatory and terrorist acts of

the defendants but also their medical plots to murder officials. There's no point in concealing the sins of our enemies from the workers. Furthermore, let so-called 'Europe' know that the repressions against counterrevolutionary medical personnel who are trying to poison and murder their Communist patients are completely 'justified' and pale before the criminal activity of these counterrevolutionary scoundrels. We request that you coordinate your trial strategy with Moscow.[51]

As we can see, this telegram gives a sense of recommendation, or request, and even an apparent attempt by the author to justify himself.

The tone is completely different in another encoded telegram sent by Stalin to regional, oblast, and republic central committees on June 11, 1937, at 4:50 P.M.:

In connection with the ongoing trial of the spies and saboteurs Tukhachevskii, Iakir, Uborevich, and others, the Central Committee recommends that you organize rallies of workers and, where possible, peasants, as well as demonstrations in Red Army divisions, and issue a resolution supporting the supreme measure of repression. The trial should be completed tonight. The sentence will be reported in the press tomorrow, that is, June 12.[52]

Another telegram, sent to Andreev in Saratov on July 28, 1937, sounds downright businesslike, even routine: "The Central Committee concurs with your proposals to bring to trial and execute former machine-tractor station workers."[53] And one more document, also an encrypted telegram sent to Korotchenkov at the Smolensk Oblast Party Committee on August 27, 1937: "I advise you to sentence the saboteurs of Andreevsk District to execution by shooting and to publish the sentence in the local press. Secretary of the Central Committee Stalin."[54] As we can see, this is no longer a recommendation but actually an order given in the first person.

None of these documents (and there are quite a few such encrypted telegrams) contains the slightest attempt to observe the rights and guarantees declared by the Constitution of 1936 or even a hint of adherence to legal procedure.

In our view, it would be unjust to try to find the source of tyranny among the rank-and-file or even leading officials of the judicial-repressive apparatus, as was done during the period of mass rehabilitations. As a rule, these officials acted in full compliance with instructions and directives that originated with the highest Party and governmental agencies and officials. It would also be wrong, however, to see them as simply robots with no will of their own. Each individual judge and prosecutor, investigator, and policeman contributed in his own way to the wave of tyranny.

Under these conditions, a state of continual tension and terror became part of everyday life. Not only did people "tremble at the sight of the diamond shapes and the scarlet color of the collar tabs of the officers' uniforms," they also began to fear their own friends, relatives, and acquaintances, who, against their own will, could bring disaster and misery down upon their heads. The universal terror, sometimes not even experienced on a conscious level, gave rise to widespread suspicion and mistrust. S.N. Kruglov, who at that time headed the personnel department of the people's commissariat, spoke at the Second Party Conference of the NKVD of the USSR in March 1940. In his speech he noted that Soviet citizens had begun to avoid the personnel department: "After someone had been summoned into the office, his acquaintances immediately began to shun him; who knows, maybe they do have something against him if they called him in like that."[55]

The arbitrariness in the legal system that had become the norm in the country as a whole continued in the camps as well. Legislation then in effect excluded the Gulag from its sphere of influence. Everything was turned over to the NKVD. The regulatory basis for the operation of the camps was the Temporary Instruction of 1939 on the Regimen for Prisoners in Corrective-Labor Camps of the NKVD of the USSR. A similar instruction in 1940 established the regimen for prisoners in NKVD colonies. For any camp administrator, an order from the People's Commissariat of Internal Affairs had supreme legal force. Convincing evidence of the real balance of power among the various agencies can be found in an NKVD order of April 23, 1940, which reported that prisoners convicted by courts or military tribunals whose cases were under review were to be released by the administrators of their places of incarceration only upon receipt of an order from the First Special Section of the NKVD. That meant that even an order from the plenum of the Supreme Court of the USSR was invalid without a corresponding order from the First Special Section. Such orders were scrupulously observed in the camps. One prisoner, for example, V.I. Ioskevich, was held in the Gulag until 1952, in spite of a court order authorizing his release in October 1940. Ioskevich was held prisoner for an additional twelve years without any legal grounds because, for reasons that are unclear, the necessary order from the First Special Section did not reach the camp. The NKVD order of April 23, 1940, was invalidated and repealed only in 1949.

At the end of the 1930s, a new type of political structure appeared in the Gulag administration, one that was unique in world penitentiary practice. On September 26, 1937, the Central Committee of the Communist Party passed a special resolution ordering that,

> In the interests of enhancing the leadership of Party organizations in NKVD camps and improving the management of construction and the quality of political work among managerial and regular personnel, the guards, and contract construction crews in camps, a Political Section shall be established in the Chief Camp Administration of the NKVD of the USSR, to be charged with the management of camps and construction projects by Party organizations.

On September 15, 1939, the Orgburo* of the Central Committee of the Communist Party approved a standard regulation concerning the Political Section of the Chief Administration of the NKVD of the USSR. In December the "Instruction on the Work of Political Sections in the Gulag" was approved.[56]

At the end of the 1930s the Party began to base its activities on joint resolutions of the Central Committee and the Sovnarkom regulating punitive policy. Particularly noteworthy among the joint documents that played a significant role in the practice of repressions are the 1938 resolutions "On Arrests, Prosecutorial Oversight, and the Conduct of Investigations" (November 17), "On Procedures for Coordinating Arrests" (December 1), and a number of others. The joint soviet-Party directives of this period were aimed not at easing punitive policies, as it may seem at first glance, but rather at establishing regular procedures; they manifest a clear tendency to impart the external appearance of legality to repressive policy. It is well known, for example, that active torture and physical abuse of prisoners began in NKVD torture chambers in the summer of 1937. Such practices were sanctioned by official statements by Ezhov and Stalin condemning the conduct of investigations "in white gloves" and ordering more intensive work aimed at rooting out enemies of the people, and so forth. At the local level, this was interpreted as a direct instruction to use torture and to increase the severity of the regimen in prisons and camps. The Party and soviet organizations, for their part, issued no official resolutions on the subject. It was not until January 10, 1939, that the offices of the NKVD received an official instruction on the use of methods of physical coercion "in dealing with spies,

---

*A subcommittee of the Communist Party's Central Committee, the Organizational Bureau (Orgburo) was created in January 1919. Responsible for Party personnel and for dealing with administrative problems, the Orgburo facilitated Stalin's consolidation of power.—Ed.

saboteurs, terrorists, and other active enemies of the Soviet people exposed during investigations who stubbornly refuse to give the names of their accomplices or to testify about their own criminal activities." It was this order of the Central Committee of the Communist Party that was to be cited by the organs of state security as the legal justification for the use of torture.[57]

The higher Party leadership was also directly involved in decision making on all issues having to do with the "supreme measure" of punishment. Officially, death sentences, which were imposed by military tribunals and local courts, legally took effect upon confirmation by the Supreme Court of the Soviet Union. In practice, decisions of the higher court depended on the will of the Central Committee of the Communist Party. In a memorandum addressed to Stalin, Beria reported on the existing procedures for confirming a death sentence:

> Decisions of the Supreme Court of the USSR in essence are not final, since they are reviewed by a commission of the Politburo of the Central Committee of the Communist Party, which also presents its conclusions to the Central Committee of the Communist Party for approval; only after this is a final decision made in the case, which is then sent back to the Supreme Court and from there proceeds to the NKVD of the USSR for implementation.[58]

Localities declared to be under martial law were an exception to this procedure; they followed the edict of the Presidium of the Supreme Soviet of June 20, 1941, which granted front-line military councils the right to approve and immediately carry out the death sentence.

These procedures led to the accumulation in local NKVD facilities of large numbers of prisoners who had been sentenced to death and were awaiting execution, sometimes for months on end. For example, in November 1941, 796 such prisoners were being held in prisons in the North Ossetia Autonomous Soviet Socialist Republic; 467 in Khabarovsk Region; 419 in Sverdlovsk Oblast, and so forth. Overall, as of November 15, 1941, 10,645 prisoners were being detained in NKVD prisons awaiting confirmation of their death sentences. People's Commissar of Internal Affairs Beria worked to expedite the procedures for implementing the death penalty. He was in a hurry—it was not enough for him that thousands of his fellow citizens were dying every day on the fields of battle. On November 15, 1941, Beria, who was at the time in Ufa, reported to Stalin:

Given the current wartime conditions, the NKVD considers it advisable:

1. to allow the NKVD of the USSR to carry out the sentences of district military tribunals and republic, regional, and oblast courts for all prisoners sentenced to the supreme measure of punishment who are currently being held in prisons awaiting confirmation of their sentences by higher courts;
2. to grant to the Special Board of the NKVD of the USSR, with the participation of the prosecutor of the Union of SSR, the right to carry out all appropriate forms of punishment, including death by shooting, with respect to cases originating with the NKVD that involve counterrevolutionary crimes and especially dangerous crimes against government procedures of the USSR. The decision of the Special Board is to be considered final.[59]

As we well know, Stalin agreed with the people's commissar and granted his request.

After the terror of 1937–38, the number of executions sharply decreased. The primary form of punishment was a ten-year term of imprisonment in a corrective-labor camp. Prisoners streamed in a never-ending, powerful current into the Gulag. Official statistics show, for example, that over a ten-day period in November 1940, 59,493 persons were removed from prisons in the USSR and sent to camps and colonies.[60] If we assume that these were not some special "ten days that shook the world" but a typical ten-day period, it is easy to calculate the annual replenishment of the Gulag population. By the beginning of the war, official sources set the number of prisoners in camps and colonies at 2.3 million. NKVD prisons, as of January 1, 1941, held 470,693 inmates.[61]

In 1940 the Gulag system included 53 camps with thousands of branches and facilities; 425 colonies, including industrial, agricultural, and other associated colonies; along with 50 colonies for juveniles and 90 "children's homes."[62] The Gulag system did not include prisons, which were filled to nearly double their official capacity, and the over 2,000 special commandants' centers (spetskomendatury), which controlled the life and liberty of millions of people being held in labor colonies, special settlements, and other kinds of settlements all over the country. These categories of prisoners were managed by the prison administration and the Special Settlements Section of the NKVD.

Although over the years of the Gulag's existence tens of millions of citizens were directly or indirectly drawn into its orbit, the fact is, the Soviet public had only the vaguest notion of the true scale and purpose of the Gulag system. The Soviet citizen was accustomed to accept as true only what appeared in print or was broadcast over the radio. As we know, the Gulag was not discussed in print or aloud. Ordinary people instinctively avoided the topic of the camps—"just keeping out of trouble"—and did not discuss it even behind closed doors. As for the government elite, they considered the maintenance of secrecy to be one of their highest priorities. The totalitarian regime did not conceal the camps, colonies, and prisons as such—every country has a penitentiary system of some kind—and even the practice of forced labor (as it was known at the beginning of the 1930s) was not a secret. What Stalin's regime concealed was one of its most valuable institutions. The Gulag allowed the higher authorities to institute a wide variety of extraordinary measures in society, to hold the people in blind submission and slavish obedience, and to destroy the rare sprouts of dissidence and freethinking before they had a chance to bloom. The Gulag facilitated an imperial policy based on the principle of "divide and conquer," helped to regulate consumption, and eased social tensions. Finally, the Gulag served as a convenient instrument for revenge that allowed the authorities to settle scores with individuals as well as with entire peoples.

But how did they manage to keep it all secret, considering the millions of people whose lives were affected? There was a whole array of methods: from requiring people to sign statements promising not to talk, to the physical elimination of witnesses. On the eve of the war the NKVD leadership experimented with another method of preventing the possible spread of secrets: depriving former Gulag prisoners of the possibility of returning to society, to their former normal life and work. On April 30, 1941, two draft documents came before the Central Committee of the Communist Party and the Sovnarkom of the USSR— meaning Stalin and Molotov. One was the "Edict of the Presidium of the Supreme Soviet of the USSR on an Additional Measure of Punishment: Twenty-Year Exile," and the other, "Resolution of the Central Committee of the Communist Party and the Sovnarkom of the USSR 'On the Introduction of an Additional Measure of Punishment, to Be Imposed by the Special Board of the NKVD and Judicial Organs: Twenty-Year Exile.'" The document resolved the following:

> 1. The Special Commission under the NKVD of the USSR shall be granted the right:
>   a. for all persons sentenced by the Special Commission to imprisonment in corrective-labor camps or prisons for a term of five to eight years, to apply an additional measure of punishment: exile to remote locations of the USSR for twenty years upon completion of their sentence in camps or prisons;

b. to apply the twenty-year exile indicated in this provision as an independent measure of punishment for socially dangerous elements;

2. Provision #1 of this resolution shall be extended to cover all persons
previously sentenced by the OGPU Collegium, the Special Board, or
NKVD troikas to imprisonment in camps and prisons to terms of from
five to ten years, whose stipulated term of punishment expires after June
15, 1941.[63]

Obligatory exile to settlements for twenty years was also applied to
all citizens convicted in regular courts. This primarily concerned those
who had served sentences for counterrevolutionary crimes and embezzlement of socialist property. The draft Edict of the Presidium of
the Supreme Soviet officially legalized exile and regulated the terms
of its implementation.

The war interfered with the plans of the NKVD leadership, or rather,
it rendered unnecessary the introduction of an additional measure of
punishment. Literally from the first day of the conflict, all prisoners
convicted of political crimes were kept imprisoned, even if they had
completed their terms.

The methods and tactics of secret-police operations were among
the most sacred secrets of the repressive system. In principle there was
nothing unnatural about this; all special services operate in secrecy.
The secrecy policy of the NKVD, however, was unique in one respect:
quite frequently the secrecy protected not just professional functions
but also criminal activities, in particular provocations, which the Soviet
security organs developed to a virtuoso level.

In October 1956 the Secretariat of the Central Committee of the
CPSU discussed a violation of socialist legality that took place in
Khabarovsk Region in 1941–49. This concerned one of the most un-
principled and cruel provocations conducted by the organs of state
security in the Far East.[64] In the spring of 1941, with the sanction of
Deputy People's Commissar of the NKGB* I.A. Serov, the NKGB Administration for Khabarovsk Region set up a sham Soviet border post
called "Manchuria Border Police Post" and "Japanese District Military
Mission" fifty kilometers from Khabarovsk, near the village of
Kazakevichi, close to the border with Manchuria. This "false border
cordon" was nicknamed the "Mill" by officials of the state security service. Complete with sham Japanese border and intelligence services,
this simulation of a Soviet border post was established to test Soviet

---

*The NKVD and the NKGB operated separately from February through June
of 1941.

citizens who were suspected of hostile activities. A test at the notorious "Mill" began when the NKVD office invited its potential victim to carry out a crucial assignment beyond the border zone. Once the person agreed, a whole sequence of events was staged: he was conducted through the false Soviet border post and deposited onto Manchurian territory, where Japanese border authorities detained him. He was taken to the "Japanese Military Mission," where he underwent a series of interrogations by NKVD officials pretending to be officials of Japanese intelligence services and Russian White-Guard émigrés. According to the report given at the 1956 meeting of the Secretariat of the Central Committee of the CPSU, "the interrogations were aimed at inducing the 'person being tested' to reveal some information relating to 'Soviet intelligence' to the 'Japanese authorities.' The interrogations were extremely grueling; various kinds of threats and forms of physical coercion were applied in an effort to break down the person's morale." After the interrogations, which could go on for several days or even weeks, the "detainee was re-recruited by representatives of the 'Japanese intelligence service,' given an intelligence-gathering mission, and released back onto Soviet territory. The provocational game culminated in the arrest of the 'person being tested' by the NKVD. His case was turned over to the Special Board, which convicted him as a traitor and sentenced him to prolonged terms of deprivation of liberty or to execution by shooting."[65]

In one typical case involving the "Mill," during the summer of 1942, a construction engineer, S.S. Bronikovskii, came to the attention of the Khabarovsk NKVD. Suspecting him, without any basis whatsoever, to be an undercover agent of the Japanese and German intelligence services, NKVD administration personnel decided to subject him to the "test." They offered him a reconnaissance mission that involved crossing the cordon, and naturally he agreed. On September 1, he was sent "across the border." According to his NKVD script, he was to tell the Japanese the truth about his life, his arrest in 1937, and his prison term and then to declare that he had decided to run away to Manchuria.

After being left on the "contiguous side," Bronikovskii was detained by the "Japanese-Manchurian border police." He was held for almost a month in prison and subjected to continual interrogations as a deserter. Bronikovskii remained steadfast and maintained his dignity throughout the interrogations, saying nothing about his recruitment by the NKVD or about the assignment he had been given. Events developed according to the established pattern: the "representative of Japanese intelligence" recruited Bronikovskii to work for Japan and "sent him back across" into the USSR.

Although Bronikovskii went immediately upon his return to the NKVD and reported on the failure of his mission, openly admitting his recruitment by the "Japanese," and although his behavior "in captivity" confirmed beyond a shadow of a doubt that he had had absolutely no contact with the intelligence services of enemy states, the NKVD arrested him in October 1942. The official reason given for his arrest was the fact that, during his interrogation by the "Japanese," he had divulged some information about Khabarovsk.

From the beginning, when they prepared the "materials" for Bronikovskii's arrest, and throughout the investigation of his case, NKVD officials crudely falsified documents. In the summation for the prosecution, the provocation at the "border post" was presented as though Bronikovskii had actually been sent abroad with a real reconnaissance task. A separate envelope was appended to the case containing information not to be divulged. Confident of the integrity of the state security service, the prosecutor confirmed the guilty verdict and sent the case on to the Special Board. On April 24, 1943, the NKVD Special Board sentenced Bronikovskii to death, and on April 26 he was shot.

The "Mill" worked flawlessly for several years, until it broke down in 1947. A cook for the "border post," an ethnically Chinese Soviet citizen, could not stand the abuses going on around him and went berserk, breaking all the dishes and kitchen utensils from Japan in a personal act of protest. Fearing exposure, the section chief A.S. Popov ordered his aide, who was also Chinese, to shoot the mutinous cook. In November of the same year, and for the same reason, two other men in service at the "border post" were executed.

Staff members of the Khabarovsk NKVD Administration A.I. Orev, D.A. Antonov, and I.A. Slobodianiuk played the role of White Guards at the "Mill." In 1941 they had been convicted by a military tribunal of violating socialist law and sentenced, correspondingly, to eight, seven, and five years of deprivation of liberty. The former Chekists were held in the camps until 1943. They were granted early release from prison based on a petition from the Khabarovsk Region NKVD Administration and assigned to work in the "border post."

The duties of the head of the "Japanese District Military Mission" were performed by a Japanese spy from the Kwantoon Army named Tomita, who had been arrested in 1937 by Soviet border guards. In 1940 a military tribunal had sentenced him to death, but by decision of the Presidium of the Supreme Soviet of the USSR the sentence was commuted to ten years of deprivation of liberty. One can only imagine the zeal of the Japanese spy, convicted by a Soviet court, as he interrogated and tortured Soviet citizens.

Only a small circle of officials in the central apparatus of the NKVD and the Khabarovsk NKVD Administration knew of the existence of the "Mill." All its activities were conducted in strictest secrecy. Occasionally people deduced the real purpose of the "border post" and were physically destroyed. For example, F.F. Akimov, chief of the Khabarovsk Administration, reported on January 29, 1944, to B.Z. Kobulov on M.I. Bochkov's behavior at the "Mill": "If he [Bochkov] is sentenced to a term of imprisonment, then while in the camps he naturally will expand his provocational activity and make it difficult to maintain secrecy in connection with these operations."[66] Akimov requested that this be taken into account and that Bochkov be shot. The NKVD leadership sent the Bochkov case from the court to the Special Board, which then decided against him, and he was executed.

Between 1941 and 1949, the state security service processed 148 Soviet citizens through the Far East "Mill," none of whom were guilty. Lieutenant-General P.V. Fedotov, the former chief of the Second Administration (for internal security and counterintelligence) of the NKVD of the USSR, was assumed to have been one of the organizers and the person directly in charge of all the operations of this sophisticated provocation. The activities of the "Mill" were regularly reported to Beria, V.N. Merkulov, and several other leading officials of the NKVD–NKGB.

Reading the materials relating to the provocational activity of the Khabarovsk state security officials brings on a peculiar feeling of bitterness and perplexity: the country was at war, people were losing their lives, and here these smug, well-fed officials, insulated from the realities of the draft and front-line duty and at a loss for something useful to do, sought some means to justify their existence. They spent substantial amounts of state money on activities directed against the state, fabricating false accusations and spurious cases against honest Soviet citizens.

War did not bring an end to the activities of the internal-affairs organs. On December 28, 1941, General Commissar for State Security Beria issued an order "On the Establishment of Special Camps for Former Red Army Servicemen Who Spent Time as Prisoners of War or Were Behind Enemy Lines."[67] Within a ten-day period, building on the experience they had gained with the Gulag, the NKVD organized ten such camps in the European part of the USSR, each covering a specific group of fronts. Four NKVD convoy regiments were assigned to transport the former soldiers to the special camps from assembly points.

Special sections of the NKVD were created to investigate former Red Army soldiers in the camps and ferret out traitors to the Motherland, spies, and deserters. Depending on the results of the investigations, soldiers were either turned over to territorial military commissariats or arrested, and their cases were sent to the Special Board. All the camps were located near industrial centers, where the former Red Army men, except for the officers, worked while their cases were pending. During the repatriation period, the number of these "identification-screening" camps tripled. In January 1946 they were officially made part of the Gulag system. The NKVD also created a network of identification and screening points for citizens returning to the Motherland. The conditions in these camps were purposely kept similar to those in the prisons and camps of the Gulag. In all, during the war and postwar periods, some 6 million citizens passed through this identification and screening system; at least a half-million of them were sent on to the Gulag, and many were shot.

At the height of the war, official prisoners serving hard labor made their appearance in our country. In April 1943, the Presidium of the Supreme Soviet of the USSR passed an edict "On Measures of Punishment for Traitors to the Motherland and Turncoats, and on the Introduction of Hard Labor as Punishment for These Persons." The first NKVD hard-labor divisions were organized by the People's Commissariat of Internal Affairs in the Vorkuta and Northeast camps. At the end of 1944 there were already five hard-labor camps in the Gulag, with some 6,000 prisoners. By September 1947, the number of prisoners exceeded 60,000.

It was no accident that penal servitude made its appearance in 1943. One of the reasons was the initiation of work associated with the atomic bomb project. Uranium is not coal; you cannot send simple camp prisoners to mine it, although it is likely they did. The hard-labor convicts were another matter altogether; it was perfectly natural to keep them completely isolated and force them to do grueling work underground that guaranteed them an early grave. Among the achievements that the NKVD listed at its Fourth Party Conference at the end of 1944 was its 100 percent contribution to radium production in the country.[68] It is not difficult to deduce who it was that mined and processed the radioactive ore.

The overwhelming majority of the residents of the separate country behind barbed wire accepted the blows of fate without active resistance, although not necessarily submissively. There were escape attempts, but only the most desperate took this step. It was not too difficult to escape from a convoy, but it was practically impossible to hide in a country where even children were aware of what the NKVD meant and where generation after generation was inculcated with a feeling of visceral hatred toward "enemies of the people." In any event, given the locations of the camps, there was simply no place to go. Pavel Negretov, who was imprisoned at Vorkuta from 1945 through 1955, recalls:

> When I was working at the sixth mine, which was surrounded by barbed-wire fencing, from time to time prisoners would escape from the work zone, which had a railroad line running through it. A prisoner would have to be out of his mind to attempt such an escape; no one was ever brought back alive after doing so. They would be left lying out there, stripped down to their underdrawers, for two or three days afterward, near the guard stations where all the prisoners could get a good long look at them on their way to and from the mines: "Here's what you can expect if you try to escape."[69]

Nevertheless, acts of protest did take place, and some of them became legendary. One of the first armed uprisings of Gulag prisoners that we know about took place in Vorkuta in January 1942. One Saturday, the prisoners persuaded the majority of the guards to go into the bathhouse for a bath. They then disarmed the remaining sentries, seized all the weapons in the camp, opened the gate to the secured zone, and invited all the other prisoners to join them. Eighty-two rose to the challenge. They stocked up on food and warm clothing, took the weapons, and headed for the regional center of Ust-Usa. By evening of the same day, the escapees had seized the regional center office of Ust-Usa and were joined by twelve more men they freed from the local NKVD office.

Over the next few days, real battles took place between NKVD troops and "Special Designation Detachment #41," as the rebels called themselves. The prisoners attempted to break through to the reindeer herds, hoping to use them to escape into the polar tundra, but they were turned in by a local hunter. The authorities spent the next month rounding up and destroying small bands of rebels. The losses were great on both sides. Of the insurgents, forty-eight were killed, six committed suicide, and eight were recaptured. According to the investigation records, "The forces that fought against the rebels suffered serious losses: thirty-three men were killed outright or were mortally wounded, twenty were wounded, and fifty-two were disabled by frostbite."[70]

If the materials from the investigation are to be believed, "the counter-revolutionary insurgency organization was formed in October 1941 by Trotskyites serving sentences in the camp." Witnesses wrote down their testimony as dictated to them by the investigators. In all, of sixty-eight men convicted of armed insurrection in the case—although they themselves had not participated—forty-nine were sentenced to death; of these, thirty-eight already had a political record.[71]

On August 20, 1942, all the camps and colonies of the Gulag received an official memorandum from Moscow, "On the Increase in Counterrevolutionary Activities in NKVD Corrective-Labor Camps," which ordered the "removal of the counterrevolutionary and anti-Soviet element" within two weeks. This initiated large-scale operations aimed at seeking out and destroying counterrevolutionary organizations such as "The Committee of People's Liberation" at the Vorkuta Industrial Coal Complex, "The Russian Society for Vengeance against the Bolsheviks" in Colony #1 of Omsk Oblast, and others. One of the Gulag reports notes, "Between 1941 and 1944, 603 insurgency organizations and groups, with a total of 4,640 active participants, were discovered and eliminated in camps and colonies."[72]

In our view, these underground counterrevolutionary organizations existed only on paper, in the case files of the Cheka branch offices of the camps. And indeed, why were "counterrevolutionary and insurgency organizations" never mentioned by NKVD officials in their internal correspondence and at Party and Komsomol meetings where internal Gulag problems were discussed? Instead, they always discussed ordinary or armed escape attempts by individuals or groups and so-called "*volynki*"—the frequent strikes and work slowdowns organized by powerful criminal convicts as a way of solving their own particular problems. One such uprising took place in Vorkuta in the winter of 1942. It is mentioned in a character evaluation of M.P. Gagarinov, an NKVD officer since 1939. Gagarinov had been serving as a

> security officer in the Ust-Usa branch of the Komi ASSR Ministry of Internal Affairs when, in January 1942, an armed work slowdown and strike broke out. Although he was the officer on duty, Gagarinov displayed cowardice and fled, abandoning Deputy Chief Selkov of the district branch of the Ministry of Internal Affairs wounded and helpless; as a result, Selkov bled to death. Gagarinov was demoted for cowardice to simple operations officer and held under arrest for five days.

As we can see, there is not a word, no emotional reaction to the "armed insurrection against Soviet power" reported in the investigation; it is all business as usual—just another "armed work slowdown." By the way, Gagarinov rose in rank to lieutenant-colonel; while serving as a senior investigator of the MVD Administration for Grozny Oblast in 1946, he was placed in detention for ten days and reprimanded publicly by the Party for beating up prisoners during interrogations. In 1949 he "worked himself into" a fibrous lung condition. According to his co-workers, "he frequently drank himself into a stupor while on duty," and in the intervals between drunken binges he wrote denunciations against his bosses. In September 1953, "in the interests of maintaining his health," the MVD leadership issued Gagarinov a two-month pass to a Yalta sanatorium. A most typical career path for a Gulag worker.

Beginning in 1943, German, Italian, Romanian, Hungarian, and other prisoners of war began to join the Soviet prisoners. During the first part of the war, eight camps were organized for them, containing around 40,000 prisoners. Initially they were not put to work. On February 24, 1943, Beria ordered a fundamental restructuring of the administration of prisoners' affairs, introducing mandatory use of their labor and improving Cheka operations in prisoner-of-war camps. By the end of 1944, 75 camps had been established on the territory of the USSR, with 719 branches and a total capacity of 1,100,000 prisoners. An additional reserve capacity was created for 935,000 prisoners in response to the eagerness with which the Czechs, Slovaks, Yugoslavs, and representatives of other nationalities who had been forced into service in the Fascist army turned themselves over to Soviet forces.[73] As of May 11, 1945, there were 2,070,000 prisoners of war of several dozen nationalities held in the USSR. The experience of the Gulag enabled the Soviet command to "process" this huge human mass within a very short period of time.

The Soviet victory in the war did not bring liberation for political prisoners, nor any easing of their fate. In fact, the severity of punitive policies increased during the initial postwar years and was particularly harsh against people who had, under various circumstances, come into contact with or collaborated with the enemy. In 1946 the MGB* began to arrest those demobilized soldiers who, after being forced to collaborate with the Germans, had gone over to the partisans, joined the Red Army, and fought in its ranks until the final victory. Many of them had been decorated or wounded and were confident that they had completely expiated their guilt. The MGB thought otherwise. To increase the severity of the charges, investigators often resorted to falsifications, transforming ordinary citizens who had been forced against their will

*The NKVD and the NKGB were divided for a second time on June 1, 1943; on March 15, 1946, the NKVD and the NKGB were renamed the MVD and the MGB (Ministry of State Security).

to serve as foremen, rural policemen, chairmen of street committees, house managers, and so on, into vicious murderers on paper.

Before the 1950s, those convicted in such cases generally received sentences of from five to ten years in the camps; in 1952, however, the situation changed abruptly. The tribunals, with only very rare exceptions, began to sentence former front-line soldiers who had been recruited to serve the Germans in occupied territories to twenty-five-year camp sentences. The reason for this intensification of the repressions was a "clarification" issued by the chief military prosecutor's office concerning cases of special jurisdiction (*spetspodsudnost'*). In 1952, E. Varskoi, the deputy chief military prosecutor, declared at a representative meeting of officials of prosecutors' offices and tribunals that prosecutors do not have the right in court to recommend a reduction in the severity of a sentence, even if the defendant had partially expiated his guilt by fighting against the Germans. That took care of it; from then on all "traitors" got twenty-five-year sentences.

Later on, when they began reexamining the cases of special jurisdiction, the commissions treated such sentences gingerly, often leaving them unchanged or, less frequently, decreasing the term to five to ten years; they practically never overturned a sentence completely. Here is a typical example: On May 29, 1954, the Military Collegium examined the case of A.M. Khovanov, who had worked as an assistant to the village elder and had been sentenced for treason to twenty-five years in a corrective-labor camp. Discovering that Khovanov had been forced to work for the elder under duress and had served in the Soviet Army from February 1943 through July 1946, had fought at the front and been wounded twice, had been decorated five times, and afterward had worked honestly for six years on a collective farm, the collegium decided to decrease his sentence to ten years. How can such "generosity" be explained? Could it be that the same dark affairs of the past were weighing on every leading official in the judicial system?

Many lives were also destroyed as a result of another secret "clarification," issued in response to requests from military prosecutors involved in "special jurisdiction." The MGB and the MVD were asked to provide a detailed exposition of the charges against an accused, listing all the facts connected with his criminal activity. Unwilling to confront the all-powerful agencies, Deputy General Prosecutor of the USSR A.P. Vavilov explained in October 1948 that "a listing of specific facts in presentation of charges in cases involving state criminals could interfere with the exposure of the criminal and the discovery of all his hostile activity." After this authoritative clarification, the military tribunals stopped giving defendants copies of the case summaries with the guilty verdict and sentences, as was required by the Criminal Code, and simply familiarized them with their contents. Instead of copies, the newly convicted prisoners received short extracts. This practice not only ran counter to the requirements of the law but it also deprived defendants of the opportunity to exercise their right to a defense, pursuant to Article III of the Constitution of the USSR, since the defendant could not do so, even in court, without a copy of the guilty verdict. Without a copy of the sentence, the defendant was unable, in any appeal of the sentence, to challenge the arguments and reasons listed in it.

The Soviet system of repression was unique in primarily basing its activity not on law but on secret instructions, clarifications, supplements, and commentaries that originated primarily in bodies that did not have any legal rights. Quite naturally, neither the common man nor the Soviet public at large, not to mention the international community, was aware of the existence of a whole series of directives that grossly violated the constitution and human rights. Judicial practitioners, investigators, MVD and MGB officials, as well as a small circle of Soviet and Party officials—that is, people responsible for enforcing the law—were the only ones who knew the procedures for applying them.

Even official legislation was not always publicly known. Many decrees of the Presidium of the Supreme Soviet of the USSR that affected the fates of hundreds of thousands of people were labeled "not for publication." After the passage of such a law, the Council of Ministers of the USSR would adopt a secret resolution clarifying the procedures for its enforcement, and the MVD and the MGB would then follow up with secret orders and instructions.

The very concept of "legal rights" developed its own particular meaning in Soviet society. The masses identified it not with the constitution or laws, much less with the natural rights of man, but rather with the specific activity of various law-enforcement agencies. The population's absolute ignorance of legal matters substantially eased the work of the system of repressions, since it virtually excluded the possibility of any form of official protest.

The postwar years were marked by the publication of a number of extraordinarily cruel and immoral decrees, both secret and open. Repressive, draconian laws that affected all layers of the population and all aspects of life tied society into one tight knot. In an effort to deflect any tendencies to make overtures to the Western world, the government issued an edict on February 15, 1947, prohibiting marriages between citizens of the USSR and foreigners. This gross interference of the state in the personal lives of its subjects not only shattered dreams and fates but gave investigatory bodies considerable latitude in enforcement. A significant number of Soviet citizens, especially young people, were sent to the Gulag for having contacts with foreigners.

Still, to quote Alexander Solzhenitsyn, this was just a "small stream." Another matter entirely was the edict of June 4, 1947, after which "entire divisions of village and city residents were sent off to cultivate the islands of the Gulag, replacing the locals who had died out."[74] This was the notorious edict "On Criminal Accountability for Theft of State Property," which supplanted all earlier laws and decrees on the subject. Its superiority lay primarily in its "freshness" and the longer terms of punishment it envisioned. As a result of this decree, a typical—if not the typical—inhabitant of the Gulag became "the collective farmer who stole a sack of potatoes."

The decree strictly distinguished state from public property. If theft, misappropriation, or waste of the former earned seven to twenty-five years in the camps depending on the circumstances, misappropriation of collective farm or cooperative property was punished less severely by the courts: from five to twelve years in the camps. For the first time, punishment was instituted for failure to report misappropriation of state or public property: from two to three years of deprivation of liberty or five to seven years of exile.[75]

The MVD chose to begin its active struggle against theft during the famine of 1946–47, when the population of the majority of the oblasts of the Black Earth zone, the Northern and Southern Volga, the Southern Urals, Western Siberia, Ukraine, and the neighboring oblasts of Belorussia and Moldavia were giving in to the instinct of self-preservation and resorting to any means in their struggle to save themselves from starvation and death.

In 1946, 181,913 people were arrested for theft of socialist property; during 1947, that number had grown to 337,751; of these, 8,444 were arrested for theft in state trade; 6,534 in consumer cooperatives; 24,803 in food-services enterprises; 25,224 at "Zagotzerno" grain facilities and mills; 177,331 on state and collective farms; 22,518 in non-food-related industrial enterprises; and 2,805 in industrial cooperatives and those for the disabled. Some 55 percent of the overall number of accused thieves, 183,909 people, were arrested pursuant to the edict of June 4, 1947.[76] Of the number of people arrested for theft, over half (52.5 percent) were peasants, that is, direct producers of grain, whom the severe government policies left essentially without the means for subsistence. The contemporary Russian researcher V.F. Zima, analyzing Soviet agrarian policies between 1945 and 1953, came to an unambiguous conclusion: "It was within the state's power to save starving people and curtail the growth of crime. There were substantial reserves of food supplies (grain, butter, sugar, etc.). The Kremlin leadership, however, continued to engage in the punitive practices that had become the norm during the 1930s."[77]

The systematic victimization of peasants during the postwar years is striking for its cynicism and cruelty. Here are a few typical examples from the people's courts of Belgorod, Mikoyan, and Tomarov districts of Belgorod Oblast. An excerpt from the sentence imposed by the Mikoyan District Court in the case of M.F. Kazakova—a farm worker on the Proletariat Collective Farm, aged forty-seven years, illiterate, a widow with two children, five and nineteen years old. On July 14, 1947, "the court investigation established that on July 1, 1947, the defendant Mariia Fedorovna Kazakova committed theft of sugar beets belonging to the Proletariat Collective Farm totaling five kilograms and ears of rye totaling 600 grams. After the theft the defendant Kazakova was detained and the beets and rye were confiscated and turned over to the Proletariat Collective Farm.* "The judicial inquest of the people's court sentenced the defendant M.F. Kazakova to the term of punishment stipulated in Article 3 of the edict of the Presidium of the Supreme Soviet of June 4, 1947: incarceration in corrective-labor camps for a period of five years without disenfranchisement upon completion of the sentence and without confiscation of property in view of the absence of such. The five-year-old child is to be turned over to the defendant's brother, V.F. Kazakov, to be cared for."[78]

On July 16, 1947, the Tomarov District Court sentenced two young peasant women from the "Country of the Soviets" Collective Farm to six years in corrective-labor camps for the theft of about four kilograms of potatoes. The court determined that the two of them had made an "agreement" that constituted an aggravating circumstance. E.G. Propashkina and T.N. Maslieva appealed to the oblast level, contesting the decision of the district court. The Collegium for Criminal Cases answered:

> The court's determination of the *corpus delicti* of the convicted was correct, and the punishment was commensurate with the crime committed.

---

*The Proletariat Collective Farm of Mikoyan District comprised peasants from three villages (seventy-six able-bodied women and ten men). On average every female collective-farm worker worked 215 days over the course of a year and was issued 300 grams of bread, 1.8 kilograms of straw and chaff, and 1.2 kilograms of hay for each working day.

In their appeals, the defendants Propashkina and Maslieva ask that the court take into account their material situation, which is not normal given the destruction of their households by the German occupiers. The request of the defendants Propashkina and Maslieva cannot be granted, since their criminal actions were aimed at weakening the economic strength of the collective farm.[79]

M.A. Marchenko, a barely literate peasant woman from the Stalin Collective Farm, convicted and sentenced by the Belgorod District Court to five years in corrective-labor camps without confiscation of property "for stealing ears of rye totaling 850 grams, which were discovered in her possession during a search," explained to the court that she had committed the aforesaid crime "due to difficult material circumstances, since she was supporting her invalid seventy-three-year-old mother." The court considered these arguments to be immaterial and upheld the conviction.[80]

Such sentences can be found everywhere in the judicial practice of the postwar years, and not only in cases involving collective farmers. The literature contains descriptions of a number of cases in which people were sent to the camps for stealing from their workplace a spool of thread, a pair of stockings, or two or three dozen cigarettes. For the sake of fairness it should be noted that not all court verdicts were that severe. Taking into account individual circumstances of the case, courts gave a suspended sentence or imposed a sentence lighter than that recommended by the decree in approximately twenty-three cases out of a hundred. Such judicial practice provoked severe reprimands from Party oversight bodies, which remarked on the "weakness of judicial repression" and demanded an "increase in the level of punishments imposed by the courts."

Based on data from the office of the prosecutor of the RSFSR, in 1950 the number of people convicted under the edict of June 4, 1947 (theft of state and public property), came to 117,641, or 25.3 percent of the total convictions for the year; in 1951, 97,583, or 21.4 percent; in 1952, 103,161, or 20.9 percent of the overall number of people convicted. The total material losses related to cases completed and turned over to courts in 1951 amounted to over 661 million rubles; in 1952, 689 million. Of these losses, only 46 percent and 49.5 percent, respectively, were compensated. The highest level of misappropriation and theft occurred in state trade and consumer cooperatives, where losses amounted to tens of millions of rubles. Although collective farms and local industry were quite low on the list, they accounted for the highest proportion of convictions.

Propaganda allowed no one to doubt even for a minute the correctness of the Soviet court; no one dared to challenge the humanity of the Soviet government. What did it take to cripple human consciousness to the point where a person never tired of "licking the hand that beat him"? A prisoner, Mariia Shulgina, gave a speech at a rally in the Kargopolskii Camp on the occasion of the amnesty of March 1953.* "The decree illustrates the great power and justice of the Soviet state," said the prisoner. "While working on the collective farm, I committed an offense and received a five-year sentence. Now I am being released because I am a mother. I want to work so much harder and better, so that I can express my heartfelt gratitude to our own dear Soviet state." Note that even at the emotional peak of her made-to-order effusions of gratitude this woman could not muster the strength to call her "action" a crime, referring to it instead as an "offense." Five years of forced labor in a camp for an "offense"—is this humane or reasonable?

As an example of a typical decree of the Soviet totalitarian state we note the edict of the Presidium of the Supreme Soviet of the USSR of June 9, 1947, "On Accountability for Divulging State Secrets and for the Loss of Documents Containing State Secrets," which supplanted a similar edict of November 15, 1943, and introduced new terms of punishment. If the edict of the war years envisioned, for divulging state secrets, a term of five years (ten years in serious cases) for officials and three years for private individuals, the 1947 edict called for far more severe punishments. For divulging state secrets, officials received from eight to ten years in corrective-labor camps; military personnel, ten to twenty years; and private individuals, five to ten years in the camps.[81] All this applied in cases involving a simple slip of the tongue, negligence, or incautious publication, not an intentional communication of information to interested parties; in such cases divulging information was treated as treason and espionage, with the appropriate consequences.

The new decree "concerned itself" with the academic world as well. Giving information abroad about any scientific discoveries made on the territory of the USSR was punishable by ten to fifteen years in corrective-labor camps. All cases relating to this edict were subject to trial by a military tribunal. On the eve of the adoption of the edict, the Council of Ministers of the USSR approved a list of information considered to be state secrets.[82] This list, which included military, economic, and "other" information, was compiled in such a way as to cover prac-

---

*Amnesty of March 1953: That is, the amnesty decreed immediately after Stalin's death.—Ed.

tically all spheres of human activity, thus turning all citizens of the USSR into potential criminals.

In 1948 a new blow awaited the countryside, which had not yet recovered from war and famine. On June 2 the Presidium of the Supreme Soviet of the USSR issued a decree on the resettlement of collective farmers who had not worked the obligatory minimum number of working days. In the same year, over 23,000 collective farmers, including 12,000 from the Russian Federation, were exiled to remote regions for terms of up to eight years, without trial or investigation.[83]

The postwar policy of "establishing order" found its logical continuation in the reorganization of the repressive system. On January 21, 1948, Stalin was presented with a document that was to have a profound effect on the fates of hundreds of thousands of prisoners. "In accordance with your instructions," reported V. Abakumov, minister of state security, and S. Kruglov, minister of internal affairs, to the generalissimo, "we present a draft decision of the Central Committee of the Communist Party on the organization of special regimen camps and prisons for incarcerating particularly dangerous state criminals and on sending them after the completion of their terms of punishment to settlements in remote locations of the USSR. We request your decision."[84]

The first paragraph of this document reads:

> The MVD (Kruglov) shall be required:
> a. within a six-month period, to organize special camps for the incarceration of agents of foreign intelligence services, saboteurs, terrorists, Trotskyites, Rightists, Mensheviks, SRs, anarchists, nationalists, White émigrés, and other participants in anti-Soviet organizations and groups, as well as persons whose anti-Soviet ties and hostile activities present a danger, who have been sentenced to deprivation of liberty. The camps are to have an overall capacity of 100,000 persons, including [space] for 30,000 in Kolyma Region in the Far North; for 6,000 in Norilsk; for 6,000 in the Komi ASSR; for 10,000 in Elabug in the Tatar ASSR; for 20,000 in Temniki, in the Mordovian ASSR; for 10,000 in the region of the cities of Griazovets and Cherepovets in Vologda Oblast; for 12,000 in the regions of Iuzh and Iurevets in Ivanovo Oblast; for 6,000 in the region of Karaganda; and special prisons for 5,000 persons in the cities of Vladimir, Aleksandrovsk, and Verkhne-Uralsk;
> b. to transfer all convicts of the above-listed categories from general-profile corrective-labor camps and prisons to the above-indicated special camps and prisons for a six-month term, except for those who are seriously ill, who are suffering from incurable chronic diseases, or who are disabled; to prohibit the incarceration in special camps and prisons of those convicted of other crimes;
> c. to build, by the middle of 1949, additional special camps with a capacity of 45,000 prisoners at construction sites for the Baikal–Amur Railroad in remote areas (in Irkutsk Oblast and Khabarovsk Region).[85]

The resolution prescribed a severe regime for the special camps, banning all privileges and requiring all able-bodied prisoners to perform heavy physical labor, in effect proposing to turn all political prisoners into hard-labor convicts—which is in fact what happened. An investigatory commission from the Presidium of the Supreme Soviet of the USSR reported in 1955 on one of the special camps (Stepnoi): "Until 1954, under the so-called 'penal-servitude' regime, conditions in the camp were practically unbearable physically and utterly degrading to human dignity. Prisoners wore large numbers on their clothing, were locked at night in barracks packed beyond capacity, and were deprived of their rations if they did not fulfill their work quota."[86] Former prisoners of the special camps recall a terrible and pervasive "dead-end feeling"; many prisoners were kept imprisoned even after the completion of their sentences—a phenomenon called "overstaying their welcome" (*peresizhivanie*). The draft resolution of the Central Committee of the Communist Party cited above contained a provision that in effect legalized this phenomenon. It reads: "Convicts shall be sent for incarceration in special camps at locations determined by the MGB; the MVD shall coordinate with the MGB the release of prisoners upon completion of their terms. The MGB shall be granted the right, when necessary, to delay the release of prisoners, with subsequent processing according to legally established procedures."[87]

We can get a sense of the scale of the phenomenon of "overstaying their welcome" from a letter written by a former convict laborer, E.L. Vladimirova, who arrived in 1948 with a group of disabled prisoners from Kolyma at the Spasskii branch camp, which, at various times, was part of Steplag, Luchlag, and Peschlag. We should note in passing how difficult it was for exhausted, ill people to endure the intense heat and dust of the Kazakh steppe after the frosts of Kolyma. "Many dozens of people," reported E.L. Vladimirova in 1954 to the Central Committee of the CPSU, "having completed their sentences (and free by law), were kept in the camp for indefinite periods of time, occasionally 'sitting' for several more years; some of them died there while awaiting release. There was a special brigade of such people. The authorities who came to the camp did not believe that this could have happened. In some cases these 'overstayers' went on a hunger strike, but to no avail." It is unlikely that the situation in other special camps was any better.

The Ministry of Internal Affairs referred to the experience of prerevolutionary Russia in developing the regulation on the special camps and prisons. The draft resolution of the Central Committee of the CPSU contains a reference to the following tsarist provision on penal servitude: "After deduction of the cost of materials, hard-labor convicts shall be issued one-tenth of the proceeds; of the remainder [of revenue—G.I.], 50 percent shall go into the treasury, and 50 percent shall be returned to the prison for its own use. Half of the earnings may be turned over to the prisoner during his time in prison, with 50 percent paid upon release." It is worth noting that Soviet prison policymakers considered tsarist practice too liberal. The corresponding provision in the Stalinist version of the resolution required that "special camps shall be maintained with funds from the state budget of the USSR. The MVD shall be permitted to retain for camp use 50 percent of the income produced by special camps, after deducting the cost of materials. . . . The remaining 50 percent shall be turned over to the state budget as revenue."[88] As we can see, prisoners of special camps did not even receive the miniscule earnings that convicts were granted under the tsarist regime.

The special camps were established in the spring of 1948, after a secret resolution issued by the Council of Ministers of the USSR on February 21, 1948, followed by two related orders from the MVD. These documents provided for additional financing and technical support for the construction and maintenance of special camps and determined staffing sources, the number of personnel required, and a number of other questions. The new "strict-regime camps for incarcerating especially dangerous state criminals" were given attractive, sometimes even poetic names: camp #1, Mineral; #2, Mountain; #3, Oak; #4, Steppe; #5, Seashore; #6, River; #7, Lake; #8, Sand; #9, Meadow; #10, Rushes; #11, Far Away; #12, Watershed—for what reason, it is not clear, unless it had to do with maintaining secrecy.[89]

At the same time as the resolution of the Council of Ministers, the Presidium of the Supreme Soviet of the USSR issued its edict "On Exiling Especially Dangerous State Criminals to Remote Locations in the USSR upon Completion of Their Sentences." This legal act of the state, whose initial variant had been discussed before the war, stipulated that:

1. The Ministry of Internal Affairs of the USSR shall be required to exile under the administration of the MGB, upon completion of their terms of punishment in special camps and prisons under the supervision of the Ministry of State Security of the USSR, spies, saboteurs, terrorists, Trotskyites, Rightists, Mensheviks, SRs, anarchists, nationalists, White émigrés, members of other anti-Soviet organizations and groups, and persons whose anti-Soviet ties and hostile activities present a danger, as determined by the MGB. These settlements are located
   — in Kolyma Region in the Far North;
   — in Krasnoiarsk Region and Novosibirsk Oblast, located fifty kilometers north of the Trans-Siberian Railway;
   — in the Kazakh SSR, except for the Alma-Ata, Gurev, South Kazakhstan, Aktubinsk, East Kazakhstan, and Semipalatinsk oblasts.

2. The Ministry of State Security of the USSR shall be required to exile the state criminals listed in Article 1 who have been released upon completion of their terms of punishment in corrective-labor camps and prisons since the end of the Great Patriotic War.

   Procedures for exiling these persons to settlements shall be based on decisions of the Special Board of the MGB of the USSR.[90]

In the fall of 1948, after the publication of the secret directive of the MGB of the USSR and the general public prosecutor of the USSR, prisoners who had been released after the end of the war began to be rearrested. All "repeat offenders" were charged under the same articles of the Criminal Code as before. Investigations of these cases were simplified and conducted without review of the previous evidence. The primary documents used by the Special Board in its decisions relating to exile were the summary reports of archived case files from the investigations of the past "anti-Soviet" activity of these people.

This edict and the practices associated with it blatantly violated existing legislation, which both prohibited repeated punishment for one and the same crime and established a scale of punishment that envisioned specific sentences; that is, a Soviet court did not have the right to impose an indefinite term of punishment such as life imprisonment or indefinite exile. But this "occurred" to people only after the death of Stalin.

In September 1953, extrajudiciary procedures were abolished. Nevertheless, a great many prisoners convicted of counterrevolutionary crimes remained imprisoned as before, and after serving their terms they were sent directly from prisons and camps into permanent exile. The edict of February 21, 1948, was not officially repealed until March 10, 1956, after which over 60,000 "especially dangerous state criminals" were released from exile.

In 1948 the Presidium of the Supreme Soviet of the USSR issued another edict, which might very well be the cruelest and most inhumane law of the Stalinist era. This was the edict of November 26, 1948, "On Criminal Accountability for Escapes from Places of Compulsory and Permanent Settlement by Persons Exiled to Remote Regions of the Soviet Union during the Period of the Great Patriotic War." Dispensing with preambles, the edict stated succinctly that those peoples who had been relocated to special settlements during the war* were to

---

*Peoples relocated during the war refers mainly to the deportation of whole peoples from their historic homelands. In September 1941, Stalin, as a "prophylactic" measure, ordered the deportation of the Volga Germans to Central Asia and Siberia, ostensibly because he feared they might constitute a fifth column. In 1943–44, he banished the Crimean Tatars, Chechens, Ingushi, Karachai, Balkars, Kalmyks, Meskhetians, and others, about a million people in all, to Kazakhstan and Central Asia. Hundreds of thousands perished along the way.—Ed.

remain there in perpetuity; a term of twenty years at hard labor was stipulated for escapes from a compulsory settlement. All adults were compelled to sign statements that they were aware of these regulations. Several special-regime settlements were organized on the territory of the Iakutsk ASSR and Krasnoiarsk Region for exiles considered to present an escape risk. One should not interpret the word "escape," as used here, literally. This could be something so simple as an unauthorized, that is, unrecorded, absence, for example, to visit a relative in a neighboring district, a friend in the next village, and so forth. Within a single year some 10,000 people were convicted under the new law. In all during this period there were over two and a half million people registered in 2,123 special commandants' facilities, nearly 70 percent of them women and children. The overwhelming majority (82 percent) of repressed people were considered to be exiled in perpetuity.

Several dozen nationalities under guard! And yet where were the protests, the public indignation? Did anyone come out and say directly that the USSR was a veritable prison of entire nationalities? And was there any criticism of a government that proclaimed equal rights for all its citizens under the Socialist Constitution?

One of the Party archives yields a document that can help explain the mentality of the people under Stalin and their attitude to the Soviet version of apartheid. On July 21, 1954, the Chechen writer M. Mamakaev, from the town of Igarki in Krasnoiarsk Region, wrote an open letter to the members of the Presidium of the Central Committee of the CPSU, addressed personally to N.S. Khrushchev. Mamakaev writes, "I have endured many different punishments." At the time of his last arrest, in Bukhara in 1949, one of his interrogators, State Security Captain Epishev, predicted, "You will never get your Soviet passport back, even as a Chechen." The reason for his letter to the higher Party level was his concern and anguish for the fate of the Chechen-Ingush people. Mamakaev writes:

> Personally I believed then and continue to believe that it was wrong to act so cruelly toward an entire people. It was possible, and perhaps even necessary, to destroy half or three-fourths of the republic's population. But it was cruel and senseless to sacrifice the lives of hundreds of thousands of innocent children, defenseless women, and old people and, worst of all, to leave a legacy of contempt and mistrust, and to insult so deeply the national pride of the younger generation. . . . A people placed in this degrading position faces humiliation and insults from any chance passer-by; it suffers suspicion and censure at the slightest pretext. . . . This situa-

tion particularly disturbs me because raising such a question about an entire nation publicly degrades Soviet authority itself and the great Marxist-Leninist teaching on the nationality question. Offenders must be punished severely, but it is inconceivable that nine innocent people should be forced into the noose in an effort to punish a single offender. It seems to me that the punishment itself is demeaned by such means, and, most importantly, the most varied segments of our society experience a natural feeling of righteous discontent, and that is most undesirable.

As we can see, Mamakaev is ambivalent: he is both defending and condemning Soviet power. On the one hand, his sense of self-worth and national pride protests; on the other, his status as a Soviet writer forces him to seek reconciliation with the existing regime.

It is not this, however, that most disturbs Mamakaev. There are cases, he writes, "when certain poets and historians distort objective historical reality and publish articles debasing everything associated with the name of the Chechen-Ingush people. . . . Poets describe all Chechens and Ingush in the darkest colors and tones, not hesitating to use the crudest and most uncouth expressions." The one who was most successful in this regard, according to Mamakaev, was the poet Rasul Gamzatov, who had been a censor in the main publishing office in Dagestan. His poems on the Imam Shamil, published in the collection *Mountain Road*, aroused in his readers a feeling of disgust and contempt for the Chechen-Ingush people. Mamakaev is ready to tolerate and forgive the master's whip, but he cannot edure betrayal and humiliation from a Caucasian neighbor.

The Chechen writer concludes, not surprisingly, "I am not asking for restoration of their former territorial rights to the Chechen and Ingush people. All I want to do is express the thought that it is completely intolerable and insulting for our Soviet society to subject a man to such restrictions purely and simply on the basis of his national origin, no matter where he might be living."

While calling on the Soviet government to reexamine the plight of the Chechen and Ingush people, the writer does not even mention the similar fates of different peoples who fell victim to the discriminatory and divisive nationality policies of the totalitarian state.

One of the most noteworthy punitive decrees of 1947–48 is that of May 26, 1947, which repealed capital punishment. At first glance it might seem to be a humanitarian measure. Many researchers believe that it was this decree that brought the machine of repressions to a halt or, rather, prevented the further escalation of the terror. Others see it as one of the factors bringing the size of the population of the Gulag in 1949–50 to its highest point in the whole history of its existence; that is, those who would undoubtedly have been shot before now entered the Gulag, increasing the number of its residents. We will not attempt to judge the validity of these observations. We are more concerned with a different matter.

The fact is, the repeal of capital punishment untied the hands of the criminal world, turning the lives of many hundreds of thousands of prisoners of the Gulag into an absolute nightmare. The camp administration secretly and openly encouraged the criminal convicts to tyrannize undesirables, foremost among whom were the "enemies of the people" and "hard workers" (*rabotiagi*), enacting bloody reprisals against them and often even camp administrators as well.

From the very beginning it was the criminal world that held the real power over prisoners in the camps of the Gulag. The "thieves" had their own system of laws that controlled all aspects of life in the camps. They occupied management positions, confiscated the prisoners' belongings and money, forced them to work for them, and, above all, murdered them, senselessly, violently, and, after 1947, with impunity. Of course, murders in the camps were investigated, and if a murderer was found, which occurred very rarely, he was tried and sentenced to the mandatory ten years. For a criminal who was already serving time, often as a repeat offender, this was simply a matter of "rounding up." If a criminal had already served two or three years, that amount was added to his sentence. After 1947, murders in the camps began to occur on a mass scale. Thousands of prisoners, given no protection by local officials, inundated the higher authorities with letters begging for help and support. They wrote to writers and composers, laureates of government awards, and performing artists; they wrote to newspapers and committees, to Party and soviet agencies. It is very important to note the possibly fatal risk they took in writing such letters. The author faced the threat of reprisals not only from hardened professional criminals but also from the camp administration, which was itself often no less brutal and violent.

History has preserved for us this epistolary heritage of the Gulag, with its outpourings of pain and hope, protest and despair. Here are some lines from a letter addressed to the Presidium of the Supreme Soviet of the USSR and the Central Committee of the CPSU, which arrived in the editorial offices of *Pravda* in October 1952 "from a man who is devoted to his people, his immense Motherland, [and] his great Soviet government and Party in the name of the great ideals of Lenin and Stalin":

> We appeal to you to close down the deadly camps in Norilsk! We appeal
> to you to put an end once and for all to the tyrannical and unendurably

brutal actions of the camp administration. We appeal to you to punish all
those who have been committing these dark deeds, whoever they may be,
Zverev, Popkov, and the rest of them!

The time has come to stop shedding the blood of those who inhabit
the zone behind the barbed wire.

We await your decision and hope that it will be just!

It will take a great deal of time and money to give a complete description of the whole tragedy of the tyranny in the Norilsk Camp of the MVD
of the USSR.

Nadezhda Gorskaia [Hope of the Mountain]—this is the pseudonym
chosen by the author of the letter—goes on to recount "brutal reprisals" committed on July 14, 1952, by the camp administration, using the
hands and knives of the professional criminals, "brutalizing people
and shedding rivers of blood," with "no one lifting a hand to protect
them." As a result of this tragedy, "the wounded who were taken away
filled up two truckloads; the number of fatalities was kept secret." The
closing of the letter is worthy of note: "In the name of the honest citizens of our Motherland! In the name of those temporarily imprisoned!—Hope of the Mountains."

This letter sparked an investigation by a special commission under
the MVD of the USSR, which revealed "shortcomings in the incarceration regime" and imposed administrative sanctions against several officials. The author of the letter escaped retaliation, for although the
commission conducted a thorough check of the prisoners, it was unable to "deduce" the identity of the person behind the pseudonym.

Some of the letters sent out to the free world are almost completely
illiterate, but this only adds to their poignancy. Prisoner N.I. Ivanov
chose to address his letter to the editor of the newspaper *Izvestiia*. "As a
patriot," writes the prisoner of the Gulag,

> I address you as a Soviet citizen imprisoned. Spending around five years
> imprisoned, this is my 10th time appealing to the authorities and for this
> whole time there's no end to the terrible things that are going on in places
> of incarceration. [Vanino Port was one of the major transit points.] There
> human lives are being taken barbarically. . . . Not a single Hitlerite or Ameri-
> can in Korea or primeval barbarian ever subjected anyone to such corporal
> beatings, like the Soviet prisoners in places of incarceration. . . . Not a single
> writer or poet could ever describe this barbarity that's going on in the So-
> viet camps.

The terror caused by criminal inmates who became lackeys for the
MVD was a hundred times more terrible than any of the official measures of punishment stipulated in the camp directives and government

decrees. In his description of the rampages of the criminals, the author of the appeal notes that the criminals had had far less power before 1947 and that the administration also had been more restrained. But now, the prisoner observes,

> if some embezzler embezzled 15,000 rubles, he gets a 25-year sentence, but say some boss goes on a spree and takes a pistol into the zone while drunk and kills someone, it's nothing—like it's supposed to be that way. The wives of Greek partisans write to the great Stalin, and he gets their letters, but when I or other prisoners like me write and describe this kind of thing, nothing comes of it.

Such letters were delivered by nonprisoners, or "free hands." If the camp administration managed to intercept a complaint, the reprisals could be extremely severe. Prisoners always emphasized that they were concealing their identity not because they were afraid of accountability to the higher authorities, but because they did not trust the local administration. Ivanov's letter ends with a typical postscript: "If you need me as living proof do not inform the local authorities about this letter and about me. I can speak only with representatives of Moscow. For I want to live."

As a rule, the reaction of the authorities in the capital to the appeals that came into their field of vision was as follows: an official investigation, an attempt to seek out the letter writer, and, depending on the degree of need, punishment of the camp personnel involved (the range of sanctions was quite broad—from two days of house arrest to trial before a tribunal). The conclusions of the investigation fit a pattern: "Ivanov's report claiming that criminal prisoners are granted privileges by the administration does not correspond to reality." In fact, both the center and the camps knew the nature of this "reality" very well.

On October 11, 1953, a group of recidivist criminals in the Viatsk Camp murdered nine other prisoners. It turned out that on October 9 the criminals had pressured the prisoners into going on strike, and whoever went out to work would be killed. At the same time, they demanded that the camp administration pay the prisoners their back salaries and release all the money from their personal accounts. The administration caved in to the ultimatum. After the prisoners received their money, the recidivists demanded twenty-five rubles from each of them. Those who refused were killed.

During the second half of 1953, the central Party authorities undertook a full-scale investigation of Gulag personnel. The final report reads: "In many camps a small contingent of criminals runs the internal life of the camps and controls the living conditions of the prisoners. The camp administration encourages this element, appoints them as brigade leaders, duty officers, and managers of storehouses, cafeterias, clinics, and so forth." When ordinary prisoners were given this kind of responsibility, the criminals forced them to carry out their will, and if they refused, they were physically eliminated. In the year 1952 alone, criminals in the camps killed 105 prisoners who had been working honestly as brigade leaders and duty officers. The overall number of those killed and wounded in the camps as a result of this kind of criminal activity came to several thousand people. By the beginning of the 1950s, the situation in the camps had become so critical that the authorities were forced to take emergency measures. On January 13, 1953, an edict was issued on intensifying measures to counter especially vicious manifestations of criminal behavior among prisoners in corrective-labor camps. In 1953 fifty-two prisoners in such camps were sentenced to be shot for banditry under this edict.

Capital punishment was officially reinstated for premeditated murder on April 30, 1954. Between May and October 1954, a total of 507 people in the Union republics were sentenced to death for murder; of these, 305 were in the Russian Republic. Eight criminal recidivists were sentenced to be shot for crimes committed in the camps. A few years before, on January 12, 1950, "at the request of the workers," the death penalty had been reinstated for "traitors to the Motherland, spies, subversives, and saboteurs."[91] In 1950–53, according to official data, some 4,000 people were shot for counterrevolutionary and state crimes.[92]

At the end of the 1940s and the beginning of the 1950s, the punitive authorities began focusing their attention on the younger generation. A series of trials took place involving various "treasonous," "terrorist," and "anti-Soviet" youth organizations and groups. In 1949, the authorities of the MGB uncovered and neutralized an illegal student group in Moscow known as the Black Legion. Stalin was notified personally about this underground organization. No wonder! After all, the members of the group, according to the report of the investigation, beginning with minor offenses, "began to manifest terrorist sentiments, planned to obtain funds for weapons by robbing savings banks; they also planned to flee the country, ultimately taking refuge in the United States." All eleven participants of the Black Legion were arrested and sent to the Gulag.

Shortly thereafter, the authorities of state security, again in Moscow, uncovered another youth organization called the Commune. According to Colonel I.V. Shumakov, who was in charge of the investigation, this illegal student group was created exclusively for the purpose of imperialist reconnaissance, since it was headed by children of previously convicted spies, Trotskyites, and terrorists. And it was irrelevant to the investigators that the group's charter, "An Oath for Life," clearly stated, "The Commune is a voluntary organization of friends, united for life by a single goal: the struggle for communism." Colonel General I.A. Serov, the future chairman of the KGB, went through the documents of the investigation twice; he, too, doubted the purity of motive and high ideals of the nineteen-year-old students. It did not seem strange to him that the material proof of the anti-Soviet activity of the group was a red banner with a five-pointed star and the slogan "Forward to meet the Dawn!" that had been confiscated from the students. And thus did thirteen members of the Commune become a special contingent of the Gulag.

In Voronezh the vigilant operatives discovered an underground organization, the Communist Party of Youth. The danger it posed was obvious: after all, during the investigation, which was headed by V.N. Sukhodolskii, the MGB administration chief himself, the Chekists succeeded in proving that the Communist Party of Youth aimed to "seize political power in the USSR." The fact that the members of the party were primarily of high-school age was not taken into account, and twenty-three of them were added to the population in the barracks of the Gulag.

The executioners dealt more severely with another youth group, which called itself the Union of Struggle for the Cause of Revolution. The leaders of this Moscow youth organization—B. Slutskii, V. Furman, and E. Gurevich—were shot; the others were sentenced to ten to twenty-five years in the camps. The investigator concluded that the group had adopted as its ultimate goal "the overthrow of the existing social and state regime in the USSR by means of armed rebellion." Ninth-grader Nina Ufliand, convicted in the case and sentenced to ten years in special camps, was an absolutely apolitical and painfully shy teenager who had never been anywhere except home and school. But someone during the investigation, perhaps under torture, had given her name in the list of his acquaintances.

By the beginning of the 1950s, there was not a single large city left in the Soviet Union where the Chekists had not uncovered a hotbed of youthful sedition. What was behind all these trials? One can presume that the younger generation became the object of repressions as a consequence of its increasing social activism. Some scholars detect in the postwar youth organizations the first glimmerings of political dissidence. It is possible that democratic forces were indeed beginning to emerge in the youth milieu, forces that posed a threat—if only in the distant future—to the existing regime. Possibly. In our view, however, another explanation is more plausible: of course it was no accident that youth, or rather, a particular segment of the youth population—educated, inquisitive, psychologically mature and aware young men and women, as a rule from families of the intelligentsia—came into the field of vision of the MGB. This was rich raw material for the officials of state security, material that allowed them to make a good career within a very short period of time, to confirm their usefulness to society, and in general to do their jobs. We were led to this conclusion by an analysis of archival documents relating to the rehabilitation of people who had participated in youth organizations. The documents show that practically none of the youth groups had been serious enough to arouse concern in the MGB. As a rule, the state security authorities learned of the existence of an "underground" organization either from one of the parents, who informed in the hopes of keeping his or her son or daughter out of trouble, or from their secret informers who worked in the student milieu. It often happened that the information came belatedly, after the circle had already clearly disbanded. Then the MGB would use provocateurs to reanimate the group, in essence creating it anew. Arrests, interrogations, and testimony by witnesses would follow. Practically all the cases were built on the youths' confessions and testimony from witnesses. Usually the material proof was such that only the overdeveloped imagination of the investigators could detect anything treasonous or terrorist about it. For example, the documents of the investigation of the Red Banner Commune noted the following: "Any red flag except for the state flag constitutes treason to the Motherland." It was an easy matter to obtain a confession from a young person who had no experience in the jesuitical practices of the investigators, especially if his or her father had been shot in 1937 as a tsarist officer or Trotskyite. The operations aimed at unmasking young "anti-Soviets" would culminate in triumphant reports to the higher levels of authority, followed by the corresponding awards, expressions of gratitude, and promotions.

The contemptible goals and criminal methods of the MGB officers were clearly exposed during the reexamination of cases involving counterrevolutionary crimes. A.R. Komarov, assistant military prosecutor of the Voronezh Military District, who was working to rehabilitate the participants in the Voronezh Communist Party of Youth, sent a letter in September 1954 to the Presidium of the Central Committee of the CPSU raising the issue of the accountability of people who had been guilty of the illegal arrests. In his short summary of the course of events, Komarov wrote:

The leaders of the former oblast MGB administration, who learned about the circle only after it disbanded, initiated a criminal case even though they were aware of the inoffensive nature of the circle. It would have been sufficient to reprimand the youths and their parents, practically all of whom were important officials in the oblast, including the second secretary of the obkom of the CPSU, but the MGB officials decided to build a case based on falsified information. They tortured the defendants into signing the protocols they needed, and suddenly there appeared, out of nowhere, a counterrevolutionary, terrorist organization aimed at overthrowing the existing regime. The youths returned from prison to their shattered families, crippled morally and physically. Meanwhile Sukhodolskii and Litkens, with a multitude of dark deeds on their consciences in addition to this one, continue to occupy high official positions, as though nothing had happened.

The career of the Chekist V.N. Sukhodolskii, which began in March 1938, came to an end in February 1956. The forty-nine-year-old major general, who had made illegal arrests, had falsified evidence, had tortured, and had violated "socialist legality" in other ways, was released from his job at the KGB for health reasons and given an augmented pension. According to information from the financial planning section of the KGB, in May 1956 there were 1,160 such "pensioners," who received from 2,500 to 4,000 rubles a month. Practically all of them, in spite of serious incriminating materials, were released from the state security agencies either for health reasons or in connection with staff reductions, which allowed them to claim substantial pensions based on their years of service or disability.

The wheel of repressions turned without interruption until Stalin's death. The wave of spy mania was followed by the campaign against cosmopolitanism. The arrests of Party workers and students were followed by arrests of doctors and Jews; it seemed that the process would never end. According to official data, as of January 1, 1953, there were 2,472,247 people in the camps and colonies of the USSR.[93] The death of the dictator brought an end to the escalation of the repressions. In March 1953, Stalin's successors had already made the first tentative attempts to bring punitive policy in line with the law. On March 27 the Presidium of the Supreme Soviet of the USSR issued an amnesty releasing over a million people from camps and colonies—although only a small minority of them were political prisoners. On March 28, the Council of Ministers of the USSR resolved to move the Gulag out of the MVD, which had been merged with the MGB on March 15, and turn it over to the Ministry of Justice. The special camps, not surprisingly, did not fall under the Ministry of Justice, since they had been

removed from the Gulag system and placed under the prison administration of the MVD. The Gulag remained under the authority of the
Ministry of Justice until January 21, 1954, when it again became a part
of the administrative structure of the MVD.

Two kinds of pressures were at work in the reorganization of the
camp system. On the one hand, numerous mass protests of prisoners,
primarily in special camps, forced the leadership of the Gulag to ease
conditions there and to remove the cruelest, most odious officials from
the camp administration; on the other hand, the obvious inefficiency
of forced labor itself and the sharp decline in the economic performance of the Gulag forced the leadership to act to improve conditions
in the camps.

In 1953 a commission under the Presidium of the Supreme Soviet
of the USSR examining the work of the MVD gave a very precise description of the state of affairs in the camps at that time. The report
indicated that the camp regimen had provoked "resolute protests
among the prisoners—refusal to work, acts of hooliganism, murders,
and escape attempts. The investigation revealed low labor productivity, absenteeism, a high rate of illness, and low morale among the prisoners." The report cited the following proof: in 1953 work attendance
amounted to only 77 percent of the workforce, and the number of
workers not fulfilling their norm came to 11.9 percent.[94]

Two directives issued by the Central Committee of the CPSU in 1954
brought about fundamental changes in the Gulag system. These were the
resolutions "On the Basic Tasks of the Ministry of Internal Affairs" of
March 12 and "On Measures for Improving the Work of Corrective-
Labor Camps and Colonies of the Ministry of Internal Affairs" of July 10.
These documents, along with a number of other Party decisions aimed at
"restoring socialist legality," brought about a certain humanization in the
camp system and noticeably eased conditions for the political prisoners.
They limited the powers of staff, redirected the attention of the Gulag
administration from "counterrevolutionaries" to the "criminal-bandit element," and introduced an eight-hour workday. On July 28, 1954, E.L.
Vladimirova, a prisoner of the Peschanyi Camp, wrote to the Central Committee of the CPSU: "This spring important changes have taken place in
the camp, which have given me the opportunity to write this letter. The
special camp has been closed; they've released the first group of young-
sters and are preparing for the release of the incurably ill. There has been
a significant change in the treatment of prisoners."

The gradual release of selected political prisoners began during
1954–55. According to data from the Minister of Internal Affairs, N.P.

REPRESSION AND PUNISHMENT 67

Dudorov, there were 940,880 prisoners being held in places of deprivation of liberty as of January 1, 1956, including 781,630 in camps and colonies. Of these, 14.6 percent were prisoners convicted of counterrevolutionary crimes (113,735 people). The decrease in the overall number of prisoners led to the closure of many facilities. At the beginning of 1956 there were 46 camps operating on the territory of the USSR, including 1,398 branch camps and 524 colonies. There were 159,250 prisoners being held in 412 prisons; 1,163 of them had been sentenced to death and were awaiting confirmation of the sentence or a pardon.[95]

On April 5, 1956, N.P. Dudorov sent a lengthy report to the Central Committee of the CPSU, providing a detailed description of the current state of the repressive system and a number of proposals for its reorganization. The minister concluded, without any reservations, that "the state of affairs in corrective-labor camps and colonies has been abysmal for many years. The location of camps and the assignment of prisoners to them have been driven primarily by economic concerns, which has led to the creation of large camps and necessitated massive transfers of prisoners throughout the country. . . . The overall number of prisoners remains high." N.P. Dudorov's proposals can be summarized as follows:

> We recommend against continuing the system of corrective-labor camps; these camps should be eliminated between 1956 and 1958, with the exception of two types of places of deprivation of liberty: corrective-labor colonies and prisons. . . . As a rule prisoners being held in colonies should not be required to work on construction sites, in the forestry, coal, or mining industries, or in other work involving heavy or unskilled labor. . . . Criminals should be isolated completely in the prisons; prisoners should receive differentiated treatment.[96]

I.A. Serov, the chairman of the Committee of State Security, sharply criticized the proposals of the minister of internal affairs. His report of May 10, 1956, addressed to L.I. Brezhnev, the secretary of the Central Committee of the CPSU, who during this period looked after the activities of the agencies of internal affairs, set forth extensive arguments supporting the preservation of the existing system and rejecting all of Dudorov's proposals as "incorrect" and "unacceptable." Serov argued that a reorganization of the camp system would "necessitate additional expenditures of government funds" and would "create the impression of the presence in the USSR of a huge number of places of incarceration." Furthermore, he found several provisions in the MVD report to be "politically incorrect."[97] The subsequent changes in the camp system that were introduced under the pressure of political and economic circumstances showed that the opinion of the KGB chairman was given significant weight in policymaking.

The Twentieth Congress of the CPSU gave an ideological basis to the release of political prisoners, which intensified, although it was not always conducted in a consistent manner. The edict of the Presidium of the Supreme Soviet of the USSR of March 24, 1956, "On Evaluating Cases against Persons Serving Terms of Punishment for Political, Work-Related, and Economic Crimes," sanctioned the creation of special commissions, which were granted the right to "consider the advisability of keeping incarcerated those persons who, although guilty of anti-Soviet crimes, do not present any danger to the state or to society." The release of citizens was not always accompanied by complete judicial or, much less, Party rehabilitation. For the hundreds of thousands of surviving prisoners of the Gulag, the process of legal restitution dragged on for many long years. But not all of them needed this official "justice." F.P. Krasavin, in August 1956, wrote to a former friend from the camps:

> I'm very glad that you have managed a successful return to life. Of course I don't know why you need complete rehabilitation. Unless it's for an administrative career. This kind of false restoration of honor cannot right the wrongs committed against you as a citizen. (After all, you're not the one who needs to be rehabilitated but our innocent government);* it will not restore your health or improve your economic situation; so who the hell needs it? [98]

As we can see, the former inmate of the Gulag had absolutely no illusions as to the "triumph of justice." And where would these illusions have come from? Felix Krasavin had been given twenty-five years in the camps under Article 58 in October 1951, at the age of twenty.

Stalin's totalitarian regime ruined the lives of tens of millions of people and subjected them to terrible suffering. The social order that existed in the USSR from the 1930s to the 1950s—and that even now is practically a model social structure for certain Russian citizens—was based on a monstrous web of crimes, chief among which was the Gulag system.

---

*Initially the text contained the words "immaculate synod of archscoundrels," which were subsequently crossed out.

A 1997 photograph of the notorious Moscow Butyrskaia Prison (known as "Butyrki"), designed by architect M.F. Kazakov and built at the end of the eighteenth and the beginning of the nineteenth centuries.

A row of cells in Butyrskaia Prison in a 1994 photograph.

A 1994 photograph of the residential facility of the Ikshansk Colony for Juveniles in Moscow Oblast, featuring a monument to F.E. Dzerzhinskii at the center of the inner courtyard.

A session of a people's court in Tomsk in 1949.

A 1938 photograph of Andrei Ianuarevich Vyshinskii (1883–1954), prosecutor of the RSSR beginning in 1931, prosecutor of the USSR from 1935 to 1939. Served as state prosecutor at the show trials of the 1930s.

A general meeting of workers of the Dynamo Plant in Moscow in 1936, voting for a resolution demanding the execution of members of the "Trotsky–Zinoviev Band" (the banner reads, "Eradicate from the face of the earth the Trotsky–Zinoviev Band: Such Is the Verdict of the Working People!").

Leaders of the Soviet state, Moscow, 1943. Left to right: G.M. Malenkov, V.M. Molotov, M.I. Kalinin, L.P. Beria, A.I. Mikoyan.

Hurrying to the May Day celebrations on May 1, 1946. Left to right: I.V. Stalin, L.P. Beria, A.I. Mikoyan, G.M. Malenkov.

Gulag architecture: a strict-regime barracks in the Dalstroi Butugychag Camp, Magadan Oblast (photograph from 1989).

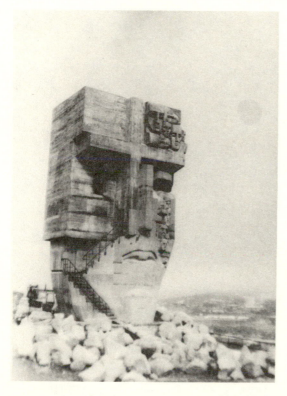

The Monument to the Victims of Stalin's Repressions, the Mask of Sorrow (by sculptor Ernst Neizvestnyi and architect Kamil Kazaev), erected in 1996 near the city of Magadan.

Traces of camp history: a guard tower dangling a section of rail at the site of a former concentration camp in Western Siberia above the Arctic Circle (1996).

Chapter 2

The Camp Economy

As a unique economic system based largely on the use of various forms of forced labor, the camp economy took shape gradually. During the early years of Soviet power, forced labor was considered to be primarily a form of punishment and only secondarily an economic force. Lenin's decrees prescribed the most "serious, unpleasant," and "onerous" hard-labor punishments to bribe takers, speculators, and other enemies of the people.[1] The special emphasis given by the Soviet authorities to building the forced-labor system can be explained by class-related factors and, later, economic considerations.

The first regulatory act concerning the labor of prisoners in places of deprivation of liberty appeared on January 24, 1918. The People's Commissariat of Justice resolution "On Prison Worker Teams" called for the formation of "teams of workers to perform work projects of national importance, with a level of difficulty not to exceed that of ordinary unskilled labor."[2]

The temporary instruction "On Deprivation of Liberty as a Measure of Punishment and Procedures for Its Implementation," issued on July 23, 1918, initiated the practice of compulsory labor in places of deprivation of liberty. Subsequent circulars from the Central Punitive Section of the People's Commissariat of Justice provided for the establishment of special prison workshops and of work projects outside prison walls.

On December 18, 1920, the interagency conference of representatives of the NKVD, the People's Commissariat of Justice, the Supreme Economic Council (VSNKh), the People's Commissariat of Labor, and the Chief Committee for General Labor Conscription resolved to require the NKVD Forced Works Section, whose authority covered forced labor camps, "to organize internal workshops and to work intensively to develop larger "production regions."[3] The VSNKh was instructed to designate a number of appropriate enterprises and facilities and to include camp workshops in the planning of the economic councils at the provincial level.

By the middle of 1921, there were 352 production workshops and 18 state farms in NKVD camps.[4] In addition, the Chief Administration of Forced Labor (GUPR) of the NKVD leased enterprises for prison labor and formed prison artels that worked under contract. It is interesting to note that the artels were permitted to accept work orders only from Soviet enterprises. The large enterprises that utilized significant amounts of convict labor included brick factories at the Kriukovo, Lianozovo, and Beskudnikovo stations outside Moscow, as well as a ceramics plant in Krasnoiarsk, two cotton-wool plants in Tula, a printing house in Moscow, and brick factories in Briansk, Vologda, Ekaterinburg, and Vladimir. In March 1922, a central economic administration was created under the GUPR to manage the production enterprises associated with the camps. It should be noted that, in spite of the relatively vigorous economic activity of the NKVD, there was absolutely no discussion of the possibility of establishing a self-sufficient economic system for the concentration camps, as prescribed under the decrees; only isolated camps managed, with great effort, to cover their own expenses.

It would be incorrect to maintain that the forced labor of prisoners played any significant role in the country's economy during the years of the Civil War or the NEP period. Nevertheless, it was during these years that the foundation was laid for the camp economy, which was to become an essential part of the economic system of the Soviet Union.

The Russian State Archive of the Economy contains a curious document, which we believe played a role in the subsequent formation and development of the slave-holding economy of the Gulag. This is a secret, strictly confidential report on the organization of prison colonies in promising economic regions, sent on November 10, 1925, by Deputy Chairman of the VSNKh of the USSR G.L. Piatakov to the chairman of the VSNKh, F.E. Dzerzhinskii.[5] Piatakov writes: "My study of geographical factors affecting industrial issues has convinced me that in order to create the most elementary conditions for a work culture, compulsory labor settlements will have to be established in certain regions. Such settlements could also relieve overcrowding in places of incarceration. The GPU should be instructed to explore these issues."

What were the economic regions that Piatakov found so promising? He had in mind, first, the area at the mouth of the Enisei River between the Arctic Circle and the seventieth parallel, north latitude, where the Kureisk graphite deposit is located. Piatakov reports: "The graphite in this region is of excellent quality. In spite of the difficulties related to transportation [Take note: he is concerned only with transportation, not mining.—G.I.], graphite from this area would be half the cost of imported graphite in Moscow."

If the work were to be organized efficiently, Piatakov believed that it would even be possible to export graphite abroad. The area also had a coal deposit, and just to the north (some 250 versts away) was the "famous Norilsk polymetallic ore deposit," which "clearly has great industrial potential. . . . The site contains an enormous amount of cobalt, nickel, platinum, osmium, iridium, and other metals. . . . Extracting the metals from these ores, not counting platinum and its associated minerals, will cover all the mining and transportation costs, and it will be like getting the platinum and its associated minerals for free." The deputy chairman of the VSNKh was convinced that, if the industrial promise of this deposit were to be recognized, appropriate facilities would have to be built in the area. Furthermore, the location of the region to the north of Turukhansk, Piatakov believed, "will undoubtedly be of great interest to the GPU in terms of establishing a settlement there."

The second promising area that Piatakov had in mind was the island of Sakhalin. He argued convincingly for the economic potential of using prison labor to exploit the island's natural riches.

The third area was the Kirgiz steppe (now part of Kazakhstan), due to its copper and polymetallic ore and large amounts of coal. Furthermore, "the geographical conditions of the region are very favorable not only for industrial mining but for all kinds of agriculture as well."

The fourth area was Nerchinsk District, famous for silver and lead deposits, which had been mined by convict labor in tsarist times. The mines had ceased production in 1907, in spite of their rich reserves of raw material. Piatakov agreed with the VSNKh on the need to reopen the lead and zinc mines in Nerchinsk District, noting that "bringing prisoners here to relieve the pressure on other places of incarceration, together with effective use of prison labor, could revitalize industrial activity in this district."

Though he limited his list to these four regions, Piatakov stressed that there were other "areas of interest from this point of view" as well. F. Dzerzhinskii, who jointly held the positions of chairman of the OGPU and chairman of the VSNKh of the USSR and who had been directly involved in the development of the economic policy of the Soviet state, did not see anything strange in Piatakov's proposal to turn prison settlements (in essence, concentration camps) into cultural and industrial centers of these enormous undeveloped territories. Dzerzhinskii assigned two OGPU officials, G.I. Blagonravov and M.F. Feldman, the task of preparing a joint decision on this matter and of providing "an official rationale for this innovation (hard-labor settlements)."[6]

Today the primary locations of the camp complexes are well known.

The largest ones were located in the regions mentioned by Piatakov. The former revolutionary could not have imagined the extent to which his abstract ideas were to be realized, the profound impact they were to have in the future, and how soon it would all happen.

At the beginning of the 1930s, forced labor became an important factor in the Soviet economy. On July 11, 1929, the Council of People's Commissars of the USSR issued a resolution, "On the Use of the Labor of Criminal Convicts," instructing the OGPU to expand the existing camps and establish new ones in the Ukhta Region and in other parts of the Soviet Union to develop and exploit their abundant natural resources by using prisoners' labor.

In 1929–31, a network of forced-labor camps was established on the territory of the USSR; by this time they had been officially renamed corrective-labor camps, many of which had already developed a clearly defined profile in various branches of industry—forestry, agriculture, oil production and coal mining, metallurgy and mining, construction, and so forth. By the beginning of 1932, the Gulag of the OGPU included fifteen camp complexes, officially called ITL (corrective-labor camp) administrations. The best known of these were the Solovetskoe, White Sea–Baltic, Ukhto-Pecherskoe, Svirskoe, Temnikovskoe, Visherskoe, Kungurskoe, Central Asian, Siberian, and Far Eastern administrations, among others. It should be noted that the terminology is not consistent; official documents use both "administration" and "camp" (*lag*) to refer to one and the same camp complex. Furthermore, a camp complex can have a number of often very dissimilar names, which complicates the task of studying the structure of the Gulag. For example, the acronym USIKMITL stands for the Administration for the Solovetskii and Karelo-Murmansk Corrective-Labor Camps; but other names are also used, such as SKITL (Solovetsko-Kem Corrective-Labor Camp), USLAG (Solovetskii Corrective-Labor Camp Administration), and a number of others, referring to a single camp complex with its administrative center in the city of Kem. Similarly, the Siberian camp complex is called sometimes simply SIBLAG and sometimes SIBULON (Siberian Administration of Special-Designation Camps).

Camp complexes as a rule consisted of several camp divisions (camps),* the number of which varied depending on the region and time period and could exceed a hundred. Camp divisions had branches—*lagpunkty, komandirovki,* and so forth—which were organized near remote work zones.

_____

*Depending on the nature of their production, camp divisions could be identified as column, mine, sluice, mine pit, phalanx, division, and so forth.

Like any Soviet institution, the Gulag underwent frequent reorganizations and name changes; camp administrations expanded, divided, and sometimes consolidated. The camp's structure, name, and even type of production could change, but its essential nature as an exploiter of human beings remained the same.

It is difficult today to say whether anyone in the Soviet Union was aware of the convention on forced and compulsory labor adopted at the meeting of the International Labor Organization in Geneva on June 28, 1930. The capitalist countries undertook to "abolish the use of forced or compulsory labor in all its forms within the shortest possible time period";[7] meanwhile, the homeland of socialism, also "within the shortest possible time period" and without public announcements, was institutionalizing the exploitation of involuntary labor in a way that was unprecedented in world history.

In spite of the rapid increase in the number of camps, the primary object of state exploitation at the beginning of the 1930s was not prisoners but special settlers, whose numbers exceeded severalfold the number of prisoners in the camps. Official data of the Special Settlements Section of the Gulag of the OGPU show that, in 1930–31 alone, 1,803,392 people were exiled to special settlements.[8] The number of prisoners being held in OGPU camps as of January 1932, according to official data, was 268,700.[9]

The camp economy actively exploited the forced labor of special settlers throughout the history of the Gulag. Settlers and exiles of various categories officially had the same rights as free contract workers as far as payment and labor conditions were concerned. In real life, however, as archival documents and the reminiscences of the victims of political repression themselves eloquently testify, the "economic use" of special settlers who were denied the right to travel freely and choose their place of residence was a form of outright exploitation.

Among the large number of documents on the "kulak exile," one in particular attracted our attention. This was a report entitled "On the Establishment of a State Farm on the Galka," prepared on March 25, 1931, by the Commandant Section of the Western Siberian Executive Committee (in Novosibirsk), addressed to the Regional Executive Committee.[10] Its author was I.I. Dolgikh, the chief of the Commandant Section, who was in charge of the relocation and economic utilization of dekulakized families. In 1930–31, the section served as a link between Siblag and the regional authorities. As of January 1, 1932, 265,846 special settlers were under its "protection." For the twenty-seven-year-old Dolgikh, who had joined the Communist Party in 1931, this was one of the initial steps on a path leading upward, to the very top of the Gulag, whose chief he became exactly twenty years later, in February 1951, at the rank of lieutenant-general. Dolgikh, like thousands of his contemporaries, built his career on the blood and tears of millions of his fellow citizens.

The report in question proposed a wild scheme to use the labor of special settlers in a radical transformation of Narymsk Region. The Commandant Section chief's attention had been attracted by a 70,000–75,000–hectare area in the basin of the Galka River, called the Galka Crests, "which were completely isolated from the local population." Dolgikh believed that the Galka Crests would serve as a perfect location for developing a "powerful model agricultural-flax and livestock and horse-breeding complex that will be able to supply not only our commandant's office but the entire Narymsk Region as well with food products, seed, livestock, purebred horses, swine, milk products, honey, and handicrafts."

The young office manager presented his economic fantasies in the form of an annual production program for the Galka State Farm Complex, complete with all the necessary projections of expenditures and income. The report concludes:

> In this way, an investment this year of some 700,000 rubles will enable the commandant's administration to create an economic and cultural center in the North. Such an ambitious project will be possible only if six to eight thousand strong and able-bodied settlers can be sent to the Galka to work intensively for two or three years; a colossal expenditure of human labor will be required to lay roads, to drain the swamps, [and] to clear the forests and rivers and make them navigable.

Dolgikh's initiative was not limited to plans on paper: by the summer of 1931, work had begun to clear hundreds of hectares of territory, an exhausting process that was done by hand. Manual labor was used to clear a tract several kilometers long through the Bakcharsk Swamps connecting the commandant's office with Tomsk, and an infrastructure was created for the "model" Siblag State Farm.

Not all the special settlers sent to the Galka made it through the two to three years of planned "intensive labor." By the end of the first year, the population of the Galka brigade had fallen by 20 percent. Of the initial 7,400 special settlers, primarily able-bodied men, 5,900 remained alive in the autumn of 1932. The Gulag authorities persisted in their single-minded pursuit of this scheme and increased the number of people in the office's control to 12,000. In spite of these reinforcements, they were ultimately unable to complete the Siblag State Farm project. Gradually the name "Galka" took on a pejorative meaning among the special settlers and came to signify pointless, exhausting labor.

During the first half of the 1930s, when the majority of the special settlers were semiliterate peasants, they were used primarily for crude, heavy labor developing the new territories. As the totalitarian regime became more firmly established, the population of settlers became more socially heterogeneous and nationally diverse. The uses of their labor became more varied, and often questions involving the use of their labor were decided at the governmental level, clearly reflecting the command-administrative nature of the Soviet economy. Thus, for example, concerned about the development of the fishing industry in Siberia and the Far East, the Central Committee of the Communist Party and the Council of Ministers of the USSR passed a joint decree on January 6, 1942, ordering the resettlement, in 1943, of five thousand able-bodied workers to work for the Iakutsk State Fishing Trust and create fishing farms. These workers were to be selected from among special settlers according to nationality: Lithuanians, Lithuanian Jews, Germans from Leningrad Oblast, and others. The state security agencies were entrusted with the task of keeping strict account of these workers and making sure that they were used only in the fishing industry.

Pursuant to this decree, fishing collectives and processing plants were established in the Iakutsk ASSR and a large number of special settlers (primarily Finns) were brought in to work at them. But since this form of the "organization of production" was based on forced labor, with "strict accounting" serving as the primary focus of management rather than material incentives to support the overall economic development of the region, the system began to collapse. Many collectives disintegrated of their own accord, and the plants experienced a catastrophic shortage of workers. In 1950, the Finns were released by official order and left Yakutia; many other special settlers risked what remained of their freedom, abandoned their work, and left the area on their own. Ultimately the local authorities, who had viewed the special settlers only as a cheap and defenseless source of labor and had made no effort to provide them with minimally acceptable living conditions and other material benefits, were left at a broken trough. By the mid-1950s, they were sounding the alarm, writing letters to the Central Committee and the government, accusing the MVD of poor management, and requesting new "state supplies of labor." But by then the times had changed, and Moscow's response was, roughly, It's your own fault. Deal with it yourselves.

The legal status of all the special settlers was such that they could be transferred at any moment from one place to another "based on production needs"; it made no difference to decision makers when these people were forced to part with the homes and other property that had cost them such effort to acquire. Few if any of the Soviet leaders could be bothered to create normal living conditions for the special settlers, although the MVD had issued orders to that effect. Special settlers were employed in various branches of the economy but primarily on hard-labor projects that were poorly paid and did not require any special skills. The widespread use of involuntary labor had a deleterious effect on production and hindered the improvement of equipment and the technologies of production.

The labor of special settlers played a significant although not decisive role in the camp economy, which was primarily based on the camps with their huge reservoir of virtually unpaid and mobile labor. During the first five-year plans, the Soviet Union built not only thousands of industrial plants but hundreds of concentration camps and colonies as well. These were an organically functioning part of the extensive Soviet economy, which was based on directives, non-economic methods of compulsion, and leveling. The lack of advanced means of production and economic incentives made labor, both free and behind barbed wire, equally ineffective and unproductive. But still, the free workers who turned out at the construction sites and plants were provided with a salary, meager though it was, whereas the prisoners worked essentially for nothing. The fact that forced labor was not paid for gave the illusion that it was cheap, which made it very attractive under a command economy that had the ability to mobilize significant manpower but lacked material incentives.

The first major work project of the camp economy was the White Sea–Baltic Canal, which was built by prisoners from two OGPU camps, the USLAG and the Belbaltlag, between 1931 and 1933. We will not go into detail on the history of this construction project, since it has been well covered in the literature;[11] we will simply note a few characteristic features.

This camp construction project (Belomor), like all those that were to follow, began without a technical plan, before the completion of topographical and geological analysis. Work began during the autumn without any dwellings, roads, machinery, trucks, or, naturally, anything else, including sufficient food. During construction, the authorities attempted to improve the provision of supplies to individual groups of prisoners, especially during the final stages of work, in the hopes of raising productivity, but working conditions remained extremely diffi-cult, and disease and starvation led to extremely high levels of mortal-ity. Documents show that many workers died after working on the canal for just two or three months.[12] Such "organization of production" be-came a tradition that remained unchanged for decades.

The first camp construction project was remarkably economical. Official data report that the canal cost 95.3 million rubles to build, as opposed to the 400 million rubles that had been projected. The sav-ings can be explained by two factors: minimal expenditures on tools and labor, and the low costs associated with maintaining the OGPU staff: only 37 career Chekists worked at the Belomor construction site, as compared to 140,000 prisoners.[13]

We believe that it was the relatively low level of state secrecy associ-ated with the project that enabled such a small number of OGPU per-sonnel to staff it. Unlike the majority of Gulag construction projects to come, which were veiled in a shroud of secrecy, there was no need to maintain several thousand professional guards, convoy troops, Chekist guards, political staff, and other camp administration officials charged with maintaining secrecy. Every single one of the many tasks involved in the canal construction, from the initial design to the guarding of prisoners, was carried out by the prisoners themselves.

The White Sea Canal project was headed by N.A. Frenkel, a former prisoner who had been amnestied, with his record cleared, in 1932. This was a man of extraordinary organizational skills, unusual resource-fulness, and legendary energy; he is unofficially credited with originat-ing the concept of the camp economy.[14] While himself a prisoner in the Solovki Concentration Camp back in the 1920s, Frenkel is said to have developed a plan for the transition of the camp to complete self-financing and had promoted it up through the chain of command to the higher authorities. Frenkel's proposals fundamentally changed the concentration-camp system and enabled the state to gain maximum profit from the use of prison labor. Before long, Frenkel became the chief of the economic section of the Special-Purpose Camps and sub-sequently an aide to the head of the Belomor construction site. Later his extraordinary biography included the construction of the 1930s' Baikal–Amur Mainline (BAM) Railroad and other Gulag construction projects. The camp administration showed its appreciation to the en-ergetic former prisoner. In 1936 he was granted 43,000 rubles by Deputy People's Commissar M.D. Berman to remodel and furnish his apart-ment. This sum, which was enormous by the standards of the time (the national average monthly wage for a worker during that period did not exceed 250 rubles), irritated many rank-and-file NKVD officials, and this figure was identified as "an example of wasteful spending" at Gulag Party meetings.[15] In January 1940, Frenkel took over the reconstituted Chief Administration of Railroad Construction Camps and remained in this position for seven years. He died in 1960 at the age of seventy-seven at the rank of lieutenant general in the engineering technical service.

Hydrotechnical installations were an especially valued part of the camp economy. A true Eastern despot, Stalin loved building canals. The White Sea–Baltic Canal was followed by the Moscow–Volga Canal, the Volga–Don, the Main Turkmen, the Volga–Ural Canal, and others. And all of this was done partially by hand, often without any particular economic justification, and with no regard for losses and consequences. Its primary purpose was to demonstrate Soviet might, for which instantaneous triumphs and dubious profit were sufficient.

During the first five-year plans, Party propaganda used all the means at its disposal to instill a "spirit of creative construction" (*pafos sozidaniia*) in the camps. Camp newspapers featured the hypocritical slogan "Labor in the USSR is a matter of honor, a matter of valor and glory." The life of the prisoner, torn away from family, normal work, and home, was filled with such slogans: "Camp Workers! Let us complete the ground preparation at a level of 150 percent!"; "Hail, Workers of the Fifth Camp Section Collective 'To Commemorate the Ninth Anniversary of the Death of Lenin'!"; "Better Provisions for Shock Workers!"; "The camp journalist (*Lagkor*) doesn't just expose people, he also organizes camp workers to complete their tasks." Later, public address systems were installed in the camps, adding to the Bacchanalia of slogans. A powerful loudspeaker, mounted on a tall pole to protect it from being damaged by prisoners, blared continually from morning to the end of the working day, filling the prisoners' minds with ideological cliches, phrases designed to direct their thoughts along the proper channels.

Brainwashing (*propagandistskii pressing*) through propaganda was combined with "corrective-labor brainwashing." All kinds of "initiatives," "special shifts" [*trudovye vakhty*], and "salutes" were dreamed up for the prisoners. A shock-work system, complete with a Stakhanovite movement* and worker competitions, was instituted, which, if the reports of

*The Stakhanovite movement was named after coal miner Alexei G. Stakhanov, who, in August 1935, set a new record for hewing coal, thereby launching a nationwide campaign to rationalize and raise industrial production. In conjunction with the campaign, the government introduced an array of material incentives to increase output.—Ed.

the camp administration are to be believed, reached nearly 95 percent of the prisoners.

The camp press played a significant role in the ideological "processing" of the involuntary laborers. The newspaper *Perekovka* (Reforging), for example, which began publication in 1932 at the construction sites for the Moscow–Volga Canal, saw its primary task as "inspiring the masses of prisoners in the struggle for rapid completion of the construction plan for the canal." In one of the issues of *Perekovka*, L. Kogan, chief of the camp construction project, explained to his prison laborers:

> Anyone who believes that hundreds of excavators, train engines, and so forth, are necessary for the task simply does not want to work on the canal. . . . Orient yourselves to the shovel, the wheelbarrow, the crusher, and the hand drill. . . . It's all well and good to know mathematics, but it is useless for construction if the worker doesn't know the correction coefficients for the Bolshevik will and for socialist methods of labor organization."[16]

As it strove to cultivate "worker enthusiasm" and a "spirit of creative construction" in society, propaganda practically turned the camp prisoner into a national hero. Many well-known writers contributed to the creation of this mystique, including M. Gorkii, V. Shklovskii, N. Pogodin, and others. This systematic praise of forced labor is one of the most shameful pages in the history of Soviet literature, which for many years not only remained silent about the presence of concentration camps and political prisoners in the USSR but in fact denied their existence.

D.N. Alshits, a writer and scholar imprisoned in the Kargopolsk Camp, penned a bitter reproach to his fellow writers:

> How many guards will they hire
> To keep us here behind barbed wire?
> But just guards are not complete;
> they also need people who beat,
> People who run things, administer
> Informers, too, an executioner,
> But most of all, it's not right
> without people who write!

The camp economy grew and gained strength with every passing year. Prison labor was used to build not only canals, roads, and dams but entire cities as well: Norilsk, Magadan, Dzhezkazgan, Salekhard, Komsomolsk, Nakhodka, Bratsk, Vorkuta, and dozens of others, many of which never appeared on maps but remained secret ghost towns.

How did a Gulag town get its start? Pavel Negretov, a "native" of Vorkuta, described the birth of this Gulag center as follows:

Settled life on the Vorkuta River began in 1931. The coal mine on its right bank gave the settlement its name, Rudnik, which is now one district of the town. In 1937 the Capital Mine was established on the left bank. The camp was initially located on the site of the current Moscow and Mine streets. Subsequently it was moved to the western side of the mine, and a free settlement was built on the original camp site, which in November 1943 became the city of Vorkuta. At that time there weren't very many free citizens in the new city; it was mostly populated by prisoners.

The words "camp" and "camp site" call up an image of barbed wire, but it was difficult to obtain in Vorkuta, and during its first years Rudnik was surrounded partially by wire, partially by plank fencing, and in places by nothing at all except a row of meter-high stakes with signs on them saying "Restricted Area" in red paint.[17]

During the 1930s, the Gulag expanded not only geographically. Its organizational and administrative structures also grew and adapted to cope with large-scale economic tasks as punitive policies became more severe. Beginning in the second half of the 1930s, the system of crediting workdays was discontinued and parole was abolished. All the camps began to install solitary-confinement punishment cells, whose functions, including the conditions and procedures for holding prisoners in them, were regulated by the Temporary Instruction of 1939 on Procedures for Incarcerating Prisoners in Solitary-Confinement Punishment Cells of Corrective-Labor Camps and Colonies of the NKVD of the USSR. The camp administration turned punishment cells into an ideal instrument of retribution against insubordinates and uncooperative prisoners. The prisoners were kept in solitary cells without any bedding; they were not taken out to work, and they were given hot food—swill (*balanda*)—only once every three days. The maximum term of imprisonment in a solitary cell was set at twenty days, which was beyond the endurance of many prisoners. It is interesting to note that the central Gulag administration was very critical of commandants in whose camps the number of prisoners in solitary exceeded a reasonable limit. Such overzealous prison authorities were often subjected to censure at closed Party meetings, where they were told to find other, more appropriate measures of punishment for offenders. The reason for such "humanitarianism" is absolutely clear—each prisoner in solitary meant one less worker-day, which translated into a loss to the state.

The "social status" of prisoners gradually changed as well. Up until the fall of 1937, propaganda, official correspondence, and even official documents avoided using the word "prisoner." Prisoners of the Gulag were more commonly called "foresters," "shock workers," "Stakhanovites," and so on. The term "Stakhanovite" in general was very widely used in the official lexicon of the camps during the mid-

1930s. Productive prisoners were housed in special "Stakhanovite barracks" and served rations from "Stakhanovite kettles" in the camp canteens. In 1936, the following was still a common scene at railroad stations: a prisoner transport train passes through, its cars adorned with Stakhanovite banners and slogans, as well as portraits of the leaders, Stalin and Kaganovich, and a poster saying "Stakhanovite Shock-Work Construction," and right there, for all to see, armed guards and the "Stakhanovite Shock Workers" themselves gazing through the gratings on the train windows at the free world outside. One day a high official in the camp administration witnessed one of these scenes in Petrozavodsk and realized how absurd it was, and only then did things change. In September 1937, the Culture and Education Section (*kul'turno-vospitatel'nyi otdel*) of the Gulag issued detailed orders stating that it was a glaring political error to call prisoners Stakhanovites.[18]

Before long the Gulag vocabulary lost not only the words "camp shock workers" and "heroes of the canals and construction sites" but also "camp workers" (*lagerniki*). The natural expressions "camp population," "camp society," and so on, were replaced by such administrative-bureaucratic terms as "contingent," "special contingent" (*spetskontingent*), "work pool" (*rabochii fond*), and others. Beginning with the end of the 1930s, the most common word referring to prisoners was the officially sanctioned abbreviation for the word prisoner, "z/k," in the plural "z/k z/k," and its derivatives, "zek," "zechka," "zeki."

In accordance with a directive of the political section of the Gulag of September 23, 1940, on the use of special titles for especially productive prisoners, all camp officials were instructed "henceforth not to refer to prisoners in oral form or in any documents as 'leaders of production' [*peredoviki proizvodstva*], 'the best people,' and so on, but rather to call them simply 'z/k performing at shock-work levels,' and, the highest form, 'z/k using Stakhanovite labor methods.'"[19]

By the end of the 1930s, the activities of the Gulag were completely shrouded in secrecy. The country was covered with a network of "post-office boxes," "special facilities," "units," "farms," and "forestry enterprises" with not a word about the camps or their inhabitants. The list of information constituting official state secrets in 1936 totaled 372 circulars, with 300 more added to them a year later.[20] The totalitarian censorship raged behind barbed wire as well as in the country as a whole. Each camp newspaper carried a label saying "Not to be removed from camp territory." Hundreds of censors worked vigilantly to ensure that no information, no matter how indirect, on the geographical location of the camp, the address of the editorial board, or the nature of the camp work projects filtered through to the camp press. The question of secrecy became particularly relevant in 1938–39, during the struggle with the "effects of sabotage in the NKVD system." "All the documents we are dealing with are secret, secret to varying degrees, secret nonetheless," asserted I.I. Pliner, the head of the Gulag, at a Gulag Party meeting in August 1938.[21]

Substantial material expenditures were required to ensure such a high level of secrecy; all secret correspondence was delivered by special couriers. In 1940 alone, 25 million secret packages were delivered by the NKVD field communications division. Of these, 675,000 secret packages and 537 tons in cargo of secret correspondence were delivered by the central apparatus of the communications division, for which 274 NKVD couriers received government awards.[22] Additionally, officials of the people's commissariat who had access to top-secret documents received a special bonus in pay.

"Top-secret" documents in the Gulag consisted primarily of information concerning the Third Section (operations) and the Second Section (accounts and distribution), the work of secret-service agents, sanitation and health issues, and the work of the fuel-industry section, as well as all information concerning secondary railway lines being built by prison labor, primarily in the Far East.

A significant intensification in the economic activity of the People's Commissariat of Internal Affairs occurred in 1938. The camp economy became a systematic, large-scale, and clearly expressed military-industrial entity. The number of prisoners and the length of their sentences rose sharply during this period.

If in 1936 there were thirteen camps with a total work volume of 1.2 billion rubles, by the spring of 1936 there were thirty-three, and the volume of capital construction had increased to 2.6 billion rubles. In the winter of 1937–38 alone, the NKVD established thirteen new camp complexes, primarily in the forestry industry, with a total population of new prisoners exceeding 600,000.[23] The Gulag had become, in the words of one of its officials, an "enormous complex" involved in a number of different industries, including mining, manufacturing, agriculture, and construction.

The gross volume of industrial output produced by the Gulag increased quite rapidly: in 1938, production totaled 1.5 billion rubles; in 1939, 2.5 billion; in 1940, 3.7 billion; and the 1941 plan totaled 4.7 billion rubles. The share of so-called mass-consumption goods in the overall volume of industrial output of the Gulag was relatively small, amounting to 1.1 billion rubles in the plans for 1941.[24]

On the eve of the war, the specific weight of certain types of goods produced by NKVD industrial facilities relative to the overall volume of the national economy was as follows: nickel, 46.5 percent; tin, 76 percent; cobalt, 40 percent; chrome-iron ore, 40.5 percent; gold, 60 percent; timber, 25.3 percent. The volume of camp production of non-ferrous metals amounted to 40 percent of the volume of production of the facilities of the People's Commissariat of Nonferrous Metals (*Narkomtsvetmet*). In 1940, the North Nickel (*Severonikel*) Metallurgy Mining Complex on the Kola Peninsula, along with a number of other metallurgical facilities, was turned over to the NKVD system.[25]

Timber processing in the Gulag amounted to 50 percent of the production of the corresponding commissariat. The Gulag provided the economy of the country in 1938 with 31 million cubic meters of wood, and in 1939, 44 million (of a planned total of 51 million cubic meters). In addition, a large quantity of wood was processed by the camp administration for its own needs.

NKVD coal basins provided the country in 1940 with 4.3 million tons of coal, with the 1941 plan calling for 5.3 million tons. Coal mining was carried out by four facilities of the Administration of Camps in the Fuel Industry: Raichikhlag (Amur Oblast), Bukachachlag (Chitinsk Oblast), Vorkuta (Komi ASSR), and Gusino Lake (Buriatsk ASSR). The Raichikhinsk deposit provided 85 percent of the total coal production of Khabarovsk Region during the prewar years (3.5 million tons). In 1938, 8,000 prisoners were working at this deposit, which was the largest deposit in the Soviet Union, where the coal was strip-mined.[26]

Development of fuel resources was one of the most serious problems facing the Soviet economy. The Party and government at the end of the 1930s initiated an intense program of developing the Ukhto-Pechersk Basin, using prison labor to obtain coal, oil, gas, and other energy resources. In 1938, the enormous Ukhtpechlag camp complex, located in the Arctic Circle in the expanses of the European Northeast, was divided into four independent camps, the biggest of which were the Ukhto-Izhemskii and the Vorkutinsk camps. The Party leadership of the country had high hopes for the region and invested substantial funds in its development. It was assumed that the new Ukhtinsk NKVD Complex would become the primary fuel provider for the North Sea Fleet.

The Soviet government proposed an unusually rapid increase in fuel production in Ukhtinsk Region. For example, the coal yield was to increase from 280,000 tons in 1940 to 12.5 million tons in 1945; oil production was to increase from 70,000 tons in 1940 to 1 million tons in 1944.[27] These ambitious plans were not to be realized; they would have required no less than a million additional prisoners to be sent to the Arctic Circle.

The Ukhtinsk NKVD Complex also included a radium-production facility—the only one in the Soviet Union. In 1944, 16.75 grams of radioactive radium was produced there.[28]

The camp economy retained its tradition of brick production; the NKVD system ran eighty-three brick factories. Prisoners produced 206 million bricks annually, and the Gulag leadership calculated their optimum capacity at 322 million.

The Gulag colonies prepared large quantities of so-called mass-consumption goods: shoes, knit products, aluminum kitchenware, hardware, horse harnesses, furniture, and many others. Here, as in heavy industry, production goals increased significantly. For example, the production plan for furniture increased in 1938 from 30 million rubles to 150 million. The Gulag was the country's primary and practically only supplier of industrial leather goods for the defense industry and the army. At the beginning of 1941, production of special sealing, which was to become one of the chief products of industry during the war years, began in the colonies.

Prisoners worked in agriculture as well as industry. In 1940 a large number of livestock was being raised in the Gulag for meat production: over 60,000 cattle and 290,000 sheep and swine. The country's largest meat-production enterprise was the Karagandinsk (Karlag) State Farm Camp, which contained over 150,000 sheep and some 30,000 cattle and was run using forced labor. Karlag incurred significant losses: twenty to thirty thousand rubles annually, with waste amounting to tens of thousands of livestock. In 1939 the backbreaking labor of starving Gulag prisoners provided the state with 143,000 metric centners of meat (the plan had called for 160,000 centners) and 406,000 centners of fish (compared to a plan of 500,000 centners).[29]

It is virtually impossible to list everything that the Gulag mined and produced. By 1940 the camp economy included 20 branches of the national economy, the most important of which were nonferrous metallurgy (which accounted for 32.1 percent of the overall goods production of the Gulag), forestry (16.3 percent), and the fuel industry (4.5 percent).[30]

The importance of capital construction in the Gulag ranked next to industrial production. In 1940, the NKVD accounted for 11 percent of all capital investment in the Soviet Union. In 1941, the People's Commisariat built a number of large military-industrial facilities whose overall value was estimated at 45 billion rubles. Of this sum, the NKVD was responsible for over 11 billion rubles, including 3.6 billion for capital construction of special facilities. The volume of capital construction undertaken by the NKVD increased annually: in 1938, 3.1 billion rubles; in 1939, 3.6 billion; in 1940, 4.4 billion. For the year 1941, the government budgeted 7.4 billion rubles to the NKVD for capital construction, which came to 167 percent of the actual volume of construction in 1940.[31]

In 1938, in record time (eight months), the Gulag built five pulp-and-paper plants vital to the military and industry, including the enormous Segezhsk, Solikamsk, and Arkhangelsk plants. The chief of the pulp-and-paper section of the Gulag, G.M. Orlov, received the Order of Lenin for completing the Party and government tasks on time.

The Norilsk Nickel Complex was extremely difficult to build. Construction was constantly behind schedule, and in 1939 the losses from faulty designs alone amounted to over 4 million rubles. The new director of the complex, A.P. Zaveniagin, who arrived at the construction site in April 1938, reported to Moscow on the reasons for the chronic delays: "The construction work is extremely disorganized: there is no chief engineer or the most elementary management staff. There is no one to organize production, work norms, salaries, or design. The work on site is disorganized. This is the reason for the pathetically low levels of labor productivity."[32] Things were not much better at the other large-scale camp construction projects: the phosphorous and chrome smelting (forfokhromosplav) plant in Kazakhstan, the Volgostroi construction sites for the Kuibyshev and Solikamsk hydroelectric stations, the Arkhangelsk shipyard (site No. 203), and others.

The construction of these "numbered" sites in the Gulag system was done by Glavpromstroi (Promspetsstroi). Its capital investments in 1941 made up 3.5 percent of the overall volume of capital expenditures for the country as a whole, with the entire sum of investments earmarked for military-industrial facilities. In 1940, construction work began for three aviation factories near Kuibyshev. Within a year, 850 million rubles were invested in this construction, which was unprecedented; this was the first time that over 400 million rubles had ever been invested anywhere.

A large amount of work was done on railroad and highway construction. In 1940, the camp administrations provided 1,731 kilometers of rail lines and 1,480 kilometers of highway for permanent and temporary use. The railroad construction plan for 1941 was nearly double that of 1940.

In setting markedly higher production targets for 1941, the government was counting not only on a rise in the number of prisoners and a greater reliance on their labor but also on a significant improvement in labor productivity. Sovnarkom economists believed that greater efficiency in the use of prison labor would result from the powerful growth planned for the material and technical base of the camp economy. If in April 1938 Gulag officials had complained at Party meetings that "the camps have no machinery whatsoever," by April 1941, at the Third Party Conference of the NKVD, S.N. Kruglov noted with satisfaction, "Over the past two years the government of the USSR has provided a large amount of equipment and vehicles for NKVD construction projects, which now have on site 636 excavators, 20,811 trucks, 658 cement mixers, 997 stone crushers, and a large number of solution mixers, compressors, scrapers, asphalt mixers, and so forth."[33]

In spite of the intensive efforts aimed at improving the technical level of Gulag construction sites and facilities, the majority of them failed to fulfill their state planning goals, and not only because there were practically no estimates or designs. In 1939, the Gulag completed only 88 percent of its construction plan, and the productivity level of prisoners' labor came to only 88–89 percent of the target. In 1940, the overall NKVD new-facilities plan was completed only at the level of 82.3 percent, the Gulag timber industry plan at 37.7 percent; Glavpromstroi at 60.6 percent, the Gulag fuel-industry plan at 85 percent, and so on. Only the Chief Administration of the Railroad Construction Administration and Dalstroi met their plan targets in individual areas of production.[34] The daily work productivity for a single prisoner under the Chief Administration of Special Industrial Production in 1940 was set at 46 rubles 27 kopecks, but the actual average level was 41 rubles 80 kopecks. The plan goal in railroad construction was set at 35 rubles 60 kopecks, but the actual productivity of prisoners working on the railroads came to 30 rubles 70 kopecks.[35]

Why was it that the dreams of the state planning officials for a significant increase in labor productivity in the NKVD system did not come true? Of course, the main reason was that no one had factored in the involuntary nature of the labor or the predatory, wasteful nature of the camp economy. Involuntary forced labor was markedly less efficient than the same work done by free workers. According to the data of the Gulag chief V.G. Nasedkin, in January 1941 labor productivity in construction and assembly work in the Gulag was 23 rubles 50 kopecks, whereas labor productivity under the Union People's Commissariats was 44 rubles 98 kopecks; in February the levels were 24 rubles 80 kopecks and 49 rubles 67 kopecks, respectively. Labor productivity on NKVD construction sites was an average of 50 percent lower than at construction projects under the Union People's Commissariats. Daily productivity per worker in the camps differed greatly from that under the civilian People's Commissariats: in the Chief Administration of Camps for Railroad Construction it was 64 percent lower than in the NKPS; in the Chief Administration of Camps for Industrial Production, 55 percent lower than in Narkomstroi; in the NKVD's Chief Administration of Camps for Hydroelectric Construction, 39 percent lower than the Glavgidrospetsstroi of the People's Commissariat of Construction.[36] A similar situation could be observed in all branches of the camp economy.

The Gulag was also unable to achieve plan goals for lowering the cost of manufacturing. Often the actual cost of camp production was several times more than the planned cost. For example, one cubic meter of land for the construction of the northern route of the Chibiu-Krutai was estimated to cost 1 ruble 6 kopecks, but its actual cost, based on calculations of camp economists, came to a minimum of 6 rubles. In 1940, the Gulag incurred a 22 million–ruble overexpenditure due exclusively to the increased cost of camp production. The camp economy had a predatory effect not only on people but on machinery as well. For example, in the Eastern Siberia Trust of the Chief Administration of Camps for Highway Construction, ninety-four trucks were completely destroyed within three years. The machinery on location at camp facilities and construction projects was seriously underutilized. There were many reasons for this, but the underlying one was that the basic concept of the camp economy was incompatible with qualified, productive, and conscientious labor.

During the prewar period, a number of industrial camp complexes were created in the USSR, along with enormous expanses of undeveloped territory set aside for them. The NKVD Far East Complex was in charge in Kolyma and Chukotka; the NKVD Ukhtinsk Complex, on the Pechora and Ukhta; the NKVD White Sea–Baltic Complex (BBK), in Karelia, and so forth.

The Council of People's Commissars' resolution of August 17, 1933, on the formation of the BBK read, "Belbaltkombinat shall be granted a monopoly right to the use of the canal and the natural riches of the adjacent regions." There followed a comprehensive list of tasks and authorities granted to the complex. All the enterprises located on the territory of the regions under development were turned over to BBK control, and all its operations were exempted from any taxation and duties until January 1, 1936. The resolution strictly provided that "no institutions or persons are to have the right without the special permission of the SNK of the USSR to interfere in the administrative management and operational activities of the complex."[37] It is worth noting here that the NKVD White Sea–Baltic Complex operated on the territory of an autonomous republic that had its own sovnarkom and oblast Party organizations.

Documents confirm that the BBK was a real "state within the state," which had control of a large territory with unlimited resources of labor, military subunits, industry, agriculture, transportation, schools, a theater, and so forth. During the prewar period, this "state" was headed by Senior Major of State Security M.M. Timofeev, the future head of the Chief Administration of Camps of the Timber Industry. The complex owed its existence to the White Sea–Baltic corrective labor camps of the OGPU–NKVD, established in 1931. As of January 1, 1939, there were 86,567 prisoners being held in the Belbaltlag, plus 27,856 special settlers (8,505 families), who had been exiled here during the dekulakization drive and lived in twenty-one settlements.[38] This was that very "work pool" that enabled the BBK to contribute to the achievements of socialist construction. The camp economy in this region was very productive. Prisoners built not only the famous White Sea–Baltic Canal and the Segezhskii Pulp-and-Paper Complex but also the Sorokskai-Obezerskaia Railroad Line, the Pindushsk Shipyard, the Sorokskii Port, the Povenetskii Ship Repair Facility, and many other facilities.

A great deal could be written about the development of the camp economy and its "achievements," but the picture will remain incomplete without providing the perspective of the Gulag personnel themselves, the people who organized production and managed, monitored, guarded, and escorted prisoners. We have a unique source that supplements the official production statistics with information of a different nature. This source is the materials (protocols, transcripts, etc.) of general and closed Party meetings of the Gulag, at which the rank-and-file personnel and the higher officials of the central Gulag apparatus, who enthusiastically supported the economic activities of their agency, engaged in criticism and self-criticism and expressed their opinions relatively freely.

We will not provide the names of the speakers—who they are in this case is not important. We will also refrain from commentary, since the point of the statements is quite clear as it is. We will only indicate the dates of the meetings at which the statements were made:

April 1937

"We know that there were times when prisoners in the camps worked without any days off, a month at a time."

"Who gives us the right to mock people? Our main task is not only to use people and their physical strength but also to reeducate them."[39]

April 1938

"The root evil is that the government did not provide the necessary funds when the forestry camps were established. . . . There are not enough horses, and machinery supplies are inadequate."

"There is chaos and disorder in the Ukhtinsk section. . . . Norilsk was planned wrong, and a lot of money has gone to waste."

"Wrecking in Kargopollag: tractors were sent, but no oil; but our camp chief is resourceful: he can get the tractors to run without oil."

"The Gulag cannot boast of success, especially where forestry is concerned. Given our expenditures, we should have had better results. . . . Our camps were organized without any systematic planning; some of the buildings were built in a swamp, and now they have to be moved."

"We are not rushing the work but operating at Bolshevik speed. We can't organize the camps to work gradually and carefully."

"We have to produce good-quality furniture. The machine shop of the Dmitrovsk Plant is supposed to produce 4 million rubles' worth of furniture. A review revealed that the furniture being produced according to Gulag designs is unsatisfactory."

"Things are very bad at Norilsk. Matveev did not complete his task."

"Wrecking took place in the assembly process at Volgostroi. In Norilsk, due to poor organization and delays in the construction of residential space, people had to live in substandard conditions for prolonged periods of time. At Segezha, the new chief of operations turned out to have been a spy since 1916 who engaged in wrecking while at Segezha."[40]

June 1938

"Wrecking and espionage activity have been discovered on the BAM line. Wrecking has occurred in railway construction in Siblag, and the embankments and excavations are slipping. Wrecking has and is taking place in planning and construction in Ukhta. The construction of the railroad in Norillag has been sabotaged. Trotskyite wrecking has also been discovered in Karlag; the saboteurs caused delays in agriculture and livestock production."

"We have money. The Party and the government have provided us with substantial aid in the form of specialists. Over 1,200 people have been sent to the camps."

"The Gulag organizational structure cannot withstand any criticism; it has a 'business-as-usual' attitude. As a result of the passivity of the Gulag apparatus, we are facing unaccountability, irresponsibility, lapses of work discipline, and terrible waste and neglect literally in every area."

"Our Gulag organizations suffer from colossal overexpenditures of funds. Some of our individual camps have gone as much as 40 million rubles over budget."

"In the year 1937, the economic activity of Ukhtpechlag brought 40 million rubles' worth of losses, plus 18 million more rubles of losses over the first six months of 1938. . . . Losses are built into the initial plan. Even if the plan is completed at a level of 100 percent, there will still be a 5 million ruble loss."

"We build giant projects, but how do we go about it? In 1937 we had losses amounting to 240 million in construction alone."

"The Gulag is a 'rich uncle' who overindulges construction projects and camps with money."[41]

August 1938

"The facilities we are working on undoubtedly are of interest to foreign intelligence services."

"We work with prisoners who, with only the rarest possible exception, are hostile to Soviet power; up to 70 percent of them were convicted of counterrevolutionary crimes. . . . The workforce in our system is primarily drawn from the rejects of socialist society."

"There are incidents of wrecking: unnecessary transportation of prisoners from place to place, disorganization in the area of sanitation and health; the enemies have introduced infections, corrupted the workforce, and squandered camp funds."

"Overstockpiling of property is taking place in the camp system. It is the wreckers who turn in inflated requests. In Kuibyshev there is so much surplus equipment that two or three new construction projects could be launched there."

"In 1936 enemies in the Far East under Deribas fooled us into believing that the Volochaevka-Komsomolsk Railway was already operational, but in fact it wasn't even close."

"There is a report from Ukhta: 'Hurrah! A new oil gusher has been discovered!' In fact there are none whatsoever."

"Ukhta has simply ruined us."

"Who gave Matveev approval to build the railroad in the snow? No one gave any such permission. Meanwhile enormous amounts have gone toward the railroad, and there's not a single kilometer of completed rail to show for it."

"Incidents of wrecking from Moroz: sanitation in the camps is terrible, with lice and starvation; people were sent there for absolutely no reason, and millions of rubles of Soviet money have gone to waste."

"Raichikhlag received five Kovrovets excavators from the Dmitrovsk plant. The excavators arrived without cables and other necessary parts. We managed to get three of them working after two or three months, but the other two are just sitting there without the chains and spare parts."[42]

January 1939

"Extremely low utilization of machinery at construction sites. At Volgostroi, 53 percent utilization of excavators; trucks, 45–50 percent; cement mixers, 35 percent."

April 1939

"In 1939, the Resources Mobilization Department is to distribute 45 million rubles' worth of equipment and materials in the Gulag system."

"At the Dmitrovsk plant, an imported 320 kilowatt transformer has been standing idle for two years because it has no registration certificate, and for that whole time no one has been able to figure out what it is for."

"A plan was essentially approved for Usollag, but no living accommodations were provided. . . . At the transit point 1,500 people were being kept. Taishetlag was planned for 8,000 people, but they sent 16,000. Last year the plan for delivering food products to the camps was not fulfilled. Lokchimlag was short 345 tons of food and 341 tons of other provisions; a total of 4,080 tons of provisions were not delivered. There is high mortality at these camps."

"The Gulag has some 60 million rubles' worth of unusable products. Now we have completely free access to the safe, to state money."

"You know that the work of the northern camps was and remains to this day literally paralyzed as a result of the breakdown in deliveries last year. The food situation in these camps is extremely critical. This has seriously affected the workforce, causing widespread disability and a high rate of mortality, and disease, and so on."[43]

March 1940

"We have not fully utilized the workforce on the construction site and in production; in spite of the enormous potential, we have been unable to utilize all that we should have and could have."[44]

April 1941

"Camp administrators and the officials of the Corrective-Labor Colonies Department (OITK, *Otdel ispravitel'no-trudovykh kolonii*) do not attribute any significance to the extremely low rate of use of the camp workforce;

they orient themselves exclusively to quantity and continually demand
additional supplies of workers."[45]

May 1941

"Not a single administration fulfilled its plan in April 1941."

"There are cases when a prisoner is given only four or five hours out of
twenty-four for rest, which significantly lowers his productivity."

"Food supplies, which are so vital to the camp, need to be organized in
such a way that food, too, will serve as an incentive for raising the productivity of prisoners' labor."

August 1941

"The principal task of the Gulag is to carry out the national defense functions entrusted to it by the Party and the government."

December 1941

"In Siblag, Karlag, and a number of other economic units, large numbers of prisoners refuse to work, and the necessary measures are not
taken to address this. . . . Millions of rubles are being wasted on the keep
of these slackers; in wartime conditions this is a crime."

"The increase in disability now taking place is ominous; in some camps it
is becoming downright dangerous."[46]

Such a lengthy citation from primary sources is not simply a whim
on the part of the author; it is justified for a number of reasons. First,
because of their strictly secret nature, this set of documents (protocols,
materials, transcript reports of Party organizations within the NKVD
and the Gulag) has never been used before, either in Russian or in
foreign scholarship. Second, these documents present a realistic picture of the state of affairs in the camp economy and convey a sense of
the times; in addition, taken together they reveal the mentality of the
Gulag officials. Third, the statements quoted above are very typical
and representative. Similar statements continued to be made over the
course of more than ten years; and at the end of the 1940s and the
beginning of the 1950s, the same things were said at Party meetings of
the Gulag about the losses and waste in production, the chronic inability to complete plans, the willful deceptiveness and hugely exagger-
ated estimates, the poor utilization of the "workforce," and the need to
struggle to preserve the "work pool."

The documents cited above, due to their semiofficial and nonpublic
nature, serve, we believe, as a useful addition to the official reports
and statements by the Gulag leadership that are increasingly being
quoted in the scholarship. One of these "official" reports, for example,

is the "Report on the Work of the Chief Administration of Corrective-Labor Camps and Colonies of the NKVD of the USSR during the Years of the Great Patriotic War," presented on August 17, 1944, to People's Commissar Beria by a Gulag official, Commissar of State Security of the Third Rank V.G. Nasedkin.[47]

This document, which in a certain sense can be considered to be a kind of hymn of praise to the Gulag, in no way reflects the real state of affairs in the camps and colonies during the years of the Great Patriotic War and does not give a complete picture of the degree of exploitation and the conditions of labor, the production costs or the human losses and levels of injury, the severity of the repressions, and so forth. For example, the report says, "As early as the first year of the war, the physical profile of prisoners changed substantially, which led to a decline in their ability to work." In reality this meant:

> On the very first day of the war, all the loudspeakers were removed, all correspondence was prohibited, newspapers were banned, and there were no more parcels. The workday was set at ten or even, under a few enthusiasts, twelve hours. All days off were cancelled. And, of course, there was an immediate and severe decrease in prisoners' food rations. . . .
> Within two or three months, the camps were filled with living skeletons. Indifferent, devoid of the will and desire to live, these skeletons, bones held together by dry, gray skin, sat on their bunks and indifferently awaited death. Carts, and later sleds, would come in the mornings to haul away the practically weightless corpses to the cemetery. By the spring of 1942, the camp ceased to function. It was difficult to find people who were even able to gather firewood and bury the dead."[48]

These are the words of Lev Razgon, who miraculously survived the war behind barbed wire. What saved the surviving camp inhabitants was the realization among some people in the higher administration that wood was necessary for the war effort, for manufacturing airplanes and skis, and as a source of the cellulose necessary for the production of gunpowder. When this became clear, the forestry camps began to issue rations at the level provided to free workers, prisoners were granted permission to receive food parcels and letters, and the loudspeakers were restored. The same changes occurred in other camps as well.

Camp mortality reached its peak in 1942, when an average of over 50,000 thousand prisoners died every month. In some camps the death rate was substantially higher than in the Gulag as a whole. In Sevurallag, for example (in what the administration considered to be the worst of the camps), in 1942, 1,615 prisoners died in January alone.[49] Mortality was so high that the Gulag leadership gave official permission to bury the dead in common graves without coffins or clothing. In all, according to our calculations, which are based on official data on the location and transportation of prisoners, over 2 million people died in the camps and colonies of the Gulag during the war years; over 10,000 of these were shot based on court verdicts and decisions of the Special Board—generally for refusing to work, for escape attempts, and for anti-Soviet agitation. Our totals do not account for losses among the so-called mobilized contingents, special settlers, residents of children's labor colonies, and several other categories of citizens under the authority of the Gulag, whose mortality rates were also extremely high.

Without insisting on a comparison, we will simply note that, according to a report of the Repatriation Authority of the USSR Council of Ministers for 1946, "On Implementing the Decisions of the Government of the Union of SSR on Repatriation of Citizens of the USSR and Citizens of Foreign States During the Great Patriotic War (1941–1945)," the total number of Soviet citizens (civilians and prisoners of war) who died while imprisoned by the Fascists was 1,135,000.[50]

In all, during the war years, over 5 million prisoners passed through Gulag camps and colonies; of these, about 1 million were released early and sent to the front.

As of July 1, 1944, there were 56 camps in the Gulag that reported directly to the center and 69 regional administrations and departments of corrective-labor camps and colonies. These camp complexes included 910 individual camp divisions and 424 colonies.[51]

The war brought significant changes in the prison population. Since prisoners convicted under Article 58 were not eligible for early release and in spite of their frequent requests were not sent to the front after the completion of their terms, their proportion increased from 27 percent in 1941 to 43 percent in 1944. The relative number of female prisoners also shot up. In 1941, they made up 7 percent of the overall prison population; by the summer of 1944, that number had grown to 26 percent.[52]

The overwhelming majority of those remaining in the Gulag were ill, emaciated, and infirm. Many of them had survived purely by chance—some had been given light work, others had encountered a "good" boss or a humane doctor. It was unrealistic to expect a high level of labor productivity from these people; the camp authorities could only meet their production goals by making the working day as long as possible and maximally increasing the number of prisoners. The internally established daily routine gave prisoners three days off a month and eight hours daily for uninterrupted sleep. Prisoners were expected to work for the entire time remaining, and, in practice, were often deprived of even the minimal envisioned rest time.

From the very first days of the conflict, the Gulag contributed to the war effort; all industrial colonies were reprofiled to produce ammunition, special sealings (*spetsukuporki*), uniforms, and other military supplies. On February 18, 1942, a special department of military production was created in the Gulag, charged with the organizational and operational/technical management of all NKVD facilities that produced ammunition and special sealings. By the end of the war, the Gulag was the USSR's second-largest supplier of fragmentation land mines and ammunition sealings.

In addition to military production, the Gulag provided workers for the most important NKVD construction projects: the aircraft factories in Kuibyshev, metallurgical complexes in Lower Tagil, Cheliabinsk, Aktiubinsk, and the Transcaucasus; the Norilsk Kombinat; the Dzhidinsk Kombinat; the Bogoslovskii Aluminum Plant; the oil refinery in Kuibyshev, and many others.

Specialists and skilled workers were sought out among the prisoners and sent to work in the defense industry. During the war years the Gulag supplied workers for 640 facilities of other people's commissariats, in comparison to 350 facilities that utilized prison labor before the war.

The Gulag organized 380 special colonies to serve the most important defense facilities, holding 225,000 prisoners under the usual prison regimen. They worked producing tanks, airplanes, ammunition, armaments, and so forth.

We will not go into detail on the "achievements" of the camp economy during the war period; they are thoroughly covered in Nasedkin's report. We will note only that for millions of humiliated, morally crushed, and physically tormented prisoners this was truly heroic work. But what was the point of their efforts, and who appreciated them?

The victory in the Great Patriotic War gave the Soviet leadership a real opportunity to change the structure of the national economy that had taken shape in the 1930s and to reorient it toward the needs of the people rather than the state. But the trench-war mentality and the established patterns of thinking in terms of the military threat kept the governing elite from curtailing the further growth of the military-industrial sector. The Cold War, which began the year after the victory, and the development of new types of lethal weaponry in the world seemed to confirm the course proposed by those who supported the militarization of the Soviet economy. These factors deeply affected the policy decisions relating to reconstruction and the subsequent development of the entire economy.

Stalin, Beria, and Malenkov, along with many leaders of the major industrial facilities and branches of heavy industry, supported a return to the model of economic development of the 1930s, which meant a continued low living standard for the population and a continuing escalation of state-sponsored exploitation under the cover of propagandistic slogans and appeals.

Significant financial expenditures were required to achieve these goals of developing industry, especially heavy industry. Of the 247 billion rubles budgeted by the state in 1946–50 for industrialization, 163 billion went to heavy industry, 59 billion to developing transportation and communications needs, and 25 billion to producing consumer goods.[53]

After the devastation of the war, and given the country's limited resources, such ambitious plans necessitated a widespread reliance on "voluntary" labor and compulsory methods; the role of the camp economy expanded accordingly.

Just before the war, the Gulag had created several chief camp administrations in its production departments that operated as central branch administrations: administrations of forestry (GULLP), railroad construction (GULZhDS), mining and metallurgy (GULGMP), industrial construction (Glavpromstroi), highways (GUShOSDOR), and others. These were structural divisions of the NKVD that reported directly to the people's commissar and his deputies. Their primary function was to manage the production activities of the NKVD camps, construction projects, and enterprises under their authority. The chief camp production administrations were relatively autonomous. The Gulag's functions in this area primarily had to do with the incarceration and isolation of prisoners.

In the Gulag itself, it was the Third Administration that dealt with production-related issues; it included departments for industry, planning, forestry, agriculture, capital construction, supply, and distribution. The organizational structure of the Gulag included also a number of administrations and departments charged with security, record-keeping, and distribution of prisoners; they were also responsible for the daily activity and efficient functioning of the camps and colonies. The Gulag had a particularly cumbersome management structure, with a top-heavy apparatus and a redundancy of functions spread across various departments. This was probably one of the country's most heavily bureaucratic institutions. Every day the leaders of the camp divisions would receive six or seven directives from the central board. In 1951, the Gulag apparatus received 132,738 reports from camps and colonies. They included five-day, ten-day, semimonthly, monthly, bimonthly, quarterly, and six-month reports, compiled eight times a year, as well as annual reports. An enormous amount of state funds went to maintaining the apparatus that prepared and reviewed these documents. In 1954, after the Council of Ministers pointed out "serious flaws in the organizational structure and excesses in staffing of the administrative-management apparatus of the Ministry of Internal Affairs," the number of internal reports was cut nearly sixfold with no serious effect; 136 of the 186 existing types of reports were completely abolished.

As the economic activity of the NKVD–MVD increased, newer and newer production-related administrative divisions were formed. In addition to those listed above, in the postwar years the MVD included such administrations as Glavgidrostroi, Dalstroi, Eniseistroi, Glavsliuda, Glavspetstsvetmet, Glavspetsneftestroi, Zheldorproekt, the High-Rise Building Construction Department, and a number of other departments, administrations, institutes, and design offices whose activities were associated with construction and industrial and agricultural production. In addition to these management structures, the MVD naturally also maintained a prison administration, chief administrations of the militia and convoy troops, sections for the special settlements and children's colonies, and over a dozen special sections and special directorates of various kinds. As of March 1, 1948, there were 129 primary Party organizations with 8,133 members, as well as a Komsomol organization with 1,890 members, reporting to the Party committee of the central apparatus of the MVD.[54] In 1948, the ministry's administrative and management expenditures alone came to 11,589 million rubles.[55]

Periodically the Party and government would issue appeals aimed at increasing economic efficiency, and the ministry would conduct a campaign to cut costs. As a rule, the approach was to cut staff and make changes in the administrative structure. In 1949, the head of personnel management, B.P. Obruchnikov, proudly reported at the Sixth Party Conference of the MVD:

> Working with department heads, administrators, and personnel managers, we have succeeded in returning 778,596 rubles in savings to the government by cutting staff and introducing structural changes. . . . We have been able to cut several thousand idlers, because the ministry's plan has been completed, which has resulted in a savings of over 700 million rubles.[56]

In 1952, the ministry cut annual expenses by over 800 million rubles. This was done by a government decision to abolish all forms of bonuses for rank and length of service to employees in the MVD system as well as benefits such as internships and special rations. This order did not cover militarized divisions. Some MVD employees, disturbed by the prospect of a decline in their standard of living, planned to transfer to other agencies. The situation was so serious that Minister S.N. Kruglov was forced to give a special explanation to the staff concerning the "vitally important political measure of the Party and government." His main argument was the following: "We know that the Central Committee of the Communist Party and the Soviet government have always taken care of the staff of the Ministry of Internal Affairs. We have lived well and will live even better!"[57] And in fact the minister's optimism was well founded.

As of January 1, 1949, the MVD system included 67 independent corrective-labor camps with some 10,000 camp divisions and facilities (*lagpunkty*) and 1,734 colonies containing 2,356,685 prisoners, of whom 1,963,679 were able-bodied workers. Over half (55.8 percent) consisted of convicts between the ages of seventeen and thirty; women made up 22.1 percent of the overall number of prisoners.[58]

In addition to supplying workers to its own production facilities, which utilized some three-fourths of the total number of able-bodied prisoners, the MVD provided prisoners on a contract basis to work for other ministries and agencies. In 1947, 507,800 camp slaves worked "outside."

The economic activity of the MVD was so irrational and inefficient that even such a potentially lucrative form of commercial activity as "renting out workers" did not bring the ministry any profit. The total balance of income and expenses of the MVD for 1949 shows that "income from labor supplied outside" in 1948 amounted to 6.8 billion rubles, while "expenses to maintain labor supplied outside" exceeded 8.5 billion rubles.[59] Funds were requested from the national budget to cover the losses in this category of expenses.

In addition to prisoners, civilian specialists were also hired to work in the MVD system. These were primarily engineers and technicians in various branches of industry and transportation, agricultural specialists, medical workers, lawyers, economists, and educators. These specialists were the ones credited with carrying out the grandiose tasks that the government assigned to the ministry. The place of the prisoners in the economic activity of the MVD was defined by terms such as "work pool," "workforce," and "work power."

The majority of hired specialists belonged to the intermediary level of the administrative staff and held low officers' ranks. The production activity of practically all of these specialists was to one degree or another associated with the labor of the prisoners; in fact, their material welfare often directly depended on prisoners' labor. Still, no one ever recalled or mentioned this fact.

The immorality and absurdity of the Gulag system of economic management is clearly demonstrated by a document that circulated around all the camps and colonies of the USSR in 1948 and was enthusiastically supported by its addressees. This was an "Appeal" to the "Workers, engineers, technicians, and employees of the camps and colonies of the Gulag of the MVD of the USSR" from collectives of divisions under the Administration of Corrective-Labor Camps and Colonies of the Moscow and Moscow Oblast UMVD. The document, which was adopted on the occasion of the socialist competition campaign that was under way in the country to commemorate the thirty-first anniversary of the October Revolution, reads, in part:

> Marching forward in step with the leading enterprises, the collectives of our divisions, having extensively initiated socialist and labor competition,* completed their production plan for gross production during the first half of 1948 at a level of 109.5 percent and for goods production, 113.4 percent, and, declining to accept government subsidies amounting to 5,394,000 rubles, have saved 1,021,000 rubles over the planned level. . . . The UITLiK Collective of the Moscow City and Oblast UMVD calculated its production capabilities and internal resources and took on a new, additional commitment—to provide the state by the end of the year with surplus funds amounting to 3,500,000 rubles over the planned level and to complete the annual production plan by November 1, 1948.
>
> As we take on these new, increased commitments, we challenge all the collectives of the camps and colonies of the Gulag of the MVD of the USSR to support our initiative and further expand the struggle to accumulate additional funds in savings above budget, in the awareness that each extra ruble is an investment in the national effort for the early completion of the postwar five-year plan.
>
> We are confident that our challenge will spark an enthusiastic response among the collectives of the camps and colonies of the Gulag of the MVD.[60]

As we see, there is not a word here about those who would, by their back-breaking daily labor, actually carry out these promises and appeals—not a word about the prisoners. There was nothing surprising about the fact that the "Appeal" remained silent about the prisoners, the primary productive force of the Gulag. After all, milkmaids and swineherds did not talk or think about the animals when they took on their socialist commitments to provide so much milk or meat above the planned levels. Everyone knew without being reminded that milk

---

*Labor competition (*trudovoe sorevnovanie*) is competition among prisoners.

and meat came not from farm workers but from livestock. The analogy with the Gulag is nearly perfect.

Only occasionally at closed Party meetings did the workers of the camps and colonies allow themselves to express concerns about the "decline of the physical profile of the work resources." Here are some excerpts from statements made by medical personnel in March 1948 at the Fourth Party Conference of the UITLiK of the Moscow and Moscow Oblast UMVD:

> No one has said anything about the problem of restoring the health of our contingent, which is doing the actual work to complete the production plans for which we receive awards and the Red Banner. Frequently the contingent in our facilities is worked to complete exhaustion.... All possible measures must be taken to decrease work-related injuries and illnesses and prevent the depletion of our contingent.
>
> Unless we create normal conditions for our contingent, we will be unable to restore their health. The transit prison provides our divisions with a healthy contingent. But within three or four months it can no longer work. The OLP-ITK leaders place impossible demands on people with war wounds and other physical defects, and they quickly become unable to work.[61]

We will remind you that these statements concern the camps and colonies in the area around the capital, where individual colonies, for example, the Kriukovskaia, were exempted from the usual restrictions and were open to visits from foreign delegations from Italy, England, and other countries.

One interesting detail: The conclusion of the Moscow doctor concerning the length of time the "contingent" was typically able to work is completely confirmed by the observations of Gulag prisoners themselves. Analyzing camp labor, A. Antonov-Ovseenko wrote, "A prisoner could withstand no more than three months working on road or railway construction, in stone quarries and mines and at timber sites. On average . . . I repeat: the usual term of labor behind barbed wire was three months. Himmler's statisticians arrived at the same figure for their concentration camps."[62]

This is clearly the primary factor explaining the instability of the camp labor force. For example, in 1947, 1,490,959 new convicts entered the Gulag; during the same period, 1,012,967 prisoners left the Gulag; in 1948 there were 1,078,324 new convicts in camps and colonies, with 842,036 prisoners released over the same period. A similar picture could be observed in other years as well, with the "average annual population" of camps and colonies fluctuating at around 2.5 million people.[63]

Beginning with the end of the 1930s, the region that came to symbolize the Gulag was Kolyma, and Dalstroi was synonymous with hard labor. This monster of the camp economy came under NKVD control in 1938. By this time there was no organization in Eastern Siberia that was not serving Dalstroi. During the following years, the camp economy expanded even further; in effect, it was a new and massive mining and industrial region that occupied a territory of 2.5 million square kilometers. In addition to gold, large quantities of tin, tungsten, cobalt, and other strategic metals were mined there. In 1947, there were fifty-two gold mines operating in Dalstroi, along with five gold pits, five gold-extraction plants, seven tin mines, eleven tin-concentration facilities, and twenty-five stationary electric plants. Some 3,500 kilometers of highways and railways were constructed as well.[64] Dalstroi was supplied exclusively through the port of Nagaevo in Magadan, and many of the gold mines were located a thousand or more kilometers away from the port.

The use of prison labor to mine gold by hand began in Kolyma in 1935. Until 1940, mining was concentrated in large, rich deposits, each of which contained from 70 to 120 tons of gold. Beginning in 1944, the gold reserves in the new deposits were supplemented by smaller and less concentrated fields scattered across the limitless expanses of the region. During 1946, 102 new deposits were developed, with an overall gold reserve of 25 tons, and the existing deposits continued to increase their yield at a modest rate. Before 1939, Dalstroi could extract over 20 grams of gold per cubic meter of rinsed sand. During the following years, however, the content of precious metal in rinsed sand declined steadily. In 1946, the amount was 6.8 grams and in 1947, 6.1 grams per cubic meter. In 1947, each ton of extracted gold meant over 600,000 cubic meters of processed rock mass; the annual plan required the processing of 31 million cubic meters of rocky soil. For comparison we note that the overall volume of rock and earth moved during the two-year construction of the White Sea–Baltic Canal came to 21 million cubic meters. All mining under Dalstroi was done in permafrost.

The winter of 1946–47 was harsh and long, but the gold mining continued without a break, which was unprecedented. Much of the work was done by hand. Concerned about the extremely low level of labor productivity among the Kolyma "cadres," the government attempted to mechanize the gold-mining process. On October 29, 1945, the Sovnarkom of the USSR issued a resolution requiring Dalstroi to raise the level of mechanization of specific tasks to 70–95 percent. The resolution provided for the importation of equipment, technical materials, and vehicles worth $21 million from the United States for use in Dalstroi. The Cold War intervened, however, and less than $8 million worth of the planned imports were delivered; none of the primary mining equipment was received.[65] Even the most intense exploitation of labor could not compensate for the lack of machinery. Dalstroi completed only 58.8 percent of its gold quotas for 1947.

Many of the survivors of the Gulag recalled the inhuman conditions of labor in Dalstroi. In 1954, the Central Committee of the CPSU received a letter from prisoner E.L. Vladimirova, who had previously been a journalist for the newspaper *The Cheliabinsk Worker*. The purpose of her long letter was to inform higher Party officials about the inhuman conditions endured by Soviet prisoners and to help the Party restore the justice and socialist legality that had been destroyed by enemies of the people. Vladimorova arrived in Kolyma in the autumn of 1938 and spent nine and a half years there, including three—from 1945 through August 1948—at the hard-labor camps of the Tenkinsk Mining Administration. She wrote only about what she herself had seen and experienced. What struck her most in the Dalstroi camps was the complete contempt for people, for the most elementary human rights, and often for human life as well. For example, several thousand prisoners were transported to Colorful Gravel Bay (Bukhta Pestraia Dresva), to the north of Magadan, to settle the area. This took place at the extremely dangerous transitional time of year when the Kolyma summer changes practically overnight to winter. The people were in their summer clothing and were pressured by the convoy guards to put their tents up hastily. A snowstorm that began during the night blew down all these unsteady shelters, and all the prisoners were frostbitten; many were crippled, and many others died.

People poured into the Magadan camp hospital in an uninterrupted stream from the mines and ore fields with serious heart ailments, scurvy, and dystrophy. Some of them had been working in the mines only for a short time. In many camps, prisoners starved en masse, and there was a very high mortality rate. The number of prisoners who were disabled, even in the strict camp interpretation of the word, reached 50 percent. Seasonal ailments were widespread—frostbite in the winter and diseases of the eye in the spring, brought on by the glaring sun and snow and in some cases leading to total blindness. The prisoners were supposed to be supplied with sunglasses, but of course they were not, and people went blind as a result. The camp for the disabled held a large number of people who had been blinded by the snow and moved around the camp in lines. The rate of work-related injuries was extremely high, and there were many suicides. The physically demanding nature of the work in the mines (loading and unloading was done by hand) was compounded by the twelve-hour shifts spent in the permafrost. The rations were extremely meager and monotonous. The main food was bread, provided in portions of from 650 to 1,200 grams, but this ostensibly large ration was in fact insufficient to restore the energy lost by the organism to the cold and to heavy labor. The bread itself was of very poor quality, and there were cases when it was served half-baked (on purpose, so it would weigh more); the sticky, underdone bread had to be served into the prisoners' caps, so that it would not run. Both the criminal prisoners and civilian employees, particularly the supervisors, raided the food supplies regularly. It may sound strange, but according to Vladimirova, it was the mining camps that provided the worst rations.

Things were no better with other supplies. Entire mining brigades in the Dalstroi camps wore shirts that were literally tattered, and during the winter many prisoners worked in rope sandals, so-called *chuni*. In the Butugychag camp division, an entire 200-man infirmary was held completely naked, without underwear or outer clothing, and with groups of two and three sharing a blanket; they were given clothing only when someone from the higher leadership happened to visit the camp.

A similar situation with food supplies and clothing could be observed in practically all camps of the Gulag. Robbery was only one of the reasons; the other was the Gulag supply system itself. "Over the past eight years, Gosplan has provided for only the barest minimum of the material needs of the prisoners," we read in an explanatory note to a 1949 MVD request for supplies for Gulag prisoners. "Funds issued for 1948 covered 32.5 percent of the demand for cloth for clothing, linen, and bedding; 44 percent for various forms of footwear; and 51.2 percent for felt footwear. As a result, the state of affairs with provisions is extremely critical. . . . An overwhelmingly large amount of the prisoners' personal property has been repeatedly repaired and mended."[66] Prisoners were given automobile tire treads to tie onto their feet instead of shoes. In January 1944, the government decided to release the NKVD from the requirement of turning in old automobile tires and inner tubes and to allow them to use them for footwear.

Somehow, in spite of the cold, starvation, disease, and death, the inhabitants of the Gulag continued to build, to mine, and to produce under the close watch of the armed guards. In 1948, 96.2 tons of chemically pure gold, 8.7 tons of platinum, and 38.8 tons of silver were mined in the MVD system—by convict labor.[67]

The French writer Saint-Exupéry once wrote, "Hard labor is not defined by its tools; it is not the physical demands that make it so terrible; hard labor is where the blows of the pickax are deprived of meaning, where labor does not bring people together."[68] Camp labor was devoid of meaning not only in the human sense but often in the economic sense as well. The former prisoner O. Adamova-Sliozberg recalls:

> We hollowed out ditches in the frozen ground. We worked with heavy miners' hacks in fifty-degree below zero weather. We tried to fulfill the quota. . . . It was extremely difficult work. The ground was like cement. Our breath froze in midair. Our shoulders and backs ached from the strain. But we worked honestly. Then in the spring, when the earth thawed, they sent a tractor out with a ditchdigger, and in a single hour it dug a ditch the size of the one that had taken six people two months to dig.[69]

This was punishment by means of senseless labor, an especially severe and humiliating punishment for people who had spent their lives at honest labor.

Beginning in the 1930s, a government-approved tradition developed in the camp economy: practically all construction projects were initiated and carried out without designs or financial estimates, and the financing was done based on actual expenditures. Sometimes surveying and construction work began simultaneously. Thus a plant would be built, a camp established, and prisoners brought in, and at that point it would become clear that there were only enough reserves of the raw material to last three or four months. In many cases, mines were planned and built on unprospected deposits; they would do the drilling, but there would be no oil. The western section of the BAM was built at great cost in human life and resources, and as they reached the end of construction, the workers discovered that the Taishet–Ust-Kut line of the route had been built without factoring in the planned construction of the Bratsk Hydroelectric Plant. When construction of the plant began, a substantial section of the railway had to be rerouted, resulting in a multimillion-ruble loss to the state. Many other examples could be cited.

One of the officials working in Eniseistroi, Major of the Internal Service V.N. Pavlov, studied the activity of this huge camp-industrial complex over the course of three and a half years. He reported to the Central Committee of the CPSU that in spite of the political and economic importance of the Enisei projects to the Ministry of Internal Affairs of the USSR, "very little has been done, and what has been done has been extremely inefficient in its use of government funds, resulting in cost increases and direct losses amounting to hundreds of millions of rubles, money that in some instances was simply tossed to the winds." The Central Committee commission that followed through on Pavlov's statements confirmed nearly all of his conclusions.

The ultimate symbol of senseless labor, volunteerism, and money tossed away to the winds, however, would most likely be the construction of the Salekhard–Igarka Railway. There is evidence that the originator of this pointless effort was Stalin himself, who had once stated at a meeting of the Council of Ministers that the Russian people had long dreamed of having reliable access from the mouth of the Ob River to the Arctic Ocean.[70] In April 1947, the government passed a resolution to build a railway line to a nonexistent seaport in the Ob Bay, and by May, the Ministry of Internal Affairs began organizing the construction work. Several dozen camps were established, prisoners, horses, and some machinery were brought in, and the planning and surveying work was initiated. The region where the dictator's latest "great construction project for communism" was to take shape was one of the most inaccessible and unpopulated areas of the country (with a population density of 0.05 people per square kilometer). According to Minister of Internal Affairs N.P. Dudorov, the conditions in this area—swampy polar tundra—made it a "natural prison," which enabled the prisoners to be completely isolated.[71] Because of the lack of roads and communications links and the remoteness of the area, it was impossible for the central authorities to monitor the progress of construction, which led to massive abuses of power and malfeasance by camp employees.

Nikolai P. was sent as a convict to the northern construction site after being repatriated from Germany. He was coerced by threats and lies into agreeing to serve as a Ministry of Internal Affairs prison guard. As of January 1, 1948, there were 31,900 such convicts serving in the so-called *samookhranka* (self-guard troops) in the Gulag as a whole, including a great many repatriated soldiers. Later, Nikolai P. recalled the years he had spent on the construction of the railway, which, according to Stalin, was the Russian people's cherished dream:

In the colonies I saw slave labor and abuse; there were tens and hundreds of thousands of people in death camps. . . . It seemed to me that the greater half of Russia's population was imprisoned in these camps. . . . The work quotas were humanly impossible. The few prisoners who were able to complete them were given 1,200 grams of bread; but the majority of the prisoners could not perform at that level and were given 300 grams—the meager crust called the "*gorbushka*." It was accompanied by a coarse barley soup with cod. After such rations and the exhausting labor, people died daily from various diseases. During the winter the corpses were piled up in a specially designated barracks, then loaded onto sledges pulled by their fellow prisoners; a tractor hauled them out to a pit, where they were dumped and bulldozed over. Two to three hundred people would be hauled out in a single "session."[72]

Like any slave-holding economy, the Gulag was not immune to uprisings. In 1949, some prisoners at the Abiaz Camp reached the limits of their endurance of the conditions in the polar death camps and rebelled. They disarmed and slaughtered the guards, then set off toward Vorkuta to liberate the convict miners there. Along the way, the rebels liberated camp after camp, filling their ranks as they went. According to Nikolai P., there were a total of over 70,000 rebels. A telling detail is that as they moved along they killed Evenks, Iakuts, and Zyrians for willingly turning escaped prisoners over to the authorities in exchange for money or payment in kind, or, more often, for vodka. Substantial efforts were expended in putting down the uprising. In the course of two weeks of battle, practically all the fugitives were annihilated, and the captured surviving prisoners were led off in chains to an unknown destination. After this incident, the entire Five Hundred First Stalin Construction Project was "reinforced" with guard towers and guards armed with machine guns. For some time the prisoners were held in barracks and not taken out to work, but then things calmed down, and the hunger, convoys, and construction resumed.

Stalin was regularly informed about the progress of the work. In 1952, five years after the project began, an engineering plan for the Chum–Salekhard–Igarka Railway was finally drawn up, with a projected length of 1,482 kilometers. The design, approved by a government commission, provided for the simplest technical solutions: bridges, pipes, buildings, and administrative offices—all to be made of wood, with the most basic tracks, "old-fashioned" rails, and so forth.

The polar adventure, which cost several tens of thousands of lives, ended immediately after Stalin's death. By a decision of the Council of Ministers in March 1953, construction was deemed unnecessary and discontinued. A 573–kilometer-long "dead road" remained in the tundra, without beginning or end.

The actual total expenditures on the construction of the Chum–Salekhard–Igarka Railway before the project was finally terminated came to 3.3 billion rubles, with 2.9 billion rubles of planned funding remaining unspent. It is worth noting that three years later the Ministry of Internal Affairs recalled this project and proposed establishing two strict-regime prisons there with a capacity of 20,000–25,000 prisoners for the purpose of completing the railroad. Traditional economic reasoning was brought to bear: "Taking into account that the specific weight of worker pay is estimated to be 33 percent of the construction and assembly expenses, and under the condition that these expenses will not actually have to be covered . . ."[73] and so on. But the times had changed, and such "economizing" had lost its former appeal. The state Economic Commission of the USSR rejected the ministry's proposal.

Theoreticians of the camp economy knew perfectly well what prison labor cost the state. It was no secret for them, for example, that, as of January 1, 1949, there were 165,445 people in the militarized guard of the Gulag, 7,937 officers and 157,508 sergeants and ordinary soldiers. But the Gulag was in constant need of guards; the government had established a minimal staffing level of 9 percent of the overall number of prisoners, which came to over 200,000 people. In addition to the armed guard troops, the camps and colonies had their own permanent staff of officers and sergeants, as well as free employees, which numbered 80,674 people in 1948. For comparison we note that the civilian staff of all the USSR border troops during the same period comprised 168,000 people (and they were understaffed by 75,000).[74]

Unlike Soviet army soldiers, the ordinary guards and sergeants of the armed guard troops received a monthly salary of 250–350 rubles, plus full room and board. In 1949, the salary of a junior lieutenant platoon commander came to 1,420 rubles; the chief of a separate camp division at the rank of captain or major received a salary ranging from 2,800 to 3,000 rubles (not counting rations, housing allowances, extra pay for working in the north, and other bonuses). Supervisors received an average of 1,000 rubles; the staffing levels were set at 1.5 percent of the overall number of prisoners. For comparison, note that in 1950, the average monthly pay of workers as a whole came to 642 rubles.

The budget of the Ministry of Internal Affairs was never made public, and it is unlikely that any Soviet citizen could have imagined how much of the country's spending went to maintaining this powerful agency. The best year for balance of income and expenses in the Ministry of Internal Affairs of the USSR was 1949. MVD expenses were set at a level of 65.8 billion rubles, of which 33.5 billion rubles were to be covered internally, with the remaining 32.3 billion to come from the Union budget. The requested funds from the state budget were primarily earmarked for the maintenance of MVD agencies and troops and camps for prisoners of war and prisoners who fell under the Union budget (20 billion rubles), for paying for the expenses for the maintenance of prisoners that were not covered internally (4 billion rubles), and for capital construction (7.6 billion rubles). In return, in 1949 the MVD planned to turn over 2.7 billion rubles to the national budget, of which 2.2 billion were to come from the labor of prisoners of war and prisoners in the Gulag.[75]

In comparison with 1948, expenses financed from the national budget had increased by 5.1 billion rubles. The majority of this sum went to the creation, in the middle of 1948, of fifteen new special-designation camps, whose fences alone required eight hundred tons of barbed wire. In addition, the MVD budget for 1949 provided for a significant increase in anticipated losses due to a rise in the costs of production in Dalstroi, the mining and metallurgy enterprises, and the forestry industry under the MVD.

The camp economy as a single economic organism was able to survive only under the administrative-distributive system, under which government decrees and Party directives replaced normal economic relations and ignored the natural and logical processes involved in the development of production. Each resolution of the Council of Ministers that had to do with the economic activity of the MVD contained a number of provisions beginning with the words "shall require." Various ministries and agencies were given the obligation to supply each new MVD construction project with materials, machinery, living space for workers, transportation for prisoners, and so forth. The larger and more significant the camp-production complex, the longer the list of organizations required to work for the benefit of the MVD. For example, the government resolutions concerning Dalstroi listed dozens of such facilities. It seemed that the entire country was mobilized to support the camps in the Northeast and to provide their workers not only with materials and machinery but also with food supplies that, for security reasons, were not acknowledged publicly.

The Council of Ministers' resolution on the establishment of one of the experimental military plants specified who was to outfit the plant and with what equipment. The plant had been designated a "category one" facility, and the list included absolutely everything, from drafting sets to an Li-2 airplane. The ministry's own responsibility, as a rule, can be summarized as "to provide the facility with a workforce from the special contingent consisting of X number of workers."

During the first postwar years, prisoners were made to work primarily by force, but this method was ineffective, especially in branches of industry that used heavy physical labor. Incentives were required to stimulate the prisoners' interest in the results of their labor. With this in mind, the Council of Ministers of the USSR passed a resolution on November 26, 1947, restoring the workday accounting system for prisoners working in essential branches of the national economy. In addition, prisoners began to receive some pay for their labor in 1948. This naturally improved morale and motivation and increased labor productivity. Together with material incentives such as credit for days worked, improved rations, cash bonuses, housing in well-furnished barracks, and so forth, the camp administration instituted on a broad scale programs aimed at improving worker morale: public expressions of gratitude, certificates, red pennants on the barracks, and so on. Moscow construction sites were often adorned with so-called "lightning-bolt" posters (*plakaty-molnii*) proclaiming:

> On April 8, the Bryzgalov team over-fulfilled their task by 665 percent, earning each team member 110 rubles. Brigade No. 18 under brigade leader Podzharov over-fulfilled the day's plan by 465 percent. Hail to the masters of high productivity of labor! Meet the standard set by the leaders!
>
> Today, April 16, the Novosadov team over-fulfilled their daily norm by 800 percent. Each team member earned 159 rubles 49 kopecks. Hail to the masters of high productivity of labor![76]

There were prisoners in the "leading" camps who achieved the production plan levels for two, four, and even five years within a single year. Of course there were very few such record setters among the millions of prisoners. Hundreds of thousands of Gulag inhabitants, enfeebled and starving, continued as before, unable to complete even the very low standard norms. But the campaign conducted by the political offices in 1948, aimed at enhancing the activity of all the camp divisions of the Ministry of Internal Affairs, brought results: the peak in the growth of productivity of forced labor came during the years 1948 and 1949, along with a noticeable improvement in the economic efficiency of MVD facilities. Many camps and construction sites declined some of the planned state budget subsidies, and achievement of planned goals was practically universal.

In some branches of industry, prisoners participated in campaigns to improve production methods. In 1947, 311 proposals for changes in production methods were submitted by prisoners in Moscow and Moscow Oblast; of these, 142 were adopted, resulting in savings of over 1 million rubles. In 1949, prisoners submitted 513 rationalization proposals, of which 266 were implemented, saving nearly 6 million rubles. In 1947, 11,598 rationalization proposals were submitted by prisoners in the Gulag as a whole, resulting in savings of 48.2 million rubles.[77]

Some of the technical improvements proposed by prisoners were subsequently to be applied on a nationwide scale. For example, convict Miromanov of Camp No. 21 outside Moscow redesigned an IaK-2 press for producing breeze-block bricks, improving the machine's efficiency fivefold. This improvement was to be broadly applied in the building-materials industry as a whole. It is interesting to note that free employees in the Gulag, even those who were specialists, were not this inventive and enthusiastic.

During the second half of the 1940s and the beginning of the 1950s, prison labor was used everywhere. Postwar Moscow flourished and thrived in part because of the Gulag. Camp divisions, of which there were over fifty in Moscow Oblast, supplied workers on a contract basis to the construction sites and factories of Moscow and Moscow Oblast. Prisoners worked at the Kolomenskoe Locomotive Factory; at the Mytishchensk Plant, which produced train cars for the Moscow Metro; at the Stalin Automotive Plant; at the Tuchkovsk Brick Works, at the Coke and Gas Factory, and at dozens of other facilities that directly touched the lives of the millions of inhabitants of the capital. Camp prisoners built the Moscow Northern Waterworks, the Kurianovsk Aeration Station, the Ostankino Brewery, the huge buildings at Sokol, apartment buildings for the workers of the Stalin Automotive Plant, a nineteen-building housing complex for MVD officials in Izmailovo, hospitals, and sanitariums. One of the most prestigious of the MVD construction projects in Moscow was the huge, 16,700-square-meter building on the Kotelnicheskaia Embankment. Stalin personally followed the course of its construction, since the generals had promised to complete the building in order to open it for use on his birthday, December 20, 1951; the Gulag provided skilled workers for the project, in addition to producing a large quantity of wooden furnishings and parquet flooring. The Ministry of Internal Affairs was awarded the Stalin Prize for the innovative metal framework it provided for the building as well as its concrete shell. The Chief of Glavpromstroi, Hero of Socialist Labor A.N. Komarovskii, managed the construction of Moscow State University, which also used prison labor.

It was a rare Muscovite who, moving into his new room or apartment, knew that his building had been built by prisoners, although the MVD in Moscow was responsible for some 10 percent of all residential construction. In 1950, in the city of Moscow as a whole, 533,000 square meters of new living space was completed, of which nearly 67,000 square meters had been built by MVD construction organizations.[78]

The contributions of prison labor were not made public; state secrecy was maintained over everything connected with the Gulag. This was particularly true of a wide variety of special facilities (*spetsob"ekty*), whose number increased rapidly during the postwar years. Of the overall volume of capital construction carried out by the MVD in 1947 at a cost of 4.2 billion rubles, special construction projects accounted for over 1 billion rubles. In 1947, 140,000 prisoners worked on the construction of special facilities.[79] In 1946–52, prisoners in Saratov built a unique complex of military-industrial plants, including a plant for producing machinery and semifinished products out of refractory metals; a plant for manufacturing special lamps for radar installations, radio receivers, and televisions; a plant for producing powerful generator lamps; and a scientific-research institute for the electrovacuum industry. The construction was managed by a specially created camp administration, Saratovstroi. Since this was a part of Glavpromstroi under the MVD, military-construction units (themselves essentially involuntary) were widely used along with prison laborers. Other construction projects were going on simultaneously with the military-industrial projects. These included a modern, fifty-two-building residential complex, three ten-year schools for 2,100 pupils, a health complex, kindergartens, nurseries, stores, and a medical clinic. All the buildings were supplied with central heating, gas, light, running water, and plumbing. Thus, in the conditions of the universal postwar devastation and impoverishment, the Gulag participated in the construction of the Soviet military-industrial complex and helped it grow and gain social prestige.

Throughout the country, large-scale top-secret construction projects were under way. They were associated primarily with the development of the military-industrial complex and in particular with the atomic project. Professor I.N. Golovin, who was directly involved in the Soviet atomic bomb project during the 1940s and served as I.V. Kurchatov's* first deputy between 1950 and 1958, recalls widespread use of prison labor on the atomic project:

> Prisoners worked on all the construction sites, mines, atomic projects, even in our institute in Moscow (at the time it was called Laboratory No. 2). . . . [There was a prison in the building of the club.] It was separated from the rest of the building by a tall thick wall, with sentries in tall booths at the corners armed with machine guns. . . . The structure where the first atomic reactor was installed (at the time they called

---

*I.V. Kurchatov was the Soviet physicist ordered by Stalin to provide the Soviet Union with atomic weapons in the shortest possible time.—Ed.

it the "cauldron"), the adjoining buildings—all of them were built by
prisoners. . . . [The first builders of the International Nuclear Testing
Center in Dubno were also prisoners.] There were many thousands of
them at our construction projects. All the specialists saw them and knew
everything. . . . It is hard to believe now, but when we had a shortage of
workers and Beria said, "We'll just send in a supplementary contingent
tomorrow," no one seemed to find it strange.[80]

The primary construction projects of the Chief Administration of
Camps for Special Construction under the Ministry of Internal Affairs
were designated special-regime facilities by resolutions of the Council
of Ministers of the USSR, and all information about their location, the
level of capital investment, the time frames involved, and so forth, was
held in a "special file." The level of secrecy at these facilities was so
high that sometimes prisoners were not even given their work orders
(*nariady*), without which they could not be issued money or credited
for days worked; this was justified on the grounds that releasing the
documents would constitute a "violation of state security."

Involuntary labor was used not only in industry and construction.
The names of such prisoners as A.N. Tupolev, S.P. Korolev, V.M.
Petliakov, V.P. Glushko, V.M. Miasishchev, A.L. Mints, B.S. Stechkin,
and many other famous scientists were associated with the activity of
the Special Design Bureaus (OKB), the so-called "*sharashki.*" Secret
scientific-research and design institutes, where scientists and engineers—who as a rule had been convicted of such crimes as "sabotage
of socialist construction" and "undermining the defense capacities of
the USSR"—worked under the supervision of the state security organs,
were established in Moscow, Leningrad, Rybinsk, Taganrog, Rostov,
and at Seliger and in many other locations in the Soviet Union. Specialists and scientists, many of whom were world famous, worked "for
rations" (rations they were, though the "forty grams of butter for pro-
fessors and twenty for engineers, with black bread on the table," were
incomparably better than the usual Gulag fare).

"Why were Tupolev, Stechkin, and Korolev imprisoned?" At the beginning of the 1970s, the writer F. Chuev posed this question to V.M.
Molotov, one of the chief organizers of the repressions of the 1930s. In
his answer, the former head of the Soviet government betrayed not a
trace of doubt in the correctness of the policies of those years: "They
were all imprisoned. They talked too much. And you can well imagine
the people they associated with . . . after all, they did not support us."
The Bolshevik true believer cited the example of the aircraft designer
Tupolev to support his philosophy that the ends justify the means:

That same Tupolev could have become a dangerous enemy. He had important ties with elements of the intelligentsia that were hostile to us. . . . The Tupolevs were in their time a very difficult matter for us. For some time they were enemies, and more time was needed to draw them closer to Soviet power. . . . Tupolev is an example of that category of the intelligentsia that was essential to the Soviet state, but in their souls they were opposed to us, and the personal relationships they formed were a dangerous and corrupting influence; if they did not engage consciously in opposition, they breathed it in that environment. . . .

Things are different now, and Tupolev is a hero, but at the time the intelligentsia was opposed to Soviet power! And they needed to be brought under control. The Tupolevs were put behind bars, and the Chekists were instructed to do everything they could to create ideal conditions for them, serve them the finest food, better than what anyone else got, but not to release them. They were to work and design things for the country's military. The Chekists were told, "These are absolutely essential people; it is not the potential for open propaganda that makes them dangerous, but their personal authority and influence; at a crucial moment they can become extremely dangerous. You can't avoid this in politics. They are unable to build Communism by themselves."[81]

The Special Design Bureaus, which were a part of the Fourth Special Section of the MVD, were involved in many different kinds of activities. For example, the Leningrad OKB-172, which celebrated its ten-year anniversary in May 1948, designed artillery systems. Over the years of the bureau's existence, convict engineers developed twenty-three major designs and carried out over sixty research projects for the government. Antitank guns, artillery installations for guard towers, marine installations, and other "products" of the OKB-172 were deployed and used during the Great Patriotic War with superior results.

On the occasion of its tenth anniversary, the OKB-172 was recommended for the Red Banner of Labor Award, and ten especially distinguished specialists who had worked in the bureau for at least seven to ten years and who, after the completion of their terms of punishment, had remained in the "sharashka" as free employees were given clear records. In addition, some of these "free" design engineers and scientists were presented with government awards together with the best MVD operatives.[82]

Another group of fifty-three imprisoned specialists worked on a long-term project designing the T-117 transport aircraft. This convict engineering collective was headed by a former member of the Italian Communist Party, the imprisoned design engineer R.L. Bartini, who came to the Soviet Union in 1923. Under his leadership, the group developed several alternative designs for the aircraft: a passenger liner (an air bus and a luxury version), a transport craft, an aerial ambulance, and a troop transport. Engineering analyses conducted at the beginning of 1946 by civil and military technical institutes confirmed the plane's superior design and flight performance.[83]

Such successes might create the illusion that the camp system established a positive environment for creative work. But in fact there were more minuses than pluses in these economic and scientific achievements. Forced labor by its very nature cannot be creative; it simply follows orders automatically. No wrongfully convicted person who has been through the shock of arrest and separation from his family, has been thrown in prison, and has lived there in conditions utterly alien to his nature can work creatively or develop to his fullest potential. Under such conditions, perfect devotion occurs only in extremely rare and exceptional cases. If within a specific period of time a group of prisoners created a single airplane, a group of free engineers sharing a common approach could have produced eight during the same period. This thought was later expressed repeatedly and with regret by former prisoners who had worked in the Special Design Bureaus, notably A.N. Tupolev.

The camp economy of the postwar period was to a significant degree fueled by prison labor. As of June 1, 1946, there were 2,038,374 prisoners of war of various nationalities imprisoned in the USSR.[84] The overwhelming majority of them worked in mining, heavy industry, and construction. In spite of the extensive use of prison labor (the chief of a factory near Moscow acknowledged that he could make the Germans under his command work as long as he wanted but never less than ten hours a day), the income from the labor of prisoners of war did not cover the expenses of running their camps. In 1946, state subsidies from January to May alone came to 317 million rubles, which was due primarily to the presence of a large number of ill and disabled prisoners, whom the government tried to return to their homeland as quickly as possible. Mortality among prisoners of war was also very high in 1946—over 5,000 or 6,000 people per month.

In the hopes of utilizing the prisoners of war and internees who were skilled specialists, the Soviet government assigned the MVD to identify and remove from the camps all specialists who might have something to offer to Soviet science and the economy. By June 22, 1946, some 1,600 specialists had been identified in prisoner-of-war camps, including 111 with doctorates in the physical and mathematical sciences, chemistry, and technical sciences; 572 general mechanical and instrument-making engineers; 257 construction engineers and architects; 216 electrical engineers; 156 chemists; as well as numerous engineers with other specializations.[85]

The list of "identified" specialists included the names of major scientists, along with prominent production and mechanical managers of well-known German companies: Manfred Christian, a member of the German Academy of Sciences and a major specialist in gas turbines and jet engines; Paul Heilandt, a doctor of technical sciences and one of the leading specialists in low-temperature technologies, internal-combustion engines, and rocket aggregates; Ernst Busse, a doctor of physics and a specialist in vacuum tubes; Ferdinand Brandner, a specialist in the production of turbine aircraft; Gerhardt Jung, a professor of physical chemistry, and others. Some ministries and scientific research institutes made requests to the MVD to provide them with specialists in specific areas of need from among the internees and prisoners of war. A resolution of the Council of Ministers granted these foreign specialists temporary residence permits for the locations where they were sent to work. They were paid the same rates as Soviet specialists with the same qualifications, with half the sum provided in the hard currency of their countries of citizenship. The MVD retained the right to require the released specialists to register every month in MVD offices, as well as the right "to reincarcerate specialists who have not conducted themselves in a positive manner at work during their first three months."[86]

There were other foreign scientists working in the USSR as well. These were specialists who had been brought involuntarily to Soviet territory in 1945 and whose research was involved primarily in the atomic bomb project.[87]

In 1947 there were 341 former prisoners of war and internees working on scientific research in the MVD system and in military research institutions. These scientists completed 114 research-based designs and inventions, many of which found application in a number of branches of industry.[88]

During the postwar years, a number of central branch administrations were created in the MVD system that were directly associated with the development of the defense industry, such as the Chief Administration of the Mica Industry, the Chief Administration of Oil Production, and others. The MVD held a monopoly on the mining of diamonds, asbestos, and apatite; there was a sharp increase in the exploration for and mining of nonferrous metals, especially lead. "Our economic tasks are military tasks; they are not routine matters, and it is impossible to follow traditional management methods with them," commented Minister of Internal Affairs S.N. Kruglov.[89]

Kruglov gave a speech at the Seventh Party Conference of the MVD of the USSR on March 31, 1950, in which he listed the unique features of the economic activities of his agency that made it unlike any other ministry:

> First of all, we are involved in an extraordinary variety of kinds of industrial production, in which we have to rely on the labor of prisoners in our corrective-labor camps and colonies. . . . We also have to work in the fuel industry, nonferrous metallurgy, railroad construction, metalworking, forestry, timber processing, leather production, and the shoe, apparel, and wool industries; we work on highways and railroads and engage in large-scale agriculture as well.
>
> Second, we carry out this multifaceted program of industrial capital construction primarily in extremely remote, unsettled territories of the Far North and Far East. . . .
>
> Third, the workforce used by the Ministry of Internal Affairs is fundamentally different from that used by other ministries. Our use of labor has to be in harmony with the goals of state security, but we also have to work for the interests of the state; at the same time, we have to deal with the conditions of the prison regime and to maintain security.[90]

In 1949, the level of industrial production in the MVD came to nearly 20 billion rubles. It accounted for 100 percent of the total yield of platinum, mica, and diamonds; over 90 percent of the gold; over 70 percent of the tin; 40 percent of the copper; over 35 percent of the carbon black; 33 percent of the nickel; and 13 percent of the timber. The gross industrial production of the MVD of the USSR in 1949 came to over 10 percent of the industrial production in the country as a whole.[91]

The distinguishing feature of the camp economy throughout the years of its existence was manual labor. After the war, a significant amount of modern technology was introduced to the construction sites and facilities of the MVD, but the prisoners continued to labor as they had ten or twenty years before, with the pick, crowbar, shovel, and wheelbarrow. At the end of 1944, the economic managers complained that, of the overall 189,000 units of equipment on hand, 85,000 were sitting idle. Equipment would lie unassembled in the camps for one or two years.[92] In 1948, the chairman of the forestry-industry camps gave a report at the Fifth Party Conference of the MVD on the work of his central branch administration: "None of the processes are mechanized, we have received no machinery at all, and there are no signs that we will any time soon; for over a year now we have been unable to utilize one hundred electrical saws because of the lack of mobile electric generators." There followed the traditional request for help, "because we cannot cope with our expanding program by muscle power and horses alone."[93]

Even horses and muscle power would have been an improvement; often the timber sites lacked both. The former prisoner at hard labor E.L. Vladimirova gave a detailed presentation to the higher Party leadership on conditions at timber-processing sites in Kolyma, specifically, in the women's camp with the playful name Bacchante. In her letter to the Central Committee of the CPSU, the former death-row convict laborer wrote:

> The timber site at "Bacchante" was at a five-to-ten kilometer distance from the camp complex itself. The ten-to-twenty kilometer journey added a terrible extra burden to the work itself. The work entailed hauling; two women would be harnessed together to a sledge with a cross beam across their chests and would pull *balans* [logs with the bark still attached— G.I.] for a distance of several kilometers at a time. So, for example, a special brigade of weakened prisoners who worked a short (five-hour) shift would haul one load of wood per day for a distance of five kilometers, making the whole trip, including the way to the site with the empty sledge, ten kilometers. Regular workers' brigades, of course, were assigned a greater workload. Brigades that failed to fulfill their quota would occasionally remain in the woods on a moonlit winter night until midnight.

Sometimes "bacchantes" would die of a ruptured diaphragm. Such deaths were recorded as work-related trauma due to violations of safety procedures. They did not raise the camp's official mortality rate, since they were entered in a different column in the record books. The mortality statistics in the Gulag were so idiosyncratic (there were separate columns for deaths in the camps, hospitals, colonies, at work, in prison, while attempting to escape, etc.) that it is still impossible to establish the precise number of prisoners who died in the camps; the official data do not give the total number of deaths among the prisoners of the Gulag.

The average level of mechanization in the timber industry in 1949 was 18.8 percent. It was only by cruel exploitation of human labor that the Chief Administration of the Camps in the Forestry Industry managed to provide the government with 75 million cubic meters of wood during the postwar five-year-plan period, exceeding the planned 71 million.[94] This considerable figure, which later was to be numbered among the main achievements of the Soviet economy, was in fact a disgrace and was one of its greatest crimes.

The MVD leadership attempted to solve the problem of mechanization by traditional means, using government orders. In 1948, the minister issued two orders aimed at improving the performance of machinery, but they had no effect. In every report, the administrators of enterprises and construction projects identified poor labor productivity and poor utilization of machinery as the primary reasons for falling behind on their plan. According to Eniseistroi reports, as of the end of 1952, its facilities (not counting the special administration) had 7,950 units of machinery, of which 3,556 were out of service. As for the working machinery, as a rule it, too, stood idle due to a lack of fuel and electrical power, and minor breakdowns that were difficult to repair because of the lack of skilled workers.

The cost of Gulag production was substantially higher than production costs in local industry, even given the lack of expenditures on labor. For example, in a large facility such as Eniseistroi, the actual cost of producing a thousand bricks was 631 rubles, as compared to a projected cost of 250 rubles; in the local regional industry, the cost of the same quantity of bricks was 210 rubles 49 kopecks. The estimated cost of a ton of lime was set at 85 rubles; but the actual cost was 170 rubles 60 kopecks, as opposed to 93 rubles 48 kopecks in local industry.

The Achinsk Brick Factory exceeded the permissible threshold for defective production sixfold and produced only 40 to 50 percent of its quota. The Iulinsk Lead Enterprise fulfilled only 38 percent of its quota for 1952, with losses amounting to 4.9 million rubles. This situation was practically universal. Some 30 percent of prisoners and 17 percent of free workers were unable to fulfill quotas that were set at intentionally low levels; at some mines these figures reached 52 percent. These low results had no effect on the material welfare of the free workers of Eniseistroi, since this camp industrial complex was financed on the basis of actual expenditures.

The camp production system caused material losses not only to the national economy; it was also destructive to the environment. Of course, none of the industrial enterprises was furnished with the necessary pollution-control equipment, and they were notoriously reckless in their use of natural resources. The Sorskii Molybdenum Complex, for example, in violation of all rules and technical procedures, emptied its production wastes into the flood plain of the Sora River (Khakasia). The plant design had provided for the installation of special waste depositories, but there was no time to build them. Everyone understood that this was a gross violation, but no one attempted to rectify it. The Gulag was indiscriminating in the harm it inflicted on both people and nature.

Wishing to avoid the negative consequences that would ensue from their inability to fulfill their plan, and in the hopes of covering up expenses, theft, and illegal payments, administrators of camp construction sites and enterprises quite often would simply report enormously inflated production figures. One of the oversight commissions laconically commented, "The level of completed construction work was considerably inflated." In monetary terms, this massive fraud against the government came to tens of millions of rubles.

In the hopes of documenting the completion of their work plans and earning rewards, administrators grossly inflated production figures for the construction of Artificial Liquid Fuel Production Kombinat No. 16 (in the city of Angarsk, Irkutsk Oblast), which was run by Lieutenant-General S.N. Burdakov. Kombinat No. 16 included fifteen different specialized plants, for which four hundred complex industrial facilities needed to be built, complete with 95 kilometers of railway, 130 kilometers of external piping, and many other elements. This was one of the MVD's major construction projects and was of great military-industrial importance. But here, too, of the 350 priority shops planned for 1952, primary construction was completed on only 139. The plan was disastrously underfulfilled, involving expenses and losses in the hundreds of millions of rubles.

The quality of construction also remained extremely low. As a rule, this did not give rise to any particular objections from the client, since everyone was well aware who was doing the construction and under what conditions. Defects were usually repaired only after the facility had entered service. But this was not always the case. At the end of 1952, the government instructed the MVD Glavspetsstroi to build three industrial buildings and two residential buildings for Defense Industry Plant No. 82 in Tushino outside Moscow. The construction and assembly work was managed by the Bakovskii Corrective-Labor Camp (Moscow Oblast), jointly with MVD military construction divisions. In spite of the high priority of this construction project, the deadlines for completion were repeatedly violated and extended, and two and a half years after the beginning of construction, several metal structures unexpectedly collapsed, threatening the integrity of the entire roof. It turned out that the design calculations had been grossly violated during the installation of the load-bearing structures. The prison laborers also left enormous defects in the residential buildings: they neglected to install smoke flues, which rendered it impossible to use stoves; plumbing pipes emptied into basements, and so on. Driven to despair, plant director Aremaev appealed to the Central Committee of the CPSU, and the question of the quality of MVD construction projects became the subject of special discussion.

As we have already noted, the economic activity of the Ministry of Internal Affairs was extraordinarily varied. In 1950, the MVD system included 1,300 state farms and subsidiary farms with 656,000 hectares of land under cultivation and 700,000 head of producing livestock. One example of a "genuine giant of socialist agriculture," as it was called in the production reports of the MVD, was the Karagandinsk Camp, with 101,000 hectares of land under cultivation. This was one of the largest farms in the country, with 26,000 head of cattle, 146,000 sheep, and 6,500 swine. A hundred or so camp facilities and an equal number of animal farms were located on a total territory of 13,000 square kilometers. Over 30,000 prisoners worked in this camp agricultural facility.

It would be misleading to imply uniform loss levels for all the agricultural camps. There were instances, of course, when the harvest of potatoes came to less than the amount that had been planted in the spring. At times, for various reasons, planting dragged on for two or three months instead of the necessary two or three weeks, with the harvesting taking place after snowfall. But at the same time, Gulag agricultural camps raised pedigreed livestock, obtained record levels of milk, and developed new varieties of seed. And no wonder: after all, among the imprisoned agronomists and livestock specialists there were numerous first-class experts who had been arrested during the attacks on Soviet biological science.*

The Gulag also made a significant contribution—one that is not recorded in the literature—to the exploration and development of virgin and fallow lands. Under government assignment, prisoners built thirty-five new grain-producing state farms in 1954–55, primarily in the Kazakh SSR, where new camps were organized and new groups of prisoners were specially brought in to do the construction and assembly work. Gulag prisoners built residential buildings, dormitories, cafeterias, and bakeries for the future settlers of the virgin lands, in addition to grain silos, storage buildings, and many other facilities.

The MVD developed and supported its network of subsidiary agricultural facilities in many ways, demonstrating a touching concern for its staff: "The officer corps, the workers, and the employees of the camps, especially those of the Far East, are in dire need of the produce from

---

*During the late 1940s, several branches of Soviet science and other disciplines were subjected to state-backed ideological interventions. Soviet biology suffered tremendous setbacks when, in July 1948, agronomist Trofim Lysenko conspired with Stalin to purge the Academy of Agricultural Sciences. Classical genetics was attacked as a bourgeois falsification and was replaced by Lysenko's crackpot theories.—Ed.

subsidiary farms," noted the Seventh Party Conference of the MIA. "Is it really possible for the children of workers in the northern camps to receive milk from anywhere except the subsidiary farms?"[95]

Professor Owen Lattimore of the U.S. War Information Administration accompanied Vice President Henry Wallace on his visit to Kolyma in 1944. Lattimore approvingly noted in his report that officials of Dalstroi were most solicitous of the state of the greenhouses there, where they grew tomatoes, cucumbers, and even melons, in order to ensure that their miners received enough vitamins.[96] The American professor was very gullible: the vitamins did not make it to the miners. The majority of the camp's agricultural output was turned over to the state, some of it went to the camp administration, and only occasionally did miniscule amounts of fresh vegetables reach the digestive systems of the ill and weakened zeks.

It cannot be said that the MVD staff was completely indifferent to the quality of life of the prisoners. For example, they were quite concerned about work-related injuries. Gulag chief I.I. Dolgikh expressed his opinion on this issue at the Eighth Party Conference of the MVD in March 1951:

> The central branch administrations are doing a bad job of maintaining their workforce. Our production branches have an extremely unsatisfactory approach to preserving labor. I will not quote the numbers here; you are well aware of them.* But labor losses due to work-related injury and mortality are particularly high in the production branches of the Dobrovolskii,** Gidrostroi, Dalstroi, and forestry camps. The work-safety situation is particularly serious in Kizellag, Ustvymlag, Viatlag, Sevurallag, Nyroblag, Vorkutlag, Norillag, Ukhtizhemlag, Angarlag, Nizhneamurlag, and a number of others. . . . If the Timofeev Trust had not had such losses, it would have provided 100,000 additional cubic meters of wood (one cubic meter per person).[97]

The Gulag chief's last sentence allows one to draw the conclusion that "production losses" in the forestry-industry camps amounted to 100,000 people per year.

The Chekist managers also expressed concern about the poor nutrition of the prisoners. In their opinion, there were two reasons for this: either the camp administration was economizing on food or the

---

*A classic example of "vigilance," since invited guests from other agencies were present at the conference.

**N.A. Dobrovolskii headed the Chief Administration of Camps in the Mining and Metallurgy Industry.

staff was stealing it. In any case, "this situation leads to a weakening of the physical condition of the special contingent and has a deleterious effect on planned labor use."[98]

The problem of "labor use of the special contingent" became especially serious in the beginning of the 1950s, when the economic crisis in the camp economy became obvious. The MVD was disastrously unable to cope with the increasing volume of work, although Gulag budget expenditures had already reached the level of several billion rubles. "The great construction projects of communism" required enormous amounts of labor—conscientious, skilled labor, which the Gulag prisoners could not provide. It was clear that without introducing sophisticated and varied forms of technology it would be practically impossible to complete any of the ministry's tasks. The expensive equipment that was being installed at construction sites and facilities required reliable, skilled workers who were adequately trained and motivated. Clearly the camp economy did not have such personnel. Like any slave-holding economy, the Gulag was helpless in the face of the growth of the forces of production.

The MVD officials were themselves well aware of these difficulties. S.N. Kruglov noted in a speech: "We have to understand that we cannot rely exclusively on prison labor for those branches of the economy that are under our administration. . . . When we were engaged in rough physical labor and clearing the land, we needed the prisoners, but now we are working with high-quality machinery."[99]

In 1951–52, not a single camp production administration completed its plan. "The greatest construction projects of the nation's prosperity" were opened for production only partially completed, with huge gaps, and substantially off schedule. The flagship of the camp economy—Glavpromstroi—managed to complete only 85 percent of its plan for 1952, even though it was always given priority in workforce allocations. Its losses were enormous. Analyzing the reasons for this, Glavpromstroi chief A.N. Komarovskii reached an unambiguous conclusion: "The primary reason is the low level of labor productivity."[100] In spite of all the efforts of the camp and production administration, a substantial number of prisoners, for various reasons, did not complete their work quotas.

Issues related to the use of prisoners' labor were the subject of continual disagreements between the Gulag and the production branches. The managers accused the Gulag of not caring about their production needs. The camp administrators expressed their own countercomplaints. I.I. Dolgikh, in his speech at the Eighth Party Conference of the MIA, noted:

> The greatest manifestations of banditry, losses, and disorder are in the branch administrations. As a rule, the plans are unrealistic; the requests for workers exceed that required for the plan severalfold, but the Gulag grants these requests, that is, in other words, the branch administrations do not value their workforce; they believe that, since the Gulag is right there with a ready reserve of workers, they can be wasteful with the workforce, to use it at any time and in any way they wish.[101]

Of course the Gulag chief was right. Each branch administration, according to Minister Kruglov, was predatory in its treatment of workers.

> Take Comrade Komarovskii. He has almost half a million workers, but he wants us to send him three hundred thousand more every single month to work on more and more government tasks. Take any branch administration—say, for example, Comrade Dobrovolskii's; he also has three hundred thousand workers; or Comrade Timofeev's, with two hundred fifty thousand.[102]

And there were still not enough workers.

In dealing with the growing shortage of workers, the MVD resorted more and more often to free laborers, most of whom were former prisoners. Upon the request of the MVD, the USSR Council of Ministers issued a special resolution aimed at securing free workers for MVD enterprises and construction projects, taking them from among released prisoners. It was perfectly natural that the work of such "free workers" would be no more efficient than that of prisoners; furthermore, they would seize every opportunity to transfer to work in civil agencies, where, in Kruglov's words, "the work quotas are lower, and the pay is better."

An intermediary layer between prisoners and free workers was the military construction units. For a number of reasons, the labor productivity of this category of workers was even lower than that of prisoners; their labor was nevertheless widely used in the MVD system, especially on road construction and military-industrial facilities. The MVD GUShOSDOR was the primary, if not the only, organization in the country engaged in highway construction. A special road-construction corps, or, rather, three road-construction units with a total of one hundred workers, was created in this unit. Maintained completely at state expense and supplied with machinery and construction materials, the corps still "performed unsatisfactorily" and "did not conserve the people's kopecks." According to the chief of the central financial section of the MIA, G.K. Karmanov, "for every ruble spent, the corps produced five kopecks worth of income." Although Kruglov believed that this was an exaggeration, he set the following task to the military construction workers: "Cut expenses by 30 percent and increase income by 30 percent in the corps, so that a ruble spent will produce not five kopecks but seventy-five kopecks worth of income."[103]

The difficulties of the camp economy were exacerbated by the amnesty of March 1953, according to which 1,181,264 prisoners were to be released from camps and colonies. As of July 10, 1953, 972,829 people arrived in cities, workers' settlements, and agricultural sites; of these, 821,780 were hired within a short period of time, and 47,056 could not be hired due to disability. Another 62,000 citizens freed under the amnesty remained near the camps to work as free laborers in industry and construction. Of the 50,000 or so prisoners released from Dalstroi camps, for example, 16,725 contracted to work in the Far North.

The month of March 1953 also decided the fate of a number of camp construction projects. On March 21, 1953, L.P. Beria, the minister of internal affairs of the USSR as well as the first deputy chairman of the Council of Ministers, sent a draft resolution to the Presidium of the Council of Ministers:

> In view of the fact that the construction of a number of hydrotechnical installations, railroads, highways, and factories mandated by previously adopted government resolutions is not justified by the needs of the economy, the Council of Ministers resolves to discontinue the construction of the following facilities:
>   (a) hydrotechnical installations:
>   — the Main Turkmenian Canal, the Volga–Ural Canal, the Volga–Baltic Waterway, the water engineering system on the Lower Don, the Ust-Donetsk Port;
>   (b) railways and highways:
>   — the Chum–Salekhard–Igarka, the Komsomolsk–Pobedino, and so on, a total of over twenty large-scale projects in all.[104]

Beria carried his plans for relieving the national economy of unproductive enterprises further. On June 16, he made a proposal to the Council of Ministers of the USSR and the Presidium of the Central Committee of the CPSU "to abolish the existing system of forced labor due to its economic inefficiency and lack of potential."[105]

Everyone who had any direct experience of the camp economy was aware of its inefficiency and the enormous material losses it caused the state; but the topic was discussed openly only after Stalin's death. During the second half of 1953, the Central Committee of the CPSU undertook a series of analyses of the Gulag aimed at determining its economic value. According to data from Rybanov, the deputy chief of the Financial Section of the Gulag, the maintenance of camps and colonies had for a number of years not been covered by income from the use of prisoners' labor, and the Gulag received substantial annual subsidies from the state budget. In 1952, the state budget provided 2,397 million rubles, or 16.4 percent of its overall allocations, for the maintenance of camps and colonies; during the first half of 1953, 1,052 million rubles, or 10.8 percent. In addition, the Gulag illegally confiscated 23 million rubles from the personal accounts of prisoners (from their salaries). Other MVD branch administrations also shamelessly picked the pockets of prisoners. In all, 126 million rubles were illegally confiscated from prisoners as of June 1, 1953.

The Gulag's baneful influence extended beyond purely material losses. The camp economy instilled a negative attitude toward labor in millions of Soviet citizens. "Chiseling" (*tufta*—decoded by the zeks as "techniques for recording fictitious labor")—became the norm for production activity not only in the Gulag but in the country as a whole. In 1961, in an attempt to somehow limit the dissemination of false economic indicators, the Supreme Soviet passed an edict "On Accountability for Inflated Numbers and Other Distortions in Reports on the Completion of Plans," which provided for a punishment of up to three years of deprivation of liberty. But it was not that simple to eliminate the *tufta*.

The Gulag instilled in Soviet society the thought that people could work without receiving any reward for their labor and trained the Soviet people, particularly scientists and specialists, to reconcile themselves to beggars' wages and not to demand acceptable working conditions. The Gulag's suspension of the development of productive forces was to have a long-term effect on the Soviet economy, and the master–slave production relations of the camps corrupted large segments of Soviet society. Hundreds of thousands of people who served as guards, managers, political workers, and so forth, in the Gulag system considered it completely normal to live off the daily exploitation of their fellow citizens and treat them like beasts of burden. Their children were raised in an atmosphere in which it was natural to be ruthless toward their fellow men; they grew up to scorn honest labor and to accept calmly as their due the good things in life obtained through lies, violence, and denunciations. Furthermore, the nether regions of the camp economy incubated a special variety of Soviet manager and exploiter, who valued and nurtured everything except for the human being. This unique type of manager was to go on to play a significant role in the economic policymaking of the Party and the government.

Analyzing the economic distortions of the socialist system of management, Academician A.D. Sakharov wrote:

In Stalin's time, the slave labor of millions of prisoners who perished in
the monstrous system of the Gulag played a substantial economic role,
especially in settling the semiwild regions of the East and North. Of course,
the system was not only infinitely inhuman and criminal, but it was ineffective as well; this was a part of the extensive and wasteful economy of
that time, not to mention the long-term consequences of the barbaric
destruction of the human potential of the country.[106]

The process of reorganizing the MVD that began in March 1953 affected all aspects of camp life, including the camp economy. On March
18, the Council of Ministers of the USSR issued a resolution transferring
the economic production and construction organizations of the MVD to
other ministries. In all, eighteen structural divisions were transferred out
of the Ministry of Internal Affairs, including such giants as Dalstroi, the
forestry camps, GUShOSDOR, and others. After the transfer of the camps
and colonies to civil agencies, production indicators noticeably worsened;
there was an increase in the number of strikes and massive acts of insubordination, and banditry intensified in the camps. The reason for these
specific changes lay not so much in the new managers' lack of experience
with repression (which is how the apologists for the old MVD system attempted to explain it) as in the overall crisis of the camp system due to
the change in the political climate in the country.

The processes of reorganizing the camp economy went on for several years. In March 1955, the Ministry of Internal Affairs parted with
one of its oldest branch administrations—Glavpromstroi, which was
transferred to the Ministry of Midsized Machine Building. The question of the transfer of all production management and construction
organizations to other agencies was decided in February 1956 at a
meeting of the Presidium of the Central Committee of the CPSU. This
did not mean that prison labor was no longer used in the economy. On
the whole, however, by the middle of the 1950s, the camp economy as
a special economic organism based primarily on the use of various
forms of forced labor, primarily that of prisoners, had ceased to exist.
Its symbolic end came on July 4, 1956, when the Presidium of the Supreme Soviet of the USSR ratified the convention of the International
Organization of Labor on the abolition of all forms of forced and compulsory labor. We should note that this international document had
been adopted in Geneva back in 1930. In addition, on September 7,
1956, the Soviet Union signed the convention on the abolition of slavery, the slave trade, and institutions and customs associated with slavery. This planted the hope that the camp economy was gone for good.

An interior view of the Moscow Northern Waterworks in 1955. The Chief Administration of Camps for Hydrotechnical Construction was reestablished in 1947 to manage its construction. Over 10,000 prisoners labored to build it, working by hand under grueling conditions.

The largest camp construction project of 1948–52, the high-rise building on Moscow's Kotelnicheskaia Embankment.

The Moscow–Volga Canal (the Moscow Canal) was built by prisoners. Left to right: K.E. Voroshilov, V.M. Molotov, I.V. Stalin, and N.I. Ezhov, inspecting the achievements of the camp economy in 1937.

NKVD officials and Moscow Party leaders inspecting the construction site of the Moscow–Volga Canal in 1935. Center: People's Commissar of Internal Affairs G.G. Iagoda; behind him is First Secretary of the Moscow Committee of the Communist Party, N.S. Khrushchev.

Prison laborers at the Moscow–Volga Canal construction site in 1935.

The Moscow–Volga Canal in 1957.

A "dead" locomotive on a "dead" railroad. At the end of the 1940s and the beginning of the 1950s, by the will of the dictator Stalin, prisoners labored to build the completely unnecessary Salekhard–Igarka Railroad through the Arctic swamps (photograph from 1996).

Chapter 3

Gulag Personnel

During their years spent migrating from one camp to another, prisoners would encounter dozens of prison officials of all kinds; "some were more cruel, others less; some were just clock-punchers, others fanatical about their calling."[1] Their characters and professional abilities were the deciding factor not only in the level of physical and psychological suffering of the prisoners, but often in their very survival. The memoirs of former prisoners contain hundreds of portraits of camp officials of all ranks and titles. Dark colors do not always predominate; even the depths of the Gulag harbored administrators who had not lost their humanity and kindness. Their virtue was, of course, relative. Lev Razgon, who for some fifteen years served as an object of the professional activity of camp officials, noted, "If these good people had received an order to burn us alive, they would have done so, though of course they would have shed some tears. And they would have agreed to establish socialist competitions among themselves to see who would complete the task first."[2]

The "staff of the Gulag" is a voluminous and composite concept. In our understanding it is not limited to people who worked in the Chief Camp Administration, but includes a broader circle of people whose professional duties were in one way or another associated with the implementation of the punitive policy and the activities of the totalitarian state's repressive organs.

Communist propaganda made active use of mythmaking to form a socialist, revolutionary worldview among citizens of the Soviet Union and to develop specific ideological positions. One of the most widely cultivated myths had to do with the image of the Chekist as a morally pure, self-sacrificing revolutionary, a proletarian knight, a ruthlessly aggressive fighter, but one who was scrupulously fair even in his treatment of his enemies. This myth was not at all based on reality. The legend of the crystal-pure Chekist evidently drew upon those emotional revolutionary declarations that were made by prominent figures of the Communist Party during the early period of revolutionary euphoria.

One Chekist instruction, written by F.E. Dzerzhinskii, contained the following exhortations: "Everyone who is charged with conducting a search, depriving people of liberty, and holding them in prison is to treat them with care; officers should be more polite with them than with their own loved ones, remembering that a person in prison cannot defend himself and is in their power."[3] The Cheka leader's good intentions were utopian. It was that very circumstance—that an arrested person was completely under the power of the punitive organs and could not defend himself—that corrupted the Chekists and gave rise to tyranny, violence, and unjustified cruelty. Criminal actions by Cheka officials were widespread, particularly in the provinces. In their attempts to reform the Chekists, whose numbers reached over 30,000 by 1921, revolutionary tribunals periodically executed the culprits. Such attempts to reform the repressive apparatus, however, failed.

At the beginning of 1921, an appeal arrived at the Central Committee of the Russian Communist Party from officials of the special section of the Turkestani front. The appeal concerned "unjust executions of Communists working in special sections and the Cheka." This document, which, according to Dzerzhinskii, gave "the impression of people with pain in their hearts,"[4] contained a number of very interesting observations and generalizations about the real state of affairs in the ranks of the Chekists. Officials of the special section wrote:

> Sad as it may be, we have to admit that a Communist working in a punitive facility ceases to be a human being and turns into an automaton who operates mechanically. . . . If we look at the Communists working in proletarian punitive organs, we will see that they are separated from the political life of the republic. The long time they have spent serving in the punitive agencies, the monotonous, difficult, mechanical nature of their work, which consists exclusively in seeking out and destroying criminals, gradually turns them, against their will, into individuals living a life apart. They begin to develop negative tendencies, such as arrogance, ambition, cruelty, crude egoism, and so on, and gradually, without realizing it, they break away from our Party family and form their own special caste, which resembles the former police force. The Party organizations regard them as they did the old *okhranka* [that is, the tsarist secret police—Ed.], with fear and contempt.

As we can see, this insightful characterization of the Chekists has nothing in common with the mythical image of the "proletarian knight." In order to rectify the situation, the *osobisty*** proposed that Commu-

---

*Osobists were members of the Cheka's Special Departments that were attached to Red Army units during the Civil War. The Osobists operated in the front zone with the goal of eliminating threats to Soviet power and of monitoring security within the armed forces themselves.—Ed.

nists be periodically recalled from the punitive organs and sent to work in other agencies, replacing them with fresh staff from the Party. "In this way," wrote the authors of the letter, "all the Party members who have spent time working in punitive facilities and left them for other agencies will not hold in contempt Communists who work in these agencies but will respect them as true martyrs for the revolution."[5]

It should be noted that relations between the punitive organs and Party organizations remained troubled for a number of years. Not wishing to mix with rank-and-file Party members from whom they felt estranged, some Chekists refused altogether to enter the ranks of the Communist Party. They took comfort in the fairly widespread opinion during the 1920s that a real Chekist did not have to join the Party. For their part, the Party organizations, whose role in the OGPU–NKVD system was relatively insignificant, repeatedly discussed the question of "Chekist arrogance." Later on, when they spoke at Party meetings during exercises in self-criticism, some Chekists confessed, "We believed ourselves to be a special category of people, who were crystal pure. We were not oriented toward the Party: you were first a Chekist and only then a Communist. There were comrades in our milieu who were not Party members, who worked in the NKVD for fifteen years and stubbornly refused to join."[6]

Relations between the Party and the punitive organs underwent a noticeable change during the second half of the 1930s, when N.I. Ezhov, the secretary of the Central Committee and chairman of the Party Control Commission, took over the leadership of the NKVD. Taking their cue from the people's commissar, who stated that the task of any Party committee is the "education of its cadres," Party organizations of the NKVD began an active campaign to "build closer relations" with the staff of the Chief Administration of State Security (GUGB).

Today's apologists of "revolutionary legality" deny any direct line of succession between the punitive organs of the early years of the Soviet regime and the repressive apparatus of the 1930s and 1940s, attempting to draw a clear boundary between the activity of the Cheka and that of the NKVD. In our view, the distinction drawn between the activities of these repressive agencies is fairly arbitrary, and the continuity between them is quite obvious. It is not a simple matter of the retention of the term "Chekist" itself or the fact that the organs of the NKVD drew attention to their connections with the Cheka and took pride in them; the continuity can be identified primarily in the so-called "Chekist traditions," most notably the massive nonjudicial reprisals; the repressions against dissidents; the total control over the army, social organizations, and the population; and the widespread use of secret agents, provocations, and censorship of the postal and telegraph services for "information gathering." Naturally, the punitive organs reacted to changes in the social climate, but their essence remained the same: they continued to be the most important component of Soviet authority and served as a reliable support for the totalitarian regime.

Conscious of their special status and political significance, GUGB officials began to call themselves workers of "the core of the only special instrument of revolutionary vigilance in the country, an organ of our Bolshevik Party in the Soviet state system, whose mission it is to serve as the drawn sword of the dictatorship of the proletariat, striking the enemies of the working class, all and sundry, without a single false blow."[7] This pretentious self-designation was repeated over and over, with slight variations, at all Chekist Party meetings; it is reminiscent of medieval oaths, which also featured the image of a punitive sword. It is interesting to note that initially not all Chekists had a sense of the real scale of the terror that had begun in the country. We find evidence for this in a speech made by an NKVD official at an election meeting of the GUGB Party organization, which was attended by over eight hundred people: "They say that, metaphorically speaking, the sword of the dictatorship of the proletariat has lost its sharp edge. No, it has not; it has simply gone a little rusty from disuse. We must flush all the vermin out of the underground and corner all the 'intelligence services' and 'gestapos' that still lurk there, in spite of our twenty-year history."[8] This meeting took place on May 7, 1937, when the machinery of repression was running full blast, and the comments made by the four-year veteran of the Cheka fell far short of the bloody reality.

Caught up in the martial spirit of their rivalry with the gestapo, GUGB officials did not notice that their "crystal pure Chekist milieu" was turning into a filthy swamp of intrigues, denunciations, slanders, and treachery. After Stalin's People's Commissar Ezhov assigned the Chief Administration of State Security the task of "pulverizing the rotten theory planted by our enemies which claims that there cannot be traitors and criminals among the Chekists" and challenged the GUGB to "increase the revolutionary vigilance of the Chekist collective,"[9] all members of the repressive agency found themselves in immediate danger. "Chekist arrogance" yielded to public expressions of repentance, self-flagellation, and frenzied critical attacks that crossed the line into threats and abuse. The term of abuse "scum" (*svoloch*) became one of the most commonly used words in the daily conversations of the state security officials; it was applied particularly in reference to old Chekists, such as G.I. Bokii, A.A. Slutskii, and many others. Slutskii had been accused of doing a poor job of "processing" Leon Trotsky after his departure from Paris.

Within a single year (from May 1937 to May 1938), Party meetings of the GUGB, which was directly subordinate to the MGK of the Communist Party, considered 393 personal cases, 257 of which were self-initiated, that is, cases in which Party members informed the Party committee about relatives who had been arrested, or repented of insufficient Party vigilance, and so forth. Of 39 Communists expelled from the Party during this period, 17 were later arrested.[10] The grounds for expulsion were quite varied: for aiding enemies, for social and political corruption, for violation of secrecy, for veiled enmity to the Party, and so forth and so on. One rather unusual accusation was made in the case of S.B. Ioffe, whose case document states, "In all her many years of work in the Party, she did not uncover a single class 'alien' or a single enemy of the Party; she submitted overly flattering reports concerning very suspicious elements. As a rotten liberal who has completely dissipated her Bolshevik Party spirit, Ioffe is expelled from the Party."[11] In our examination of the case documents of dismissed officials, we also encountered notes such as the following: "Confirm the Party Committee's decision to expel Kolesnikov. Take note of his absence from the case review due to suicide."[12]

Over the course of the year, "the administrative purging process" resulted in the dismissal of 439 officials from the GUGB apparatus; 59 were transferred to other administrations. New officials came to take their place—366 people were brought in from the provinces, and 162 employees were sent by the Central Committee of the Communist Party. Thus the state security administration staff had a 50 percent turnover in 1937–38.[13]

As of May 1, 1938, there were 2,159 staff members in the central apparatus of the GUGB; of these, 1,316 were Communist Party members, 328 belonged to the Komsomol, and 515 were not in the Party. We have data on the social class, nationality, gender, and age of the members of the GUGB Party organization, as well as their educational level and number of years in the Party. Since practically all security officers and administrative personnel were Party members, these figures can be used to provide a general characterization of the Cheka cadres.

In social origin, all staff members were traditionally divided into three categories: peasants made up 10.2 percent; white-collar workers, 43.5 percent; and members of the working class, 46.3 percent. In fact, these divisions did not give a true picture of their social origins, since many staff members were from the petty merchant class, the petite bourgeoisie, lower officer ranks, craftsmen, the clergy, and so on. We do not know under which of these three categories they were recorded.

The largest group by age—66.3 percent—was made up of mature officials between the ages of thirty-one and forty.

The number of women in the GUGB apparatus—10.3 percent—was about the same as in other state administrative offices.

The educational level of the majority of the staff was low: 8.8 percent had received some form of higher education; 22.4 percent had graduated from high school; 7.9 percent had continued their studies in various institutes of higher learning; the remainder (60.9 percent) had attended high school for varying lengths of time. The NKVD ran literacy schools for those who had not learned to read and write (and there were some).

The majority of staffers (64 percent) had been Party members for over ten years; forty-two (3.2 percent) had previously been members of other political parties.

The national composition of the management and security staff of the GUGB was rather varied. The largest group was made up of Russians, 64 percent; the second-largest was Jews, 16.6 percent; then Ukrainians, 7 percent; Latvians, 3.3 percent; Belorussians, 2.1 percent; Armenians, 1.5 percent. The remaining 5.5 percent included some fifteen different nationalities.[14]

As for professional training, during this period the concept did not even exist in regard to GUGB security officers. The people who went to work for the GUGB were usually without skills or education, but endowed with a heightened "class sense" and a taste for the work. The following description can be taken as fairly typical: "A.D. Dubovik was illiterate when she came to work as a courier; she attended high school while continuing to work, became a Party member, and was assigned to work as a security officer."[15]

The professional service of the Chekists never went unnoticed. In 1938, 161 administrative workers of the GUGB apparatus were awarded the Order of the Soviet Union, and 811 people earned a personal expression of thanks from the "Iron Commissar."[16]

In the beginning of the 1930s, Stalin emphasized his own personal role in the OGPU and the NKVD by presiding over their most important meetings in the Kremlin. After each such meeting, so-called "receptions," with elegant luncheons or dinners, were held in the Kremlin. These banquets were organized by I.M. Ostrovskii, the chief of the management administration of the OGPU–NKVD. It was said that at one of these "receptions" Stalin proposed a toast to Ostrovskii's health, calling him a wonderful organizer and manager, "whose self-sacrificing labor provides not only the administrative staff of the OGPU but us sinners, Central Committee workers, with everything we could possibly need."[17]

State security staff never had to complain of neglect from the Party and government or from their own leadership. Even rank-and-file workers of the security sections of the NKVD enjoyed a level of material benefits that was markedly higher than the average level of consumption in the country as a whole. The Glavspetstorg [special closed shops—Ed.] system, working through the Strela orders department, provided the families of staff members not only with food but with manufactured goods as well. The Cheka newspaper *On Guard* (*Na-cheku*) published frequent reports on problems in the work of this special agency. "Problems" included the following: difficulty in getting through on the telephone to submit a request; an inadequate assortment of goods, especially of fresh fish and dairy products; unsatisfactory residential services due to the absence of special shops and kiosks in some of the buildings in which NKVD workers lived; irregular deliveries to the dacha areas where many NKVD workers vacationed in the summer; and so forth.[18] Even this simple listing of these undoubtedly justified complaints gives an idea of the standard of living of state security personnel. The Chekists were provided with special tailors and shoemaking shops, numerous cafeterias, clubs, dachas outside Moscow and in resort areas, rest homes and sanatoriums, special medical clinics, and numerous other benefits that ordinary Soviet citizens could not even dream about. Living space alone remained a problem, but only because of the continual influx of new cadres. The moral character of the newly arrived cadres allowed them to deal with the problem of living space by requisitioning the two or three rooms that had belonged to people who ended up "at Veinshtok's"* (i.e., in prison—G.I.).[19]

The NKVD leadership showed a great deal of concern for its employees' children. They vacationed in pioneer camps and children's colonies; a special "forestry school" was organized for children with delicate health; the majority of the children were educated in Menzhinskii Special School No. 233. The saying "the apple does not fall far from the tree" involuntarily comes to the mind of the researcher

---

*From November 1936 through April 1938, Ia.M. Veinshtok headed the GUGB's Prison Department. He was shot in February 1939.

who reads the secret documents concerning the discovery by the GUGB in the spring of 1937 of a children's "cheka" organization called "Beat the Bourgeoisie!" (*Bei burzhuev!*). This rowdy street gang included children of NKVD officials, among them Young Pioneers who had outgrown that organization. They entertained themselves primarily by attacking, robbing, and undressing other children.[20]

The wives of security officers were no more exemplary in moral character. By the traditions of the time, the wives of state apparatchiks were actively involved in social and community activities in the institutions where their husbands worked. The same was true of the NKVD. This allowed the wives of leading administrators to use official automobiles for their own private business, to interfere in administrative work as they pleased, and in general to feel at home in their husbands' offices. Such "wife work" (*zhenrabota*) aroused sharp criticism from rank-and-file workers, who indignantly reported at Party meetings that "the women came in all decked out in fine dresses with long trains and took over the tailor's shop, and they had a terrible falling out."[21]

The privileges and benefits that came along with the job made work for the NKVD attractive for anyone who wanted to climb to the top of the social pyramid. The careerist ambitions and casual attitude toward principle among certain categories of young people were manipulated successfully by L.P. Beria in his staffing policy. He attracted thousands of new, devoted workers into the state security agencies, while destroying the powerful layer of staff who had served as Stalin's instrument in the establishment of his personal authority.

In 1939, 7,372 people were dismissed from the security officer staff of the NKVD, including 5,607 from branch offices, 695 from the central apparatus, 752 from highway and transportation sections (DTO), and 318 from other departments. During that same time, 14,500 new Chekists were employed both at headquarters and at local branch offices. The central apparatus employed 3,460 new officials; the territorial offices, 9,332; the DTO, 1,086; and special departments, 628.[22] Seventy-six percent of the new staff came from Party and Komsomol organizations, in addition to NKVD security officer schools, which admitted students mobilized by Party organs. Over 60 percent of the new workers had attended or had graduated from an institution of higher learning. These were young, politically and socially active people, primarily Russian in nationality.

At the end of 1938, Beria had managed to secure a substantial salary raise for all the workers in the Chekist security administrations; in addition, the SNK instituted a special 15 percent bonus for serving in

NKVD troops. In 1939, workers in the central apparatus were granted 3,600 residential rooms, and construction of 13 large new apartment buildings on the Leningrad and Mozhaisk Highways and on Sukharevskaia Street on Moscow's Ring Road rapidly approached completion. These "monumental buildings, worthy of gracing the streets of the red capital," were erected by prisoners. The NKVD State Construction Trust, whose "collective" consisted of 9,000 prisoners and 1,250 free workers, began construction on a new, 867-room administrative building for the commissariat. Employees who came to Moscow from the provinces were provided with a great deal more, including a new 408-room dormitory-style hotel.

Beria's appointment as chief of the NKVD brought with it not only a rapid improvement in the standard of living of commissariat workers but also a closer relationship between the Party and the repressive organizations—which considerably raised the social status of the latter. On Beria's initiative, the Central Committee of the Communist Party resolved to introduce the position of deputy chiefs for personnel. Former obkom and gorkom secretaries and major Party and Soviet officials were appointed to these positions. In 1939, the leadership staff underwent a verification process, which resulted in the certification of 26,700 people, including 16,600 who were first-time workers in the state security agencies. It is worth noting that personal ranks were introduced in the GUGB system somewhat later than in the Red Army. As a result, a lower rank in the security agencies would correspond to a higher rank in the army. For example, the rank of "captain of state security" corresponded to the military rank of "colonel." The wholesale granting of special ranks to security officers in the NKVD changed their attitude toward their work and noticeably increased their motivation.

This was the first year that Cheka staff were processed by Party officials, who checked their qualifications and approved them for their positions. The nomenklatura of the Central Committee of the Communist Party consisted of 10,277 people. NKVD officials themselves believed that such attention from the higher Party organs instilled confidence, strengthened their position, and motivated them to do whatever they could to justify the trust placed in them by the Central Committee.[23]

The new people's commissar worked to raise the professional level of his subordinates. For the first time in the history of the state security organs, a special bureau was created to produce instructional manuals for training Chekists. By the end of 1939, security officers were given six new manuals summarizing and analyzing the battle history of the VChK–OGPU–NKVD.

The personnel policies in the NKVD system were conducted in strict accordance with Stalin's famous instructions: workers were to be selected first on the basis of political criteria and second for their professional qualifications. For a number of reasons, the second requirement was not always observed, but the first was never violated.

Beginning with the end of the 1930s, the political sections took over the selection and assignment of staff for the central and branch offices. By 1937, on the initiative of N.I. Ezhov, the Central Committee of the Communist Party resolved to create political sections within the NKVD that would report directly to the higher Party organs. It was only after Beria's rise to power, however, that they became fully operational. At the beginning of 1940, the work of administrations and departments in the commissariat was supervised by eleven political sections, with a staff of 370. The number of paid Party workers depended on the number of Party members served by each section. For example, the political section of the first (security) department had a staff of 88, whereas only 7 worked in the children's colonies political section. Such a substantial difference can be explained by the fact that the Party organization of the first section included 3,900 Communists as compared to only 248 in the children's colonies section.[24]

The political apparatus played a very strong role in the NKVD system, particularly in the Gulag. This is evidenced not only by official documents—orders and reports of various kinds issued by political sections—but also by the direct observations of people who got to know the repressive system "from the inside." Former prisoner A. Antonov-Ovseenko, who went on to research the history of the Gulag, described the structure of this new rival to the special section in the Northern Pechora (*Severo-Pechorskii*) camp-production administration:

> The political section was designated No. 1; it was the top department in the administration. For a long time it was run by Colonel Kuznetsov. His office was enormous, to match the dignity of his rank. He would summon in the chiefs of the other sections, who would line up and stand at attention, arms straight down at their sides, listening with anxious and respectful attention to his instructions. Kuznetsov had portraits of Dzerzhinskii and Beria hanging on his office walls. . . . The political section was involved in all the affairs of the cultural and educational section and in fact was completely in charge there. The other sections as well, from the technical people to the security guards, were constantly aware of the iron grip of the political section on them.[25]

The enormous power of the political section and the high rank of its leader—his post was part of the nomenklatura of the Central Committee of the Communist Party—were due to the increasingly important role of Party organizations in the NKVD system. It is clear that the higher Party leadership had developed a close interrelationship with the administrative officials of the NKVD.

The united Party organization of the People's Commissariat of Internal Affairs was formed in March and April 1939 by decision of the Eighteenth Congress of the Communist Party. In February 1940, the Party committee of the commissariat encompassed 112 primary Party organizations, with 6,731 members. The Komsomol committee included 93 primary organizations, with a total of 3,124 members. Party committees were created in all the chief administrations, including the Gulag, which further strengthened the role of the primary organizations. As we have already noted, the number of members in the primary Party organizations varied widely. For example, collective No. 32 (as the Gulag was called during this time, in the interests of maintaining secrecy) had 505 members, making up just 7.5 percent of the overall number of members of the Communist Party. It is well known that, as a rule, all the important leadership positions were occupied by Party members; they were also an absolute majority in the NKVD apparatus. Their prominence warrants an analysis of their social composition by social class, gender, age, and educational level.

The 6,731 Party members can be divided into three groups based on social origins: 42.5 percent of the Communists identified themselves as workers; 47.8 percent as white-collar workers; and 9.7 percent as peasants. As we can see, the category of "white-collar workers" had increased slightly since 1938, with a corresponding decrease in the number of "workers."

An analysis of the age composition of Party members in the NKVD shows that, as a whole, they had gotten younger. Communists between twenty-five and thirty years of age made up 31.6 percent; those between thirty-one and thirty-five, 30 percent; the group of mature Party members aged thirty-six to forty remained fairly large, 20.1 percent; and all other age categories totaled 18.3 percent.

The number of women had slightly decreased from 1938; they now made up 8.8 percent.

There was a noticeable increase in the average educational level of Party members, due to a sharp increase in the number of Communists who received a higher education. They made up 20.1 percent; 6.4 percent had attended institutions of higher learning; and 17.7 percent had a high-school education. People with lower and primary education remained the largest category, 38.9 percent; together with those who had attended some classes in high school, they made up 55.8 percent of Party members on the NKVD staff.

The majority of Communists—61.1 percent—had joined the Party between 1922 and 1932; 24 percent had become Communists between 1933 and 1940. Only 0.2 percent had been Communists since before the Revolution. The remaining 14.7 percent had joined the Party during the Civil War. The number of people who had previously been members of other parties had decreased to 15 (0.2 percent).[26]

Very significant changes had taken place in the national composition of Party members. These were not circumstantial changes; rather, they came as a result of the overall nationality policy that Stalin and his closest associates instituted quite openly on the eve of the war. We learn about the new "conception" of nationality relations from the reminiscences of the former head of the government V.M. Molotov:

> In 1939, when Litvinov was dismissed and I became minister of foreign affairs, Stalin told me, "Get the Jews out of the Commissariat." Thank God that he said it! The fact was, Jews were the absolute majority in the leadership there and among the ambassadors as well. That, of course, is not completely true: they were Latvians and Jews. . . . And each one of them was dragging a long tail behind him.[27]

Undoubtedly Lavrentii Beria received similar "words of advice" from Stalin when he took over "internal affairs." We can gauge the nationality bias in his administrative personnel policies by noting the changes that had taken place in the nationality composition of the NKVD Party organization as of the beginning of 1940. First of all, the proportion of Russians had increased sharply; they now made up 80.2 percent of the overall number of Party members on the staff. Second, there had been a significant decrease in the number of Jews, who now comprised only 6.3 percent. The proportions of Ukrainians and Belorussians remained practically the same, 7.5 percent and 2 percent, respectively. The number of Armenians had decreased to 0.9 percent. As far as representatives of other Union and autonomous republics, their numbers even before had been very small, but now they decreased to 2.7 percent. A very small number, just 0.4 percent, of other nationalities from outside the USSR, such as Germans, Poles, Estonians, Lithuanians, and so forth, remained. The number of Latvians, for example, who traditionally had been well represented in the VChK–OGPU apparatus, had dwindled to 0.1 percent.[28] Thus we can see that, in spite of its all-Union status, the People's Commissariat of Internal Affairs was staffed primarily by Russians, which was entirely consistent with the newly revived imperial traditions of the Russian state.

It should be noted that these qualitative changes, no matter how significant, cannot be compared with the quantitative changes. The rates of growth in the numbers of officials in the NKVD apparatus were far greater than those in all the other state structures and professional groups. If the overall number of blue-collar and white-collar workers in the branches of production increased by 14 percent between 1937 and 1940,[29] the NKVD staff grew by 35 percent over the same period. In 1937, the overall number of personnel working in the NKVD organs, both in the capital and in the local offices, including the internal troops, was 270,730; by 1939, this number had increased to 365,839.[30] The most significant increase in NKVD staff during the prewar period occurred in the Gulag.

The elite status of personnel in the state security organs made the situation there quite different from that in the Gulag. The problems that would come to characterize the Soviet camp system go back to the 1920s. Penitentiary workers at their congress in October 1923 complained about meager financing, a continual lack of personnel, and systematic overcrowding in places of incarceration. The 1923 report of the Chief Administration of Places of Incarceration of the NKVD of the RSFSR notes that "in spite of unemployment, to date it has not always been possible to find people willing to occupy vacancies in the prison service."[31] The difficulties involved in staffing the camps were primarily due to their inadequate standard of living. A decree of the Council of People's Commissars of June 22, 1923, established an average salary level for a white-collar worker in a place of incarceration at the state level (they were financed out of the state budget) of 17 rubles 50 kopecks, which was lower than the Russian average. Furthermore, whereas a prison or colony chief at level sixteen earned 35 rubles 70 kopecks, the salary of an eighth-level junior supervisor came to only 15 rubles 30 kopecks. In general, workers in the locally financed corrective-labor facilities experienced, in their words, "abject poverty."

The staff of workers in the central apparatus for the administration of places of incarceration comprised 85 people, with 28 positions vacant. At the oblast and provincial level, camps were administered by 54 newly created inspection agencies, with a total staff of 742. Inspectors of places of incarceration who headed the provincial apparatus were selected primarily on the basis of their Party standing. Of 54 inspectors, 38 (70.4 percent) were Party members. The largest group by age (66.6 percent) was made up of people between twenty-five and thirty-five years of age. The educational level of inspectors, here as everywhere else, was extremely low: 2 of them had a higher education; 14 had graduated from high school; the remaining 38 (70.4 percent) had only a lower education* or had been educated at home. The overall number of personnel serving all places of incarceration in Russia was rather small. In the summer of 1923, the staff list of the GUMZ, which had been approved for three hundred places of incarceration, included 11,190 workers.[32] The intensification of the repressions was accompanied by an increase in the staff of prisons, camps, and colonies, but their growth was inhibited by insufficient funds. The first large OGPU camps were practically all "self-staffed"; suffice it to say that only 37 staff members of the OGPU were employed on the construction of the White Sea–Baltic Canal. Practically all administrative, technical, and other positions in the camp and in production were filled by prisoners.

In the second half of the 1930s, the enormous increase in the number of prisoners had a serious effect on the personnel situation in the Gulag. The problem was not so much an overall lack of workers as their absolute lack of professional skills or qualities. A good sense of the situation was provided by I.I. Pliner, deputy chief of the Gulag, in an April 8, 1937, speech at an election and reporting meeting of the Gulag Party organization:

> For four or five years now we have been trying to get people for our staff, but to no avail. We get the leftovers from other sections; they send us people based on the principle "You can take what we do not need." The cream of the crop are the hopeless drunkards; once a man goes over to drink, he's dumped onto the Gulag. When I ask, "Just who do you think you're giving us?" I get the answer, "Forget it; reforming criminals is your job, and this fellow is not even completely gone yet." This is their reasoning, and it is the primary basis for the staffing of the camp apparatus. From the point of view of the NKVD apparatus, if someone commits an offense, the greatest punishment is to send him to work in a camp.[33]

Pliner, who became the chief of the Gulag in August 1937, was even more blunt in a speech made a year later:

> Before the change in the NKVD leadership, before Nikolai Ivanovich Ezhov took over, the enemies demonstrated their enmity in their approach to staffing policy; all kinds of riffraff were dumped on us, and sometimes they put it in writing: "Dismiss them from state security and send them to work in the Gulag system"; and sometimes even without this commentary.[34]

It should be noted that the approach to staffing so emotionally described by Pliner was typical, not only "before the change in leader-

---

*"Lower education" was understood, as a rule, as one or two years of primary school. In 1946, 92.6 percent of the VSO staff had a lower education.

ship" but also during all the previous and subsequent periods of the existence of the repressive agency.

Viktor Abakumov, a young security officer who had "erred," had a chance to experience the "rehabilitating effects" of the Gulag for himself. The future chief of the MGB came to work in the state security organs in 1932 at the age of twenty-four. He brought with him a reputation of being a "fine fellow," the all-but-adopted son of Nikolai Podvoiskii, one of the leaders of the October 1917 uprising. After some difficulties getting along with his superiors, Abakumov was transferred to several different offices before ending up in one of the economic administration sections of the Moscow Oblast OGPU, where he was assigned to "develop" the ceramics and silicate industries. The new official, according to his employment file, "didn't set the world on fire" and had one weakness that earned him the nickname "foxtrotter." Abakumov appreciated pretty women and enjoyed their company during his working day. When he started his new job, the newly fledged security officer set energetically to work: reports unmasking saboteurs poured in, one after the other. It became clear, however, during his first unscheduled review, that all the agents he had recruited were attractive girls from the secretarial divisions of the industrial enterprises under his administration. Abakumov met with each of them in private at a clandestine apartment; they had a good time, and afterward, without giving it much thought, the girls would sign papers presented to them by their secret beau. Naturally Viktor Semenovich was the author of the denunciations, since the "agents" had no idea about how to write them themselves and, in any case, could not have known the engineers identified in the papers. This episode in the life of a "prominent Chekist" was later recalled by M.P. Shreider, who was Abakumov's direct superior.[35] Upon his request, the talentless security officer was dismissed from the economic administration of the OGPU as degenerate and unsuitable for operative work and in fact for any state security work at all.

Abakumov's career might very well have ended here if he had not been rescued by the Gulag. Influential protectors supported the feckless "counterfeiter," and he was appointed an inspector in the Chief Administration of Camps. The Gulag workers were not especially indulgent to Abakumov; the future minister endured a great deal of criticism and numerous accusations from his colleagues at Party meetings. Here are just a few of the statements made by Party members, taken from the minutes of meetings during the first quarter of 1937: "Abakumov needs to pay more attention to his duties; he has too high

an opinion of himself"; "Abakumov is not very enthusiastic or disci-
plined"; "Our group went out of our way to make Abakumov learn
what he had to do"; and so on and so forth. In his defense, the object
of their criticism cited the permission granted him by the leadership
to educate himself, claiming, among other things, that he was busy
with his outside work in the MGK of the Communist Party.[36]

Abakumov would not seem to be a likely candidate for a successful
career or a rapid rise to the top. But things worked out differently. The
powerful fists and sadistic tendencies of the experienced forgery artist
served as a good foundation for a rise up the ladder of success in the
NKVD system. Rumors spread that Abakumov had had a hand in the
investigation of the case of the military leaders Tukhachevskii, Kork,
Iakir, and others. Soon he took over the Rostov NKVD oblast administration, where he initiated a bloody purge of the Soviet and Party leadership in the oblast. He was subsequently transferred to the central
office to head the special section, where the notorious "Smersh"*—
also headed by Abakumov—was created during the war. This is followed, in the "fox-trotter's" curriculum vitae, by the positions of deputy
minister of state security, deputy minister of defense, and, finally, in
1946, chief of the MGB. Corruption, debauchery, servile devotion to
his protectors (first and foremost to Beria), forgery, fraud, and falsification—these are the key words in V.S. Abakumov's career record.

Of course the Gulag was not staffed exclusively by sewage from the
state security organs. People came from outside as well, though rarely
of their own free will. A significant number of personnel for the camp
system was also generated during the prewar period by Party mobilization campaigns. At the beginning of 1938, over 3,000 Party members
and over 1,200 new graduates from institutes were appointed to leadership positions in the camps. Hundreds of Party members came to
work in the central apparatus of the Gulag from the Central Committee and MGK apparatuses and from the Planning Academy (*Planovaia
Akademiia*). In the words of Deputy People's Commissar of the NKVD
V.V. Chernyshev, during those years the Central Committee turned
"literally into an employment agency" that supplied cadres via district
Party committees throughout the Gulag periphery. At the end of April
1939, the staffing problem of the Gulag was the subject of a discussion
at a meeting with G.M. Malenkov, who was in charge of looking after

---

*Smersh was a military counterintelligence agency set up in 1943 to root out
spies and "counterrevolutionaries" in the Red Army and among prisoners freed by
advancing Red Army units. An abbreviation of the Russian words *smert' shpionam*
(death to spies), the name was purportedly thought up by Stalin himself.—Ed.

that agency. The secretary of the Central Committee decried the dependent position of the Gulag leadership and demanded "a solution to the question of indiscriminate hiring of staff from the Central Committee."[37]

Within one and a half or two years, over 150,000 new workers were employed in the camps and colonies, and the administrative staff of the Gulag nearly tripled. It is interesting to trace the rates of growth in the number of employees in the central apparatus of the Chief Administration of Camps of the OGPU–NKVD during the 1930s: in 1930, 87; in November 1932, 253; in September 1934, 366; in August 1935, 527; in April 1937, 633; in November 1937, 936; in May 1939, 1,562.[38] The nearly eighteenfold increase in the number of administrative staff in the Gulag's central apparatus can be explained not only by the enormous growth in the number of prisoners but also by the fact that, by the end of the 1930s, the Gulag had turned into a huge economic institution, a manufacturing complex that operated in twenty different branches of the economy. The removal of a number of production facilities, such as Glavdvigstroi, Glavpromstroi, and others, from the Gulag system led to a sharp decrease in staff from the production departments. A total of some 600 employees remained in the central apparatus of the Gulag on the eve of the war, which was about the same staffing level as in a typical branch of a people's commissariat.

The leadership of the camp agency also underwent some changes during its history. The first chief of the OGPU Camp Administration was the former head of the Solovki camps F.I. Eikhmans. After six weeks in office, in June 1930, he was replaced by L.I. Kogan. Between 1932 and 1937, the Gulag was headed by the career Chekist M.D. Berman, who was born in 1898 in Zabaikale. To his chagrin, Matvei Davidovich was unable to boast of proletarian origins: his father had owned a brick factory and a steam mill. His education as a cadet in the Irkutsk Military Academy did not help his career either, but all the rest was in the spirit of the times: he had joined the Party in 1917, and, beginning in 1918, he served in leadership positions in the organs of the VChK–OGPU–NKVD. During the Civil War, he chaired provincial branches of the Cheka in various Siberian cities. During the 1920s, he served as acting deputy representative of the OGPU in Central Asia. Given the history of the establishment of Soviet power in these regions, it is not difficult to guess at the number of bloody "heroic feats" the "proletarian knight" accumulated under his belt. At the end of 1930, Berman was transferred into the central apparatus of the OGPU in Moscow. In January 1937, he was named deputy people's commissar of the NKVD.

After Berman, the Gulag was headed by his former deputy I.I. Pliner.

Between November 1938 and February 1939, G.V. Filaretov, the former people's commissar for local industry of the RSFSR, was both Gulag chief and deputy people's commissar of the NKVD.

We will not attempt to judge the degree of wrongdoing committed by these people in their professional activity from the standpoint of human values, or the level of their guilt before the hundreds of thousands of prisoners who perished, and in fact before the entire Soviet people. From the point of view of the totalitarian regime, however, their service in the camps was completely logical, justified, and commendable. But the Soviet repressive system existed and developed according to its own canons. Following the dialectical law of the double negative (*otritsanie otritsaniia*), it destroyed its own cadres, in spite of their enthusiasm for and devotion to their work. Four of the five Gulag chiefs named above, all of them except Filaretov, were shot in 1938 and 1939.

In February 1939, Deputy People's Commissar of the NKVD Vasilii Vasilievich Chernyshev, who had previously headed the Chief Administration of the Militia, took over the leadership of the camp system. Chernyshev spent the 1930s in the Far East serving as the chief of the administration of the border guards. He had spent nearly twenty of his forty-three years in the troops and offices of the NKVD. A Party member since 1917, Chernyshev was well known as a hero of the Civil War and had been awarded the Order of the Red Banner twice. According to the reminiscences of his contemporaries, he had not been eager to probe the political implications of the repressions. He avoided conversations about the NKVD's use of torture, and he assured uneasy employees that no one was arresting innocent people.[39] Chernyshev saw his primary task as "eliminating the consequences of wrecking in the Gulag." In speeches at meetings with his colleagues, he often compared the Gulag to the Augean stables, with himself taking the role of Sisyphus (unlike the ancient Greeks, Chernyshev for some reason believed it was Sisyphus, not Heracles, who cleaned the Augean stables).

A structural reorganization of the Gulag took place under the leadership of the new chief. Security in the camps was tightened, as a result of which the number of escape attempts dropped sharply, and production became more efficient. Chernyshev was well aware of the growing economic importance of the Gulag and required his subordinates to "learn how to make full use of the prison workforce." He attempted to raise the social status of camp personnel, proposed introducing special ranks for Gulag workers, strived to increase the levels of budget financing, especially in the area of salary, and proposed introducing additional benefits and rewards. His reasoning went roughly as follows: "Our apparatus has to keep track of one and a half million prisoners, enemies of the people. . . . Our camp workers are just as important as the troops who guard our border, and this is a no less honorable and responsible task, both for the Party and for the country."[40]*

In expressing his concern about the Gulag staff, the deputy commissar understood that the system's increasing need for these people could not be satisfied without improving their standard of living and raising their social status, which traditionally was significantly lower than that of GUGB workers. Communists and Komsomol members sent to work in the NKVD were far more eager to work for the state security organs than in the Gulag. The reasons for this are clear from statements made by Gulag staffers themselves, who took every opportunity to complain about unsatisfactory working conditions and low pay. Here are some typical comments made at Party conferences and meetings over the course of several years:

1937

"Everyone received a raise on February 1, but the Gulag Chekists got nothing, not even on the first of May. In honor of the holiday they were just given their regular monthly salary. Every single improvement in the standard of living has to be fought for with blood and nerves."

"Our prison chief receives 350 rubles and 50 percent for length of service, and the division chief, who is in charge of an entire division, receives 435 rubles."

"The Gulag is seen as an administration from which everything can be demanded and nothing given in return. . . . This excessively modest way of thinking—that we are worse than everyone else—is wrong, and it allows inequities in pay, in housing, and so on, to continue."[41]

1938

"Two hundred fifty people in the Gulag have not yet received their fixed rate and have been living for nine months on advances. They work hard, without rest, and are worn to a thread; it is absolutely abnormal to work every day from ten o'clock in the morning until two in the morning. In any case, work productivity is quite low after eight or nine P.M. They spend more time sitting around than working."

"I have to comment on the bad scheduling of the workday. People work a lot, but some people manage to slip away from work at 4:30, reappearing at 11 P.M. and sitting there until four in the morning—the bosses like that."

*Taken from a speech made by V.V. Chernyshev at a Party meeting on April 22–25, 1939.

"We sit in a stuffy shed for fourteen to sixteen hours at a stretch with no ventilation; it's inhumane to sit for so long in such conditions."

"The workers are overloaded; they sit at work for twelve to sixteen hours at a time, and for what? It's exhausting."

"The salary system in the Gulag is an example of wrecking. The pay is so bad that only the prisoners stay on the job; the free specialists leave."[42]

1939

"There is blatant wrecking involving salaries: the VOKhR detachment commander, who is responsible for 150 troops, receives 380 rubles; meanwhile the camp chief's driver is earning 400."

"Free workers are impossible to find because of the low pay. A norm-setter technician gets 350 rubles; a master craftsman—300; a planning economist earns 350–400. The prisoners run things themselves. The workplace is an Augean stable, the working day is unregulated—'as much as will fit in'—and this means staying on the job every day until eleven or twelve at night, which amounts to a working day of twelve or thirteen hours."[43]

Undoubtedly, the working conditions during those years were similar to those in many other state institutions as well. The practice of "sitting through the night" was extremely widespread. The leadership liked this system, since the leadership at the next rung up liked it, and so on up to the very top.

As far as salary is concerned, it was no lower and in fact possibly even slightly higher than the average monthly salary of workers in manufacturing. But other factors were also at play in the Gulag. For example, Gulag staffers knew that the chief security officer in any camp was paid over 1,000 rubles a month and enjoyed the use of an official car and a separate apartment, and they wanted their share of the action as well.

Officials of the central apparatus of the Gulag were paid quite a bit more than those on site. Their monthly salary ranged from 700 to 1,000 rubles, but there were some individual rates of 1,400 rubles. Overall, the salary of Gulag workers was approximately half the level of those in the GUGB apparatus, which naturally caused resentment among the former.

The privileged position of security officers in the NKVD system went right up to the level of the commissariat divisions. Only after the state security organs were separated and given their own independent people's commissariat did the Gulag receive the status of "most-favored administration," which was partially due to its economic importance.

The heaviest burdens of camp service naturally rested on the shoulders of the on-site cadres. A Gulag official who made an official visit to the White Sea–Baltic Complex (BBK) was struck by the miserable conditions endured by his colleagues:

> The staff is our most important resource, and look at them. Things are indescribably bad for the people working out there. Recently I visited the BBK. I had thought that they had a lot of staff there. A single camp section chief has nine hundred prisoners and manages the whole program by himself. Considering the conditions in which he works, we have to marvel at how he manages to do his job at all. There is one clerk there, a free man, on salary. This senior clerk is the only one for all those prisoners; they all share him. He is responsible for mechanization and for preventing the padding of output to obtain better rations. The man gets five hundred rubles and works practically around the clock.[44]

The local administrators who came to Moscow from the camps and colonies never tired of complaining of their heavy burden. One camp administration representative told his colleagues:

> Our central figure is the camp chief, and he is always in a terrible position. He literally cannot have his family with him; there is no place for them to live, and the conditions in the camp might threaten their safety. Camp administrators live together with the prisoners; their salary of 450–500 rubles is not enough to make ends meet, and each one of them is responsible for several thousand prisoners.[45]

There is no reason to doubt the sincerity of these officials. But we should not be hasty with our conclusions either. Let us return to a different source and look at the camp leadership from the point of view of the beneficiaries of their "thankless toil," the prisoners themselves. "Decent people were extremely rare among those who were called the 'bosses'; they basically just observed the strict rules and regulations of the camp," wrote F.F. Kudriavtsev, a military man from a military family, who had served in three wars and, after being wounded five times, ended up in Stalin's camps.

> More commonly they were the rejects of Beria's administration—drunks and libertines corrupted by their unlimited power over people and their immunity from punishment who did not hesitate to rob the prisoners, to keep things that had been confiscated from them, to come to work with empty wallets and go home with them stuffed full, and to take all the best food, leaving the prisoners to starve. Many of them used the unpaid labor of prisoners to build and furnish their own personal dachas. Young and pretty women were also theirs for the taking.[46]

The observations of the former prisoner are completely confirmed by statistics from the personnel records of Party members working in the camps. Over 50 percent of those who were expelled from the Party or who were reprimanded were punished for "abuse of their official position for personal gain," "waste, forgery, and theft," "moral and social degeneracy," and so forth. The practice of "self-supplying" was widespread among the camp leadership everywhere, and only rarely did it attract the attention of Party or administrative oversight bodies. As a rule, cases only came to light if the administrator had offended someone and had to be removed, or if the violation was so flagrant that it came to the attention of the higher security organs.

It was not only the prisoners who were robbed by the camp administration. "The data at hand allows us to confirm the incidence of serious criminal actions and theft of the people's property, especially in NKVD camps, construction projects, and colonies," reports S.N. Kruglov, head of the personnel department of the NKVD, at the administration's Third Party Conference in April 1941. Based on the results of the planning audits of 1940, 1,515 workers were dismissed due to embezzlement and theft; disciplinary reprimands were issued for 3,547 people; 2,424 cases were turned over to investigators; and 196 people were convicted in court trials.[47] There is no doubt that the dismissed and punished camp officials made up only a very small proportion of the total number of people who, having only the vaguest notions of honor and conscience, took advantage of the universal bad management and ignorance. As the philosopher Francis Bacon, who knew a thing or two about financial machinations, wrote, the opportunity to steal is what creates the thief.

The largest group of camp staffers were the armed guards (*voenizirovannaia okhrana*, VOKhR). The ratio of guards to the camp population before 1939 had been set at 5 percent; later that norm was raised to 7 percent; and after the war to 9 percent and higher. It should be noted at the outset that practically at no time was the VOKhR fully staffed. It was primarily the difficult conditions of service and its extremely low prestige that kept people out of the guards. At the same time, there were cases when someone would refuse to serve as a convoy guard for purely moral reasons, not wanting to be a watchdog.

Former Red Army soldiers made up 95 percent of the guards. Junior Red Army commanders were looked upon by Gulag administrators as "a gold mine," and Gulag officials considered the army to be none other than "a university for all the organizations." During the establishment and growth of the camp system, the conditions of service for armed guards in the Gulag were substantially worse than in the Red Army. Because of the lack of personnel, ordinary guards were forced to serve on watch for thirteen to fifteen hours a day, often without any days off. In the event of an escape, they could be arrested and tried. Living space was scarce, and there were not enough rifles and uniforms, not to mention books, radios, or movies. The reports of political workers of the time often contain statements such as "the guards are dressed like the Red Guard in 1918"; "the soldiers have no uniforms; they go around unclothed and barefoot." The chiefs of the guards complained, "Red Army veterans come to work for us, but they are fed swill and housed in dugouts in the ground, and the men turn to drink, fraternize with the prisoners, and so on. . . . We have an extremely high suicide rate."[48] In a report on discipline and the political and psychological health of the staff, political section chief M.E. Gorbachev noted, "The guards indulge in immoral behavior and drunkenness; there are suicides. The number of guards who have been reprimanded ranges from 24 to 70 percent of the total guard staff."[49] The most common violations of work discipline were drunkenness and sleeping on watch.

In an attempt to correct the flaws in the security system of the camps, the political sections instituted the practice of so-called mass organizational work, which boiled down to propagandistic drills and studying the biography of Stalin in Party-sponsored study groups. Great efforts went into cultivating a sense of hatred in the guards toward the prisoners, impressing upon them that they were dealing with extremely dangerous criminals, the worst enemies of the Soviet people. Guards were instructed to treat the prisoners cruelly, and any hint of humane treatment was punished severely. As a result, the guards were motivated by only two feelings, animal fear and hatred, which had a terrible effect on the prisoners' quality of life. The memoir literature and archival documents contain thousands of examples of the refined tyranny that was encouraged among the guards, their cruel, inhuman treatment of prisoners, their blind, unreflective zeal for their duties, and their moral degradation. Not a single former prisoner had a kind word to say about a single guard—not because they were guards but because, as a rule, these were creatures who were embittered by their upbringing and the miserable conditions in which they lived; they were drunken degenerates and uneducated people who had never experienced anything good in their lives. I hope that any former guards among my readers will forgive me for such a blunt characterization, but it is based on documents and eyewitness reports. In all the many archival sources, we encountered only a single one that presents a VOKhR soldier in a positive light. This was an anonymous letter from a soldier in the armed guard at Dalstroi, signed by the pseudonym G. Levonets. The anonymous Soviet soldier informed G. Malenkov of his intent to "appeal to the government to bring several parasites to justice for cruelty and for murder, and for illegally recording the deaths of their victims, in keeping with common practice in the camps, as resulting from escape attempts, disease, or violence against the supervisory staff."

A brief but very revealing characterization of camp guards was provided in 1939 by a Gulag official who believed that "the people who served as guards were not second-class but fourth-class people, the very dregs."[50]

The chronic shortage of all kinds of staff forced the Gulag administration to use prisoners with professional skills and people with criminal records for administrative and technical duties. The NKVD leadership tried to overcome this problem by periodically publishing orders prohibiting the use of prisoners for particular types of work, but reality, especially the economic needs of the Gulag, was stronger than these orders. As a result, skilled workers among the prisoners continued to work as accountants, economists, engineers, technicians, doctors, and so on, though their numbers decreased.

The presence of prisoners in the apparatus of camp administrations continued to be the subject of criticism and self-criticism for two and a half decades. In March 1931, a special commission examined the work of the cultural and educational section of one division of the OGPU's Solovki Camp. The commission concluded, among other things, that

> the primary task of the KVCh in the near future is to sweep all the "*kaery*"* out of our apparatus and to staff KVCh positions with working-class prisoners or elements of the poorest peasantry, giving first preference to former Party members and prisoners convicted of social and work-related crimes. . . . All the work done by the KVCh must have a more distinctly class character and must be oriented exclusively toward the prisoners closest to us in class, those with working-class and peasant roots, poor and middle-level peasants, and the déclassé element.[51]

The Solovki Party Committee report for 1931 also addressed the issue of prisoners serving as staff members. Party Committee secretary Kontievskii observed, "One negative issue that must be noted is the fact that the majority of sector chiefs in the camp are prisoners; prisoners convicted of counterrevolutionary crimes are in charge of

---

*This word, formed from the initial letters of "counterrevolutionaries," or k-r's, refers to prisoners convicted under Article 58.

such vital sectors as agriculture, subsidiary enterprises, the fisheries, supplies, sanitation, accounting and distribution, and finances."[52]

One issue of particular importance for the new chief of the Administration of Northern Camps under the OGPU, Bukhband, was the relations between free workers and prisoners on staff. Bukhband presented his position at a meeting of the Party activists' group of USLAG in July 1933:

> You all know what the contingent of our camp is like; you know what kind of people we have working in our apparatus. These are usually counterrevolutionaries who are now enjoying an easy life, "practically saints." This should serve as an eternal warning to the Chekist staff about the need for strict vigilance, about the need to be ready at any moment to rein them in, to straighten them out, and, if necessary, to root out prisoners who forget themselves and step out of line. But walk into any department and you will see the same picture everywhere: the line dividing individual staff members and free workers from counterrevolutionary convicts working in the apparatus no longer exists. They call each other comrade, Ivan Stepanovich, Ivan Mikhailovich, and so forth. In this environment, it is easy to think that these are people who all think and work the same way and who are equally meritorious, that they form a monolithic unity. Our staff workers and prisoners try not to remind each other of their differences in rights and stations in life. This, comrades, is no good. Such relations will lead to a bad end. Such relations are alien to us Communists. What we need to do is not erase the distinction between the Chekist and the counterrevolutionary but rather draw attention to it and preserve it as it is, and as it should be, for in such a friendly atmosphere the free staff will mingle with the prisoners and inevitably will lose their sense of class identity and their focus. We cannot allow this to happen. And it is the Communists who have to take the initiative to put a stop to it.[53]

In the history of slavery there were periods when the dividing line between slave and owner was nearly eradicated and their relations were built on a businesslike, fully amicable foundation. Such periods are conventionally called "patriarchal slavery." Something of this sort can be observed in the history of the Gulag likewise. A tradition of cooperation between Chekists and skilled prisoners took shape during the construction of the White Sea–Baltic Canal. Later many camp managers emulated this model in other camps as well. At one time there were even prisoners—former and current—working in the central apparatus of the Gulag. There was a special building in Moscow, at Kuznetskii

Bridge, where they were housed. The prisoners had days off, they joined the free workers in the cafeteria for lunch, and so forth.[54] In many camps, during the first year or two after the completion of the White Sea–Baltic Canal, skilled prison workers who had been convicted under Article 58 were not even kept in prison but were housed in private apartments or even in their own residences. Pliner, who traveled to the Central Asian camps on an official inspection tour in the mid-1930s, was extremely disturbed by the arrangements that had been made with two of the prisoners in Tashkent. Galon, who had been convicted of espionage and sentenced to ten years, was chief of the planning section, and Nikolskii, who also had been convicted under Article 58, was the chief of the agricultural section of the Central Asian camps. Pliner was struck upon seeing these prisoners arrive in the morning at the administrative office with their briefcases after the tram ride from home. It turned out that they had been convicted in Tashkent and had just remained there to serve their sentences. "The camp administrator and the chief of the third section considered this to be perfectly normal," writes the indignant Pliner. Upon his request, Galon and Nikolskii were relocated to the prison.[55]

A liberal attitude toward prisoners with professional skills itself became a crime beginning in the second half of the 1930s. People could be expelled from the Party, dismissed from work, and brought to trial for "fraternizing with the prisoners." As the repressive policies grew more severe and the Gulag became stronger, relations between free workers and prisoners became restrained and formal. Often the degree of severity depended on the location and the institution involved. If a prisoner worked in a state enterprise that utilized camp labor, he could have full confidence in the good will of his "clients." F.F. Kudriavtsev recalls in his memoirs that

> they valued specialists, who often were much more highly qualified and had greater knowledge and experience. Quite a few, without saying anything out loud, were fully aware that there were many honest people in prison who had committed no crime. And they tried to help them in any way they could: they intervened on their behalf, obtained benefits for them, and tried to ease their lot; they delivered letters, brought books, and bought food for them. And they did it all at enormous risk of being taken to court "for fraternizing with prisoners."[56]

The attitude toward specialists within the camp system itself was quite different. Here they remained slaves, and their welfare depended completely on the character and temperament of the slaveowner. It was only because of the desperate need in the camps for educated, trained specialists that some prisoners found themselves doing work that was not physically demanding. The chief of the political section of the White Sea–Baltic Complex reported in January 1941 at the Central Committee of the Communist Party of the Karelo-Finnish SSR:

> Over the past three years, the administration of the Belbaltkombinat (BBK) has repeatedly appealed to the Gulag to help with its pressing need for qualified staff, which has necessitated the use of former and current prisoners in administrative positions, since there is no other source for staffing these positions.
>
> The primary administrative staffing level of the Belbaltkombinat and its camp divisions is set at 6,653 workers, whereas the actual number of personnel as of November 1, 1940, is 3,064 people.
>
> The low staffing level is primarily due to the impossibility of attracting specialists to work in the underpopulated regions where the camp complexes are located. The personnel section of the Gulag sends only a very small number of specialists. In 1939, the complex requested 647 specialists and was granted 31; in 1940, 663 specialists were requested, and only 15 were sent.[57]

A similar situation existed in other camp administrations as well. In 1940, there were 13,000 specialists with higher training in all professions working in the organs of the NKVD;[58] skilled prisoners working on staff, of course, were not included in that figure.

Following Gulag instructions, the camp leadership, as much as possible, replaced the prisoners working in skilled positions with free workers. Prisoners who had been convicted under Article 58 were replaced by prisoners serving time for crimes committed against individuals or crimes related to work or military service; these classes of prisoners were permitted by camp instructions to serve in administrative and management positions.

The dynamics of the changes that took place in the relative numbers of free workers and prisoners and their levels as compared to the prewar period can be seen in Table 1, which presents the figures for the White Sea–Baltic Camp Administration.

As we can see, the proportion of free workers in relation to the overall number of personnel at the White Sea–Baltic Complex rose steadily, without ever exceeding 50 percent. A similar situation could be observed in many other camp administrations. In some particularly remote camps, the number of prisoners in the administrative apparatus reached 90 percent. As for the free workers, in the NKVD system this was often a relative concept: "Of the overall number of free workers in

Table 1

Quantitative Composition and Proportion of Hired Workers to Prisoners on Staff in the White Sea–Baltic Camp Administration (BB Lag)

Years	Structural divisions	Free hired workers (number of people)	Prisoners on staff (number of people)	Total number of people on staff	Percentage of free workers on staff	Overall number of prisoners on staff in BB Lag
1938	Total apparatus	5,205	9,813	15,018	34.7	83,810
	VOKhR	2,423	1,566	3,989	60.7	
	Administrative apparatus	398	185	583	68.3	
1939	Total apparatus	6,523	11,266	17,789	36.6	86,567
	VOKhR	3,320	875	4,195	79.1	
	Administrative apparatus	453	148	601	75.4	
1940	Total apparatus	6,178	7,295	13,473	45.9	71,322
	VOKhR	3,191	965	4,156	76.8	
	Administrative apparatus	523	108	631	82.8	

Source: Based on *Gulag v Karelii: Sbornik dokumentov i materialov 1930–1941* (Petrozavodsk, 1992), pp. 147, 161, 185, 189.

our camp, 40 percent are former prisoners, and if the third sections,* which have the smallest number of former prisoners, are excluded from this number, the level reaches 60 percent,"[59] reported I.I. Pliner at a Gulag meeting. The NKVD leadership issued various instructions and orders prohibiting specific categories of released prisoners from leaving camp territory. They were considered "attached to the camp" and lived outside the prisoners' zone in a barracks for free workers; as a rule they worked in the same positions as before their release. Lev Razgon wrote about this category of camp personnel:

> Many of them had been arrested back at the beginning of the 1930s; they served their time and then found themselves employed in the camp—

---

*The "third sections" were the Chekist security sections.

permanently! I knew wonderful, sincere people among them who saved the lives of many prisoners, eased their physical and emotional sufferings. . . . One way or another, the ranks of the managers, and, accordingly, the prison administrators as well, came to include those of us who had served our time and were forced to stay and work in the camp: planners, norm setters, financial managers, accounting managers, clerks, senior foremen, . . . I myself belonged to this category. In spite of everything, we, too, were employees of the prison! . . . And there were people who adapted very quickly and became real prison officials—they turned informer and informed, the SOBs."[60]

The practice of keeping released prisoners at the camp was widespread during the postwar period.

During the war, significant changes took place in the staffing of the Chief Administration of Camps. The central apparatus of the Gulag, which had been transferred to the city of Chkalovsk (now Orenburg), was cut by 40 percent. Instead of the 416 staff units that had been assigned to the Gulag before the war (not including operative and political sections), 251 remained at the end of 1941. There was a substantial decrease (by 47 percent) in the Gulag Party organization: in December 1941, total staff numbered 175, including 38 (22 percent) women.[61]

During the first three years of the war, 117,000 primary camp personnel, including 93,500 people from the armed guard, were mobilized into the Red Army. In August 1944, the total number of personnel in all the Gulag divisions came to 85,000 units (not counting the armed guard), but in fact only 85 percent of staff positions were filled. Here, as everywhere, women, old people, and disabled war veterans took over the positions left by men who had gone to the front. In 1944, women made up 31 percent of the total number of camp workers. Overall, the camps and colonies of the NKVD employed over 72,000 people in administrative and management positions. Their educational levels (4 percent with a higher education, 18 percent with a high-school education, and 78 percent with a primary education) testify to the fact that it was the most backward groups of the population who were brought to work in the Gulag. The variety of nationalities represented among camp workers broadened considerably, primarily due to the increase in the number of indigenous peoples, who made up 20 percent of the total; Russians made up 68 percent and Ukrainians, 12 percent.

Only 22 percent of the prewar Gulag staff remained; the other 78 percent had less than three years of experience working for the NKVD. The changes had affected primarily the lower ranks of the Gulag apparatus; 65 percent of the administrative staff leadership had been working for the NKVD for over seven years. Party and Komsomol members made up 88 percent of the nomenklatura, whereas overall they comprised only 19 percent of camp staff.[62]

The NKVD leadership knew very well that the apolitical, uneducated, unskilled mass of camp personnel were not equal to the important tasks assigned to them by the state. At the end of 1943, in an effort to improve the authority and social status of workers in the camps and colonies, Beria issued an order conferring special titles and military officers' ranks to the Gulag staff. The junior command staff of the armed guard troops and some categories of employees in the camp sector were given ranks in the NKVD special service. In 1944, there were 37,000 such people. The administrative staff of Gulag divisions and senior VOKhR commanders were awarded the corresponding special titles in the state security service and military officers' ranks; 18,000 titles were conferred in all. The official Gulag nomenklatura in 1944 comprised 6,000 people.

The importance of the tasks assigned to workers in the repressive agency is confirmed by the fact that during the war 1,350 Gulag workers, including 89 workers of the central apparatus, were awarded medals and orders of the Soviet Union for "successful completion of government tasks."[63] As a rule, all government tasks assigned to the Gulag were associated with the construction of secret military-industrial facilities or the transportation and accommodation of deported peoples.

The guard troops of the Gulag also underwent substantial changes during the war years. Of the 135,000 VOKhR guards, 93,500, or 69 percent, were sent to the front. They were replaced by older men subject to the draft but only marginally fit for military service, as well as women. People between twenty and forty years of age now made up 38 percent of the guards, in comparison to 86 percent before the war. The number of Party and Komsomol members decreased by nearly half.

In August 1944, the Gulag guard troops comprised 110,000 people, of whom 98,000 were rank and file, 10,000 were sergeants, and 2,000 were officers. The rank-and-file and junior commander ranks were understaffed by 6,600.[64] The guard was on active-duty status and was housed in barracks. A direct consequence of the changes that had taken place in the guards was a sharp increase in the number of escape attempts by prisoners, especially criminals and recidivists. In an attempt to improve the disciplinary level and efficiency of the camp guards, the Presidium of the Supreme Soviet of the USSR issued an edict on March 11, 1942, extending the disciplinary code of the Red Army to cover the personnel of the VOKhR, which to a certain degree achieved the desired effect.

The introduction of officer ranks to the senior and middle supervisory staff (*komsostav*) and of uniform stripes to the entire staff had a noticeable effect on the psychology of camp commanders. They not only developed a sense of social importance but also came to view their service in the camps as a lifelong career, one that was difficult but prestigious and lucrative. The Gulag allotted a great deal of funds for training and preparing camp personnel, particularly VOKhR commanders. Every year they were assigned the same task: "to raise the military, political, and special-training levels of the guard troops to equal those of NKVD troops,"[65] though they never did manage to achieve this goal.

The NKVD's need for camp personnel grew as the Red Army progressed westward. By 1944, corrective-labor colony administrations had been established in all the republics, regions, and oblasts that had been liberated from German occupation; forty-four industrial colonies out of the fifty-six that had existed before the war had been reestablished, along with all forty agricultural colonies. The Gulag assigned 3,500 camp-sector workers and 6,800 armed guards and guard commanders to permanent positions in these repressive organs.[66]

The success of the aggressive punitive policy conducted by the Soviet leadership in the Western oblasts of the Ukrainian, Belorussian, and other republics depended on the presence of a sufficient number of reliable security officer personnel from the camps. During 1944, on Beria's orders, the personnel department of the NKVD sent 42,000 workers to reinforce the internal affairs offices of the Ukrainian, Belorussian, and Moldavian SSRs; of these, 22,000 people were new to the internal affairs organs.[67]

A significant number of camp personnel was needed to staff the over one thousand camp divisions that held foreign prisoners of war. In 1944, over 8,000 officers were sent from Moscow to work in prisoner-of-war camps. By the end of 1944, the staff of these camps comprised 32,000 people, and over 300 people were employed in the central apparatus of the Administration of Prisoners of War and Internees.[68]

In addition, the NKVD and NKGB jointly administered special camps and prisons in the Soviet occupation zone in Germany. They held Germans arrested at the end of the war by NKVD and NKGB agents at the fronts "in the process of purging the rear of the Soviet field army" who had not been transferred immediately to the Soviet Union due to physical weakness and unsuitability for work.[69] According to V. Abakumov, these prisoners included "old people, women with children, youth, and rank-and-file members of Fascist organizations against whom there is no evidence of actual criminal activities." V.D. Sokolovskii, the leader of the Soviet military administration in Germany, repeatedly requested a reevaluation of the categories of the prisoners in these camps, but to no avail. Only at the end of 1947 did the minister of the MGB give partial assent to Sokolovskii, proposing "to release no more than 20,000 such persons from the camps" but continuing to hold the rest.[70]

The successes of the Red Army brought NKVD activity to the territory of Eastern Europe. Powerful internal-affairs subunits followed hard on the heels of the army, rooting out and destroying national organizations and groups that opposed the Communist regime. NKVD officials also participated directly in the formation of national security services in a number of countries. In Poland, for example, where the NKVD divisions were headed by I.A. Serov, a security organization called the Urzád Bezpieczénstwa (UB) was created. Its leader, Stanisław Radkiewicz, honestly admitted in a conversation with Arthur Bliss Lane, the U.S. ambassador in Warsaw, that "the Russians had sent him two hundred NKVD instructors to help create the Polish security police based on a Soviet model."[71]

NKVD activity in Poland definitely followed a "Soviet model." General Zygmunt Berling, previously the commander of the Russian First Polish Army, a member of the Polish National Liberation Committee, wrote the leader of the Polish Workers' Party Władysław Gomułka: "Beria's minions are laying waste to the entire country, with the help of criminal elements from Radkiewicz's apparatus. During legal and illegal searches, people's things disappear; completely innocent people are deported, thrown into prison, or shot like dogs. . . . No one knows what they are accused of, who is arresting them and for what, and what is to be done with them."[72]

In May 1945, at the Plenum of the Central Committee of the Polish Workers' Party, Gomułka admitted that they had lost control of both the UB and the NKVD: "No one likes the security organs, but they seem to be turning into a state within a state. They conduct their own policies, and no one is allowed to interfere. In our prisons, they treat the prisoners like animals. The security-apparatus officials are demoralized and are leaving the service. . . . Ultimately we will become simply an insignificant organization subordinate to the NKVD."

Radkiewicz also had grave doubts about the activities of the NKVD "teachers":

> "There are signs of a crisis in the security service, which currently employs 11,000 people, with only a quarter of the positions filled. . . . A large

number of competing organizations have arisen, and morale is low. . . . It is difficult to say whether the Russian advisers have brought more benefit or more harm. During the first stage they helped us; in the second, they began to do harm. Now the situation has changed, and for the time being there is no need to get rid of them."[73]

It is hardly likely that the Polish people would have supported the opinion of their minister of security, but the organs created "based on a Soviet model" never needed their support.

NKVD advisers established a strong presence not only in Poland but in all the other "people's democracies" as well. Many of them, including Major-General V.N. Sukhodolskii, the senior adviser in Bulgaria, Colonel M.A. Ianov, the senior adviser in Czechoslovakia, and others, had an extraordinarily rich experience in the repressive system, which led to their dismissal from the Soviet security service in the mid-1950s for violations of socialist legality.

As we can see, the personnel of the NKVD in the postwar period were in demand not only in the Soviet Union but abroad as well. Nevertheless, most of the personnel resources were absorbed by the Gulag. The steady growth in the number of prisoners required continual increases in the number of camp personnel, whose primary sources of supply were the identification and screening camps. The residents of these camps were not officially considered to be prisoners, although they were held under convoy guard in conditions that were barely distinguishable from those in the Gulag camps. After identification, prisoners who did not fall under the suspicion of the state security organs were released and sent either to work in the location of their permanent residence or to staff the so-called "workers' battalions," which had been formed specially for work in industry, or they were returned to military divisions. Some of the citizens who passed through this screening process were turned over to the jurisdiction of the NKVD. As of January 1, 1946, there were 31,000 such people. Repatriates and former Red Army soldiers were usually sent to serve in the armed rifle guard troops (after the war, the acronym VOKhR was replaced by VSO). This category of guards endured extremely difficult work conditions. The majority of them had absolutely no desire to live this "dog's life" and did everything they could to get out of it.

The number of people who came into the guard service from the identification and screening camps was quite large, especially during the early postwar years, when such people made up between 16 percent and 20 percent of the total rank and file, and in some camps 80 percent. In 1950, the chief of the Political Section of the Moscow Camp

Administration N. Isaev reported to the Moscow Committee of the Communist Party:

> In some camps critical statements have been made concerning work and living conditions. Some guards, especially those who came from the identification and screening camps, do not want to continue service and do whatever they can to avoid it. . . . There are a total of 412 guards serving in the VSO system who came from the PFL;* the majority of them are undisciplined and do not want to serve, and their behavior has a negative effect on the entire staff.[74]

Protests against involuntary service in the organs of the Ministry of Internal Affairs took different forms: Radkiewicz, a guard in one of the camps near Moscow, refused to sign a document attesting to his service in the guards and turned in several official requests to resign, warning that "if he is not released in a proper manner, then he will attain release in an improper way."[75] A repatriate named Daniliuk categorically refused to serve in the guards. He explained his unusual behavior in no uncertain terms: "I do not want to serve in the organs of the Ministry of Internal Affairs at all."[76] After numerous "processing" sessions, the obstinate rifleman was finally dismissed from the guard service.

One common form of protest was suicide. Every year three or four hundred involuntary guards in the Gulag took their own lives. Analyzing these cases, camp investigatory commissions were often unable to find any specific reasons for the suicides. A typical conclusion reads: "No particular reasons leading the guard to commit such an act were established. This event is nothing more than an act of faint-heartedness related to personal experiences."[77] What were these "personal experiences"? In 1950, a guard's suicide attempt was intercepted in one of the colonies outside of Moscow. Repatriate Podoprigora, the would-be suicide victim, had spent the years between 1942 and 1949 living in the American occupation zone on German territory. The guard explained his "depressed state of mind" as follows: "Yes, I did intend to kill myself. The reason for this is the fact that I've been in the service for a very long time now, and I still have not been given a residence permit, and nearly every day a policeman comes around with an order to vacate the apartment, and this leads to quarrels in my family every single day."[78]

Soviet power had its own logic: it entrusted weapons to people it

---

*During this period, the staff of the VSO of the corrective-labor camps and colonies of Moscow and Moscow Oblast comprised 3,397 people, including 162 officers, 736 sergeants, and 2,499 rank-and-file guards.

considered untrustworthy but was afraid to entrust them with documents, that is, to grant them the rights of free citizens. Former prisoners of war and repatriates who served as guards went for years without passports, military service certificates, and residence permits. The lack of documents completely deprived a person of his rights, humiliated him, and kept him in a state of bitterness and slavish servility; his life became a continual torment. In 1948, the head of one of the camps near Moscow, Shpindel, reported to his colleagues about the state of affairs: "There are cases when entire detachments of soldiers and sergeants are not registered. Many guards and sergeants have no documents at all. People get married, but the marriages cannot be registered without documents. The children of such a marriage are considered illegitimate, since the militia refuses to register their birth."[79] We should note that these were not prisoners but people who were legally free. The situation continued, essentially unchanged, until the beginning of the 1950s.

Although former Soviet prisoners of war and repatriates serving as guards conducted themselves in a manner described by the camp administration as "confrontational" and "having a negative effect on personnel," they were not dismissed because of the critical shortage of guards. In 1947, with 157,000 people serving, the rifle guard troops of the Gulag were understaffed by 40,000.[80] As in the prewar period, the rank-and-file and sergeant positions were filled primarily by recruiting demobilized Red Army soldiers, who signed a pledge to serve in the Gulag for two or three years. Unlike soldiers called in for short terms, they received a monthly salary of 250–350 rubles, with all living expenses paid. At the beginning of the 1950s, the military registration and enlistment offices began to call up citizens unfit for combat to serve as guards in camps and colonies.

In 1947, upon the initiative of Gavrilova, the young Party secretary of Camp No. 38 outside Moscow, guards signed a pledge to "serve vigilantly in the armed guard troops until the end of the five-year plan" and challenged all the VSO guards in the Gulag as a whole to follow their example.[81] Their "Address" resonated far and wide. All the camps and colonies began to collect signatures from their guards. The political sections initiated a propaganda campaign, and within a year over 96 percent of the personnel of the VSO, which included a large number of women, signed a pledge to serve until the end of the five-year-plan period without a single violation of discipline. In its turn, the MVD leadership issued a series of orders aimed at improving the standard of living of the workers in VSO divisions. At the end of this high-profile campaign, the chiefs of camps and political sections reported cheerfully to the ministerial leadership:

> There used to be a lot of escape attempts and immoral acts; 70 percent of the staff refused to serve in the guards, but now everyone has gotten down to business for the remainder of the five-year-plan period; immoral acts have decreased to a minimum. . . . Guards used to receive worse rations than the prisoners themselves,* which led to widespread attrition in the VSO staff; discipline was weak, which led to escape attempts by prisoners. Now the guards have a good standard of living, there is no more attrition, and prisoners are no longer attempting to escape.[82]

In fact, no real changes had taken place: in one place a barracks had been repaired; in another a guard with a family was given a long-awaited room; somewhere else the food did indeed get a little better or movies started being shown more often. Overall, however, things remained unchanged; no order or political campaign could change the mentality of a guard or raise his educational level, teach him self-esteem, or instill in him a sense of respect for others.

A commission of the Central Committee of the Communist Party of the Soviet Union conducted a review of the Gulag staff at the end of 1953 and concluded: "Many workers are out of control; they go on drunken binges and commit crimes. Such behavior is especially common among the guard troops in the camps and colonies."

There followed a long list of specific examples: shooting into the air, resulting in deaths among prisoners; hooliganism; terrorizing the local population; and all of this taking place against a background of utter, unmitigated drunkenness.

The educational level of the VSO staff (both officers and the rank and file) in 1954 was as follows: 0.2 percent had graduated from or attended an institution of higher learning; 2.5 percent had graduated from high school; 18.5 percent had attended high school; 70.8 percent had a lower education; and 8 percent of the guards had no education whatsoever.[83] One might assume that the guards compensated for their lack of education with a high level of professionalism; however, this was not the case. Only rarely did a guard demonstrate any level of achievement in military or political training. We analyzed the results of a review of a weapons training drill conducted in the spring of 1948 in one of the camps near Moscow. Of the overall number of partici-

---

*In 1954, a guard was provided a daily food allowance of 4 rubles and 66 kopecks.

pants, 44.3 percent received an assessment of "bad"; 28.8 percent, "average"; and 26.9 percent, "good."[84] Frustrated division commanders often reported at meetings: "The guards do not know how to oil, clean, and take care of their weapons. . . . A female guard stands on duty with her rifle barrel stuffed with a rag. . . . Some guards take other people's rifles out on duty, leaving their own back at home because they're too lazy to clean them each time. . . . Many do not know the caliber of their own rifle and have never adjusted it."[85] And so on and so forth.

The Party organs did not seem to make any special efforts to improve the level of political awareness of the guards. In 1947, the political section of the Gulag even issued a special order: "Guards are not to be included in any political study circles."[86] Under the circumstances, it is no wonder that one of the leaders of the guards' Komsomol organization, when asked the question "What do you know about the Truman Doctrine?" answered, "That is some woman who came here from America."[87]

A description of the personnel of the VSO is incomplete without factoring in their nationality. The opinion has been expressed that the majority of the guards were not Russians but came mostly from Central Asia and other peripheral areas. This was supposedly done on purpose in order to build on the guards' presumably innately hostile attitudes toward the prisoners, among whom Russians predominated. This opinion is not supported by the facts. During the postwar period, the overwhelming majority of VSO personnel were of Russian origin. In 1945, the nationality composition of the guard troops in the camps and colonies was as follows: Russians, 91.6 percent; Ukrainians, 4.9 percent; Belorussians, 1.5 percent; Kazakhs, Uzbeks, and Azerbaidzhanis, 2 percent.[88] By the following year, the number of Russians had decreased to 84 percent, and the number of Ukrainians and Belorussians had increased to 10.8 percent (primarily due to repatriates); other nationalities accounted for 5.2 percent.[89]

The situation had fundamentally changed by the mid-1950s. We do not have precise data on the nationality of the guard troops during this period, but we do have other information. Beginning in 1955, all levels of the camp leadership, from camp administrators to the minister of internal affairs, repeat the same complaint: the newly hired guards do not know Russian or have only a weak knowledge of it, and on average they have only a second-grade education.[90] In April 1956, Minister of Internal Affairs N.P. Dudorov informed the Central Committee of the CPSU in strict confidentiality that the staff of the guard troops "is in need of substantial qualitative improvement," since many of the citizens who are being recruited into the guard service in the camps and colonies are "poorly educated, and some of them, especially those recruited from Central Asia, the Transcaucasus, and the Baltic areas, do not know Russian."[91]

Such an influx of non-Russian guards can only be explained by the fact that in 1955 men born in 1934 began to be recruited for guard service. As new research by Russian scholars has shown, it was in 1934 that the birth rate in the country was at its lowest level. In 1933, there was a decrease in the natural growth of the population. The chief losses occurred in Ukraine and Russia, although the nature of the losses in the two republics was quite different. If the negative population growth in Ukraine was due to an extremely high mortality rate, in the RSFSR the primary cause (70 percent) was a decrease in births.[92] These were the tragic consequences of irresponsible state policies during that time, of the violent collectivization and forced industrialization that led to the terrible famine of 1932–33 and the sharp decrease in the Russian birthrate.

Thus, returning to the question of the nationality of camp guards, we can note that, when it was forced to hire personnel who did not know Russian, the MVD was to a certain degree reaping the fruits of the ruthless punitive policy it had conducted against the peasantry. Citizens from the Asiatic and Caucasian republics took the places of Russian lads who were not born. The practice of recruiting non-Russians into the camp guard service subsequently expanded and even became the norm.

The supervisory staff was quite similar to the camp guards in work status and moral-intellectual level. The internal supervisory service was introduced into the Gulag in April 1944. It was staffed by guards, former prisoners, and the local population. The structure of the supervisory service included chief administrators, senior supervisors, and regular supervisors. Women made up approximately 15 to 16 percent of the total. Over half of this category of employees were people of middle age, from thirty to forty years old; people over forty made up 40.8 percent. Party and Komsomol members made up around 25 percent.[93] Membership in the Party was not considered to be an advantage; in fact, supervisors tended to view it as just an extra burden. Many newly hired members of the supervisory and general camp staff concealed their membership in the Party when they began work, or they neglected to reclaim their Party documents when they left the service and considered themselves as having voluntarily left the Communist Party.[94]

Supervisors made up the least educated group among camp personnel. In 1954, only 2 percent of them had a secondary education; the remaining 98 percent had only a lower or primary education. The Gulag leadership made repeated attempts to raise the professional and educational levels of their employees. Many camp administrations organized special classrooms for the supervisory staff, where groups of twenty-five to thirty supervisors would undergo training during their working hours. In addition there existed in the Gulag system a network of special fifteen- to twenty-day courses following a curriculum developed by the Gulag in such subjects as the biography of Stalin, the history of the Communist Party, the geography of the USSR and foreign countries, as well as special training courses.[95]

The attempts made by the Gulag leadership to improve the qualifications of camp workers were unsuccessful. In spite of the good grades they received in these courses, supervisors continued to rob the prisoners (the most widespread method was to borrow money and not pay it back), to mock and insult them, and to beat them brutally. Their abuse took many forms. For example, in the winter of 1949, supervisors in several camps, particularly mining camps near Moscow, thought up the following activity to entertain themselves: in the middle of the night, they would awaken the prisoners and start shaving them and giving them haircuts.[96] Thousands of similar examples could be cited from the memoirs of surviving Gulag prisoners.

The number and composition of camp personnel were determined by their two main functions: to guard the prisoners and enforce camp rules, and to carry out a large number of production tasks. As S.N. Kruglov, minister of internal affairs, said, Soviet "camps must be exemplary: on the one hand, a camp must be a prison; on the other, it must serve to rehabilitate prisoners through labor."[97] At different times, depending on the instructions that came down from above, the Gulag could focus primarily either on ensuring proper enforcement of camp rules and procedures or on production tasks. As the economic potential of the Gulag increased, the number of qualified personnel grew as well, primarily those with technical skills. A new term appeared: "Chekist production manager." Kruglov assured his subordinates, "We are not only soldiers, not only security officers; we need to be managers as well. We must not shun managerial work; we must develop a taste for it, because we are building a socialist economy; we are creating the economy of communism."[98] The growing need in the Communist camp economy for engineering and technical personnel remained partially unmet. In 1948, according to MVD personnel department calculations, over 6,000 positions had not been filled. At the end of the war, there were 37,000 skilled workers with a higher education or a vocational degree working for the ministry; by 1954, this number had grown to 59,774. The specialists included 20,515 engineers and technicians with expertise in various branches of industry and transportation, 19,993 medical workers, 3,791 agricultural specialists, 1,915 lawyers, 3,102 economists, and 10,458 educational and cultural workers. Eighteen percent of the overall number of specialists (some 11,000 people) were so-called "young specialists," that is, people who had graduated from institutions of higher learning and technical schools between 1952 and 1954.

The camp empire had its own scientists as well. By the beginning of 1951, the MVD system contained around ten scientific research institutes: the Scientific Research Geological Institute of Prospecting for Gold, the Chief Scientific Research Institute of the Mica Industry, the Scientific Research Institute in Magadan, the Scientific Research Institute for Apatites, and a number of others. Half of them had been established by government decision in 1950. In the same year, 116 MVD employees were awarded the Stalin Prize "for outstanding work in the area of science and invention." Hundreds of others were awarded medals and orders. The work commended included designs and plans for construction projects in permafrost conditions and other, similar work aimed at supporting the camp economy. In 1950, there were 32 doctors and candidate-doctors of science serving in the Party organization of the central apparatus of the MVD.[99]

The proportion of specialists, particularly scientists, in the free hired managerial staff of the Gulag was rather small; the blue-collar professions predominated, and they included many people with no qualifications whatsoever. The example of Glaveniseistroi, one of the largest camp production enterprises, gives a good picture of the profile of production workers in the Gulag. The data in Table 2 show the changes that took place in the staff of Glaveniseistroi between 1950 and 1953 in three categories: educational level, Party membership, and nationality. As we can see, non-Party members predominated among workers in the camp production complex, which disproves the view found in Soviet literature that the Siberian construction projects were built by Komsomol members. It is also not justified, in our opinion, to speak of a mix of different nationalities, for the absolutely overwhelming majority of personnel were Russian. The educational level of production workers, as everywhere else in the country, was low: people with incomplete secondary or lower education predominated.

As of January 1, 1953, there were 31,916 free workers, including blue-collar workers and junior service personnel, employed in divisions

Table 2

Staff of Glaveniseistroi
(not including workers and junior service personnel)

Overall number of people	January 1, 1950 3,779 people = 100 percent		January 1, 1953 7,932 people = 100 percent	
Education				
Higher education	467	12.4	920	11.6
Incomplete higher education	80	2.1	137	1.7
Vocational secondary	342	9.1	844	10.6
General secondary	508	13.4	1,725	21.8
Incomplete secondary	1,247	33.0	3,005	37.9
Lower	1,135	30.0	1,301	16.4
Party membership	3,739			
Communist Party members and candidate members	742	19.6	1,622	20.4
Komsomol members	350	9.3	1,384	17.4
Not Party members	2,687	71.1	4,926	62.2
Nationality				
Russians	3,170	83.9	7,098	89.5
Ukrainians	183	4.8	377	4.8
Belorussians	54	1.4	64	0.8
Jews	130	3.4	137	1.7
Other nationalities	242	6.5	256	3.2

Source: Compiled from data in TsKhSD, f. 5, p. 21, d. 497, ll. 89, 90.

of Glaveniseistroi. The available positions were staffed at a level of 85.6 percent. There were 1,662 engineers and technicians with diplomas; of these, 920 were engineers and 742 were technicians. The majority of specialists—1,147 people—worked in production; the other 515 served in the administrative apparatus. Mining specialists and geologists predominated. Glaveniseistroi organized the Kanskii Mining and Geological Technical School for training personnel, which had 906 students in 1952–53. The administration as a whole was understaffed by 1,048 people. In spite of the serious personnel shortage, Glaveniseistroi did not employ all those wishing to work, since many of its construction projects were closed sites. The political reliability of workers was monitored by the state security organs and the political sections. In 1952, special reviews resulted in the dismissal of 449 people; 108 people were transferred from closed sites to other locations; and "seriously compromising materials" placed 650 workers under suspicion and subject to dismissal.

A similar situation with personnel could be observed in practically every large camp production complex. The proportion of free workers to prisoners varied, although as a rule the involuntary workers predominated. For example, at the end of 1952, there were 48,000 prisoners and some 5,000 free workers—some of them in military service—engaged in constructing the Kuibyshev Hydroelectric Station, which was under the management of the Kuibyshevgidrostroi Camp Production Administration.

In a great many instances, production discipline and labor productivity among the free workers was extremely low. In 1952, over 10 percent of the workers underwent various forms of punishment (a trial by their peers, administrative sanctions, dismissal, conviction, etc.) for absenteeism. Work-related abuses, embezzlement, forgery, theft, and drunkenness were widespread among the production workers. It is not at all surprising that many administrators of camp construction projects and enterprises preferred aides chosen from among prisoners convicted under Article 58.

In July 1952, the Central Committee of the CPSU and the MVD conducted a joint review of the state of affairs on the construction site of a strictly secret facility in Irkutsk Oblast a production complex for manufacturing artificial liquid fuel. The review showed that the division heads of the project grossly violated the main principle for selecting personnel: political reliability. The review documents noted:

"Many prisoners convicted of counterrevolutionary activity are working as division chiefs, occupying civil service positions. . . . Many camp administrators are trying to reduce the number of free hired workers and replace them with prisoners." The planning, budgeting, and technical departments were headed by prisoners, who often found themselves supervising free workers who were Party or Komsomol members. The inspectors were particularly critical of the head of the mechanical shop, Ukhanov, who had completely ignored the order of General S.N. Burdakov, chief of construction, to replace prisoners with free workers: "Ukhanov took two prisoners who had been released from the camp based on a count of their working days and immediately appointed them to positions as senior engineers, although neither of them had a specialized education, and both of them had been convicted of counterrevolution," reads the report. Fairly good relations had developed between the free workers and the prisoners at this construction project. A large number of free women entered into relationships with male prisoners. Within a short period of time in 1952, six female office workers married recently released prisoners. The leaders of the camp administration even joined in the wedding celebrations. Some camp chiefs threw parties to celebrate the release of "counterrevolutionaries." This sort of behavior by camp administrators was characterized by the Party oversight reports as "utter gullibility" and "a loss of political vigilance."

Relations between free workers and prisoners were not always amicable. Many true-believing Communists, fervent crusaders for communism who were consumed by a righteous hatred for the enemies of the people, wrote denunciations of their coworkers. At the beginning of 1953, one such denunciation reached G. Malenkov, the secretary of the Central Committee of the CPSU. M.I. Agafonov, a worker in the Northern Kuzbass Corrective-Labor Camp wrote with great concern and crude grammar: "I am to declare of trouble in our facility as of the present day." What was the reason for this "trouble"? Well, of course, it was that "a whole number of persons who do not inspire trust has been axessed [sic—G.I.] to leadership as a result of a loss of vigilance and a fading of the class struggle." There followed a list of section leaders, engineers, and specialists who had been convicted in the past of counterrevolutionary activities, or had served in Kolchak's armies, or had dubious (kulak) origins, or were Jews with relatives living abroad. A total of fifteen names were listed. The author of the denunciation was very well informed. He gave a detailed listing of whose brother was repressed for what and when, who his relatives were and where they lived, and so on. The Communist Party member shared his concern and anguish with the higher Party leadership: "I believe that it is impossible and intolerable to continue working, for such generosity bordering on utter gullibility can lead to an undesirable end."

The Central Committee of the CPSU did not ignore the denunciation, but times had changed. The inquiry about all the workers listed in the letter was sent not to the state security organs, as it would have been in previous years, but to the Glavspetsles Administration of the Ministry of Forestry and the Paper Industry, which covered the Northern Kuzbass Camp. The answer came back that all the employees listed in the inquiry "have been given positive evaluations at work, and we do not consider it advisable to dismiss them from their jobs at the present before satisfactory replacements can be found." The resolution of the Central Committee of the CPSU was even more specific: "At the present time Glavspetsles does not support Agafonov's proposal concerning the replacement of section chiefs [a list of their names follows.—G.I.] due to their convictions in the past, since all of them are qualified specialists and are fully competent and productive in their performance of the work assigned them." Thus did economic interest conquer political vigilance.

The reaction of the higher Party leadership to such questions was not always so calm and reasonable. An extremely interesting anonymous denunciation addressed to Malenkov arrived at the Central Committee of the CPSU, also at the beginning of 1953. A certain Ivanov "ratted" in a businesslike and ungrammatical fashion:

> Comrade Malenkov, we request immediate measures be taken against Com. Evstigneev, chief of the Ozerlag Administration of the MIA of the USSR. Firstly, he's a careerist. Secondly, he serves the enemies of the people. We request a check of his origins and especially of his wife's. His wife, a former prisoner, signed on to serve the enemies of the people, while in prison. Taking advantage of her husband's official position, she's still doing it now. She helps former Article 58 prisoners get set up in jobs in the special camp Administration, one third of the prisoners, former repatriates, Jews with relatives in America, and other no-goods were hired because of her.

The anonymous denouncer describes S.K. Evstigneev himself as follows: "He lacks a higher education; he is dishonest, unenlightened, with a superficial knowledge of Marxism-Leninism. . . . [He is] overfed, like a landowner. He goes out hunting during work time, using the office car. He has a wife and two-year-old daughter on the side. He's morally degenerate. We request that this landowner be removed, unmasked, and brought to justice." This anonymous letter was processed by the MVD Administration for Irkutsk Oblast, which confirmed some of the facts listed in it: "As for the presence of politically untrustworthy persons in the apparatus of the Administration of Ozernyi Camp, these facts have been completely confirmed," concluded the investigatory commission. The review established that there were over 300 employees working in Ozernyi Camp against whom there was serious incriminating material: convictions for counterrevolutionary crimes, time spent as prisoners of war, and so on. They confirmed the Jew with relatives abroad, and the son of the kulaks, and all the others. The Central Committee of the CPSU demanded that the Gulag leadership "purge politically untrustworthy persons from the Administration of Ozernyi Camp of the MVD." An edict was also issued ordering the replacement of the head of the camp himself, Colonel Evstigneev. Despite the ill-wisher's denunciation, this camp administrator had a very successful career. He safely survives to the present day and was not afraid during Gorbachev's perestroika to speak out in the city of Bratsk about his "career" as head of Ozerlag. Evstigneev saw no need to justify himself. The major refrain of his presentations was the very same one used by other former workers of the repressive system: "I was a soldier of the Party."[100] Regarding the events of 1953, we cannot confirm or deny the charges made against Evstigneev by his anonymous denouncer.

We should note in all fairness, generalizing from this one specific case, however, that the description of the Ozerlag chief was consistent with the general style of camp leadership that became established in the Gulag at the end of the 1940s and the beginning of the 1950s.

Signals coming from the camps, such as these denunciations, to a certain degree prevented the camps from completely turning into "plantations" or "feudal estates." In addition, campaigns against theft and embezzlement periodically swept across the expanses of the Gulag, and "feudal lords" were unmasked, dismissed, and sometimes even brought to trial. In 1949, the case of Kanevskii, the chief of Moscow District Camp No. 49, received a great deal of attention. He was removed from his position and expelled from the Communist Party for abuses of his official position. The documents from the Party commission on this case maintained:

> Reports coming in from Communists enabled the political section to establish that Kanevskii, while serving as the head of the camp, conspired with the security guard, Ulianov, systematically to abuse their official positions and to use prisoner labor for their own personal purposes; their wives and daughters had free access to the camp, where they forced the prisoners to work for them for free, extorted money from the prisoners, threatened to have prisoners they did not like sent to other camps, and considered the camp to be their own little empire.[101]

Another criminal band, discovered by investigators in 1947, was the subject of a number of conversations among the camp leadership. Considering himself to have unlimited powers, Minskii, the procurator of the Moscow Camp Administration, with the support of the head of Camp No. 19, Timoshenkov, had a dacha built near Moscow, whose value was assessed by experts at 120,000 rubles. The investigation established that the dacha had been built by prisoners and that all the construction materials had been obtained fraudulently under the pretense of supplying the camp.[102]

Often officials involved criminal convicts in their schemes, using their help to steal clothing, food products, building materials, manufactured goods, and so forth, from storage. Along with petty swindlers, the camp production administration also harbored large-scale wheeler-dealers in the "shadow economy." Some of them were unmasked during the monetary reform of 1947. The case of Major A.S. Sviridov, the chief of Karagandazhilstroi, was widely publicized. A few days before the reform, Sviridov had deposited nearly a quarter of a million rubles in his bank account, and after the new currency was issued, his wife deposited some 7,000 more rubles. Naturally this attracted the attention of the appropriate officials. In the course of the investigation, it turned out that, during and after the war, Sviridov had bought up furniture and other goods made by prisoners in the camps or sent to them from home for practically nothing and had resold them through the commission store.[103] In April 1948, he was removed from office for admitting to "illegal capital investment."

In spite of the fact that the names of dozens of employees caught stealing were listed at the annual reporting and election meetings of the Party in each camp, in general the self-appraisals of Gulag workers were fairly high: "It should be kept in mind that jobs in the Ministry of Internal Affairs are not handed out to just anybody; nowhere else are employees more carefully selected. We should be proud of the fact that we are entrusted with jobs in the MVD organs,"[104] was the opinion of the leaders of the camp administration in the capital. No less patriotic declarations came from camps outside the center: "There is no need to prove," wrote an employee of the North Urals Camp to the Central Committee of the CPSU, "that workers in the Gulag system are themselves the most devoted servants of their people; it is difficult to overestimate their role in the cause of strengthening the Soviet state. These tireless workers are doing very useful, but also very difficult and sometimes unpleasant or even dangerous, work aimed at isolating and rehabilitating criminal elements." Undoubtedly these people would have been happy to have the Soviet calendar adorned with a national holiday, "Camp and Colony Staffers' Day." It seems strange that there was still no such holiday.

The camp world held over 300,000 employees of all levels and specialties in its orbit. Each year several thousand more people came to work in the Gulag. In 1947, for example, 25,824 people were hired to work in the camps and colonies, and 6,156 were dismissed.[105] In all, during this period, the Gulag employed (not counting the guards) over 80,000 camp personnel. The most important and influential category of camp workers was the camp administration: heads of administrations, sections, camps, colonies, their deputies, and so forth. To characterize this category of camp employees, we used data on delegates at several Party conferences of corrective-labor camps and colonies of the MVD Administration of the city of Moscow and Moscow Oblast. As we explained before, Party statistics can be used to provide an accurate description of the Gulag leadership; practically the entire camp leadership consisted of Party members, and the delegates chosen to attend Party conferences were usually representatives of the camp administration, Party secretaries, political workers, and VSO commanders.

The data in Table 3 show that the proportion of women in the leadership of the Gulag was extremely small, with a slight increase occurring only in the second half of 1953. The figures showing the social origins of camp leaders are worth noting. By 1950, there had been a sharp decrease in the number of people of peasant background, accompanied by a correspondingly sharp increase in those with white-collar origins. These changes can be explained by the large-scale reduction in staff that took place in the MVD system in 1948–49, particularly affecting middle-range managers. The employees dismissed were primarily people with a weak educational background, alcoholics, and "socially inert workers"; these people were mainly of peasant background. As for the data for 1953, most likely there had been a change in the concepts of "origin" and "status." In all probability, delegates indicated their social status in the questionnaires based on their current occupation. The ratio of 90 percent white-collar workers to 10 percent workers corresponds to the actual division of labor in the Gulag as a whole.

The changes that took place in the national composition of the camp leadership reflect the chauvinistic campaign conducted by the Party against "cosmopolitanism." During this period, many Jews were dismissed from the MVD and the number of Russian personnel increased substantially.

The educational level of camp administrators was somewhat higher than that of the staff as a whole. Table 4 gives a more complete picture of the educational levels of administrative personnel. As we can see, the lowest educational level is that of deputy political officers and the command staff of guard troops. Management personnel of the camp administration had the highest educational level.

The data in Tables 3 and 4 relate to corrective-labor camps and colonies of the MVD Administration of Moscow and Moscow Oblast. We believe that it is justifiable to extrapolate data about "the Moscow Gulag" to the camps and colonies of Russia as a whole. According to the head of the political section of the Gulag, Colonel L.D. Lukoianov, "The conditions of the UITLiK divisions of Moscow Oblast are somewhat different from conditions in the other camps. Here the staff is stronger; the prisoners are different from those in the remote corrective-labor camps, and the local Party organizations contribute more."[106]

Table 3

Delegates at Party Conferences of Corrective-Labor Camps and Colonies of the MVD Administration of the City of Moscow and Moscow Oblast
(in percent)

Date of conference	March 1948	May 1950	September 1953
Overall number of delegates	205	196	186
Sex			
Male	90.7	91.3	87.6
Female	9.3	8.7	12.4
Social Origins			
Peasants	63.4	3.6	—
Workers	27.8	35.7	10.2
White-collar	8.8	60.7	89.8
Education			
Higher and incomplete higher	15.6	18.4	17.2
Secondary	39.0	34.7	33.9
Incomplete secondary, primary, or no education	45.4	46.9	48.9
Nationality			
Russians	74.6	83.2	87.1
Ukrainians	10.8	8.7	7.5
Belorussians	2.0	1.5	1.6
Jews	10.2	4.6	2.7
Others	2.4	2.0	1.1
Occupations			
Camp-production administration	37.6	53.0	no data
VSO officers	27.8	19.9	no data

Source: Compiled from data in TsAODM, f.2264, op.1, d. 44, ll. 108–109; d. 72; ll. 74–76; op. 5, d. 1, ll. 22–23.

If, according to Solzhenitsyn, Kolyma "is the polar extreme of cruelty of this amazing Gulag country, which geography has shredded into an archipelago, but psychology has bound into a continent," then the "Moscow Gulag" is something like the "red corner" of the Gulag, the exemplary part it puts on display. It is no accident that some colonies of Moscow Oblast were opened, by special permission, to visits by foreign delegations. But if in this "red corner" in the Moscow corrective-labor camps and colonies, with their "strong personnel," about half of the management personnel had only a lower education, hundreds of officials were reprimanded for drunkenness, theft, and embezzlement, and the heads of camps turned them into their own little empires, then what must have been the situation in the depths of the Gulag, at the "polar extreme of cruelty"?

Table 4

Educational Level of Core Party Members (*aktiv*) in the Production Administrations of Corrective-Labor Camps and Colonies of the City of Moscow and Moscow Oblast (in percent)

Administrative personnel	Higher; incomplete higher	Secondary	Incomplete secondary; primary
Heads of colonies and camps	20.5	15.4	64.1
Heads of administrative sections and their deputies	33.3	37.1	29.6
Secretaries of Party organizations	9.3	37.0	53.7
Commanders of divisions, deputy political officers [*zampolity*]	5.8	16.3	77.9
Overall Party organization	12.1	16.9	71.0

Source: Compiled from data in TsAODM, f. 2264, op. 1, d. 25, ll. 7, 13, 31; d. 26, l. 2, 3; d. 33, l. 23, 24.

The remote camps of the north often served as the last refuge for officers and managers of the Gulag who had become hopeless alcoholics and moral degenerates. In 1951, the Nemnyrsk Corrective-Labor Camp was founded under the "Aldansliuda" Trust on the territory of the Iakutsk Autonomous Soviet Republic. Nemnyrsk reported to the Chief Administration of the Mica Industry of the Ministry of Internal Affairs of the USSR. The Gulag sent 136 management personnel to staff the new camp. Over 30 of these people were notorious idlers, hopeless drunkards, and degraded individuals who had been dismissed and banished from everywhere else they had worked. When they were given complete control of camps four hundred to six hundred kilometers away from the Administration of Corrective-Labor Camps without any direct supervision over their activities, these people let themselves go completely, treating the lives, health, and property of the prisoners as raw material to use for the satisfaction of their basest needs and whims. The behavior of this group of camp administrators was so immoral and criminal that it led to a special investigation in the Central Committee of the CPSU in 1953.

The Nemnyrsk Camp was not an exception; similar situations could be observed everywhere. For example, in the Ivdelsk Camp in Sverdlovsk Oblast, headed by a drunken lieutenant-colonel of the internal service, D.N. Liutanov, 1,800 crimes and immoral acts by camp workers were recorded in just four months, from April to July 1953. It is interesting to note that the staffing reductions in camps and colonies that took place as a result of the amnesty in the spring of 1953 had practically no effect on the so-called regular staff of the Gulag, since the chief of the Gulag, I.I. Dolgikh, had ordered that the staff reductions begin with the local population, reserve officers of the Red Army, and petty officers and sergeants serving on a contract basis.

It was the massive unrest that swept through the Gulag in 1953 that forced the higher Party leadership to address the abuses and tyranny of camp personnel. In the Chusovsk section of the Nyrobsk Camp, Akhverdov, a convoy leader, and Shorokhov, a dog handler, decided to throw their weight around. They forced a group of prisoners whom they were taking back under convoy to the residential zone of the camp to lie down on the ground and do the leopard crawl in the mud. Then the petty tyrants loosed a guard dog on the exhausted, worn-out prisoners, threatening the whole time to open fire. In this same camp, platoon commander Tereshkov systematically used to beat up prisoners, humiliate them, illegally handcuff them, and lock them up in solitary-confinement cells. When the prisoners wrote complaints to the higher authorities, Tereshkov removed their letters from the mailbox and returned them to their authors with threats. This caused an uprising in the prison, and the prisoners went on strike.

In Kizelovsk Camp in February 1953, for no reason whatsoever, a guard named Gasiukov fired point-blank at Onorin, a prisoner, and killed him. This sparked a protest in which 300 prisoners refused to go to work.

During the May Day holidays in 1953, prisoners of Camp Division No. 9 of the Krasnoiarsk Camp—over six hundred people—announced a hunger strike and demanded a meeting with a representative of the Gulag. The reason for the conflict was the disorderly behavior of a camp security officer, Captain Lovchev, who incited a brawl on the evening of the first of May in the cafeteria where prisoners were having dinner. To establish his authority, Lovchev overturned a half-eaten bowl of kasha on the head of prisoner Bessmertnyi.

In many camps, strikes came about as a result of unjustified actions by the camp administration, such as miscalculations of prisoners' salaries, delays in paying prisoners the money they had earned, serving spoiled food, turning a blind eye to banditry and terrorism in the camps, and so forth. The local leadership did its best to conceal the real reasons for the protests and provoked fights between groups of prisoners, which resulted in dozens of deaths. Between April and September 1953, thirty cases of mass acts of insubordination and unrest were recorded in the Gulag; during that same period, over two hundred prisoners were killed or wounded. Sometimes, in order to avoid bloody confrontations, prisoners drove individual camp workers out of the residential zones of the camp for "inability to behave properly." In the Viatsk Camp, for example, this was the fate of Shulakov and Morozov, employees in the educational and cultural section, who, for systematic extortion and abuses, were driven out of the residential zone by the prisoners and barred from reentering in the future.

Occasionally people with records of convictions for work-related, economic, or criminal offenses were appointed to administrative positions in the Gulag. They served their terms of punishment in the camps and colonies, then took jobs in the camps after their release, making a career for themselves in the Gulag system. Major I.A. Zhelonkin, in spite of his low educational level and criminal record, worked as head of the administration of the Lower Amur Camp. Lieutenant Colonel N.A. Ivanov, who had a similar record, worked his way up to a position as chief of the corrective-labor colony department in Orlov (Orel) Oblast. Major S.S. Sretenskii, also a former prisoner with only a minimal education, was appointed deputy head of the Administration of the Selenginsk Camp in May 1953.

Based on a tradition that had been in place since the 1920s, many officers dismissed for gross violations of Soviet law—for abuse of their official position and other offenses—were appointed to administrative work in the Gulag. High officials of the MVD, the Ministry of State Security, and the Gulag easily found a common language and supported each other in every way during critical staff readjustments and mass purges. Lieutenant Colonel of the Internal Service Chizhikov ("a drunk and an idler," according to the Party organization's evaluation), after being dismissed from his position as deputy minister of internal affairs of the Moldavian SSR, was hired in the Gulag with the support of Deputy Chief of the Gulag for Personnel V.M. Kozyrev and appointed chief of the camp procedures and operations department of the Northern Kuzbass Camp.

Lieutenant Colonel P.P. Sokolskii, dismissed from the MVD and the MGB for violation of revolutionary law, careerism, and abuse of his official position, was given an important job as head of the operations section of the Ust-Vymsk Camp in May 1953. He received the personal support of his former colleague Dolgikh, chief of the Gulag. By the time Sokolskii's official approval for this position came through, he had already been responsible for the deaths of thirty-four prisoners in the camp and for thirty instances of the violation of Soviet law by the supervisory staff.

Colonel Sh.I. Bokuchava was repeatedly removed from positions in the MVD. In June 1952, he was dismissed from the position of minister of internal affairs of the Abkhaz ASSR for gross violation of socialist legality. The Central Committee of the Communist Party of Georgia issued him a stern reprimand and warning. V.M. Kozyrev saved the colonel's career by getting him a position as head of the operations department of the Nyrobsk Camp.

Practically every high camp administrator had committed acts in the past that were essentially crimes, though they were labeled, by Soviet tradition, "violations of legality." Major General A.V. Shamarin began his career as a Chekist in the roads and transportation department of the NKVD of the Tomsk Railroad. It was here in 1937–39 that he manifested his extraordinary talents as a falsifier and stool pigeon. The young security officer uncovered a series of counterrevolutionary crimes, one after the other. But one time he miscalculated. Shamarin had managed yet again to get an NKVD troika to sentence five defendants to death, when suddenly and unexpectedly higher officials requested their case files. At this point it became clear that there were no case files—Shamarin had simply not bothered to record them. The Novosibirsk Oblast Party Committee dismissed the falsifier from his position. S.R. Milshtein, however, who was then head of the Chief Administration of Transportation of the NKVD, intervened on his behalf. Beria took Shamarin back into the NKVD and in 1943 named him chief of the NKVD Administration for Kemerovo Oblast. In 1948, he was dismissed from this position for gross violations of socialist legality and sent to administrative work in the Gulag. Shamarin's exclusive reliance on the so-called criminal-bandit element during his time in the camps repeatedly earned him reprimands from the Party. The major general ended his career as the acting head of the Poliansk Camp in Krasnoiarsk Region.

Not all MVD generals whose previous criminal records came to light were forced to leave their ministerial offices for remote Siberian camps; many managed to find comfortable positions in the central apparatus of the Gulag. The former minister of internal affairs of the Moldavian SSR, and subsequently of the Mariisk ASSR, Major General M.I. Markeev, was dismissed "for failure to perform his duties satisfactorily and for unjustified arrests of citizens." In spite of this record, however, Markeev was given a position as inspector in the central apparatus in June 1953. Leadership positions in the Gulag system were entrusted to Generals I.I. Vradii and V.P. Rogov, who had been dismissed from the Ministry of State Security apparatus. Major General I.G. Popkov, who formerly had been head of the Kuibyshev and Sverdlovsk oblast MVD administrations, also found a place in the reserves of the Gulag.

During the personnel reshufflings and dismissals that began after the death of Stalin, when Beria took over the combined MVD, eight generals, thirty-four colonels, and a number of lower-ranking officers who had been removed for various reasons from responsible positions in the organs of the MVD and MGB were appointed to leadership positions in the Gulag system.

The personnel situation in the Gulag obviously contradicted the new policies aimed at "restoring socialist legality." In the fall of 1953, Gulag personnel issues were taken over by the higher Party organs. The Secretariat of the Central Committee of the CPSU met on November 2, 1953, to discuss the staffing policy of the camp agency, which at that time was subordinate to the Ministry of Justice of the USSR. The Secretariat concluded that the current policy was unsatisfactory and adopted a resolution that read:

> Incorrect actions were taken by Deputy Minister of Justice of the USSR Comrade Kudriavtsev and the head of the Chief Administration of Camps Comrade Dolgikh when they issued orders on April 8, 1953, and March 29, 1953, obligating chiefs of the ITL, UITL, and OITK to dismiss the entire staff of master sergeants and sergeants, along with reserve Soviet Army officers, in order to replace them with people from the Gulag administration who were left without a job due to the staff cuts in the camps. The directives issued by Comrades Kudriavtsev and Dolgikh gave cause to dismiss good and conscientious workers from the officer reserves of the Soviet Army without an assessment of their merits and faults.[107]

The Secretariat of the Central Committee of the CPSU recommended that Minister of Justice K.P. Gorshenin revoke the improper orders and take measures to correct the injustices that had resulted.

In November and December 1953, the administrative section of the Central Committee of the CPSU undertook a thorough evaluation of the work of the Gulag. A Central Committee commission studied seventy-nine reports from the camps, visited dozens of Gulag sites, and familiarized themselves with hundreds of individual cases and personnel files. All the facts pointed to "an extremely bad state of affairs" in the Chief Administration of Camps. The commission paid particular attention to the question of personnel. The report memorandum of the administrative section of the Central Committee noted the following:

> The evaluation revealed that Party guidelines for the selection of staff have been grossly violated in this administration, and a certain propor-

tion of unsatisfactory MVD and MGB employees have been transferred into the Gulag system. Individual workers who are unable to carry out their assigned tasks have been given positive evaluations and promoted.

During the layoffs, a significant number of reserve officers were dismissed without a proper evaluation of their merits and faults, while many others who were idlers and drunkards kept their positions in the Gulag. A number of people hold administrative positions in the camps who, while working for the MVD, had arrested completely innocent Soviet citizens and falsified cases accusing them of grave counterrevolutionary crimes.

The results of the first and only large-scale evaluation of the Gulag evidently baffled not only the MVD officials but the higher Party leadership as well. In our view, it is these materials that led to the adoption in 1954 of a number of important Party resolutions aimed at reorganizing the repressive system and easing punitive policy. During 1954, 2,790 divisions in the MIA system were reduced and reorganized, including 39 camp administrations and 16 prisons that were closed. The number of regular staff in the MVD was reduced to 16,300, including 600 in the central apparatus. Administrative and management expenditures for the MVD apparatus were cut to 250 million rubles. This structural reorganization of the repressive system was accompanied by a wholesale replacement of the leadership. In the hopes of improving the personnel situation, local Party and Komsomol organizations sent 3,035 people to work for the Ministry of Internal Affairs, many of them in leadership positions. In the same year, 498 new administrators were hired in the Gulag system, and the middle level of management was restaffed: 1,639 new workers, 636 of them specialists, took positions in the lower camp divisions. The central Gulag apparatus replaced 29 people in administrative positions. There was a nearly 50 percent turnover in the command staff of Party organizations. These changes in personnel resulted in an increase in the educational level of the leadership. The number of officials with a secondary or higher education increased by 15 percent over the 1952 level.

The reorganization of the repressive system was accompanied by several primarily administrative measures aimed at restoring legality. The USSR Minister of Internal Affairs ordered the dismissal of the deputy minister of internal affairs of the Azerbaidzhiani SSR, Atakishiev; the head of the Peschanyi Corrective-Labor Camp, Sergienko; the former senior investigator of the investigative division for especially important cases of the Armenian SSR, Grigorian; division heads of camp administrations Bystrov of Mineralnyi, Vradii of Ukhto-Izhemsk, and Gladkov of Stepnoi; Ruchkin, deputy head of the Mineralnyi Corrective Labor Camp; Novikov, the head of the militia administration of Cheliabinsk Oblast; Semenov, deputy minister of internal affairs of the Belorussian SSR. Upon the request of the MVD, the Council of Ministers of the USSR issued a resolution on January 3, 1955, demoting all these people, plus B.P. Obruchnikov, former head of the personnel administration of the MVD, from the rank of general for discrediting themselves during their work for the MVD and the MGB. In 1954, 358 people in leadership positions were dismissed for past violations of Soviet law; a significant number of them were in the Gulag leadership.

Among the people dismissed was the head of the Chief Administration of Camps I.I. Dolgikh. In February 1956, after an annual review conducted by the chief military prosecutor of the USSR, he was stripped of his general's rank, dismissed "based on evidence discrediting the high rank of chief of staff in the MVD," and assigned a reduced pension of 840 rubles a month.

The career path of the fifty-two-year-old demoted lieutenant general was extremely simple and at the same time quite typical: six years in the Komsomol, twenty-five years in the Party, and thirty-six years working in Soviet, trade-union, and administrative positions, twenty-eight of them in the MVD. The biography of Dolgikh cannot be called unusual, nor was his career path unusually quick or out of the ordinary, but everything fits. "Thanks to our Party and Soviet power, I, the son of a poor shoemaker, a peasant, followed a path that took me from secretary of the local soviet, a junior GPU agent, to minister of internal affairs of the Kazakh SSR, head of the Chief Administration of Camps, and a member of the collegium of the MVD and the Ministry of Justice," writes Dolgikh of his career path. What was it that allowed a man without education, profession, special talents, or merits to progress so inexorably up the career ladder? Dolgikh gave an unambiguous explanation for his successes: "I grew with the help of our Party."

The young OGPU official became a Communist Party member in 1931. By that time he had already ceased to view special settlers and prisoners as people; they had become for him a "workforce" and "labor supply." Between the autumn of 1931 and the autumn of 1932, he worked 1,500 special settlers to death, forcing them to realize his careerist office-desk plan of transforming the Narym region.[108] But it was not this "achievement" that caused the general to lose his high rank. There were other "feats" in his work record.

In 1937–38, he headed the investigatory section of the NKVD road and transportation department of the Southern Railway in Kharkov. It is here that the future head of the Gulag demonstrated his power. Be-

tween August and November 1937 alone, the leaders of this department arrested 1,800 people. The valuable railroad workers were destroyed on such a large scale that it provoked a critical reaction from
the NKVD leadership.

A review of a number of falsified cases brought to light numerous
instances of unjustified arrests, cruel beatings of people under investigation, all kinds of abuses and provocations, and in general everything
that official terminology labels "gross violations of socialist legality."
DTO head D.S. Leopold was shot during that period, in 1939. His deputy
K.S. Kurpas was dismissed from the NKVD later, but Dolgikh, the head
of the investigation department and a direct participant in all these
crimes, survived unharmed, in spite of numerous requests from the
Kharkov prosecutor's office for his arrest and trial. Whenever he moved
to a new position—as a rule, with a promotion—Dolgikh greeted his
new colleagues by emphasizing that he had "no record of Party or administrative infractions." For him this was the most important thing,
and it was a matter of no interest to anyone that criminal cases had
been brought against him on three different occasions and then suspended for no apparent reason.

Many secrets came to light in 1956. Not wanting to accept his dismissal, Dolgikh appealed to the Central Committee of the CPSU. He
completely denied the accusations against him and desperately attempted to prove that he had always followed Party directives and acted
in the spirit of the times. To a certain degree he was correct. Never
having experienced real labor, without any special skills, Dolgikh was
most concerned with the prospect of having nothing to live on. "I know
from the experience of other NKVD workers what it means to be dismissed on the basis of incriminating evidence, especially from the
MVD," he wrote in his appeal to the Central Committee of the CPSU.
"Even a certificate of release from a place of incarceration is considered by many managers to be a more positive document in an employment application than something like this from the MVD or the MGB."
Dolgikh's request, basically, was "to retire from the MVD based on years
of service." At that time the Central Committee of the CPSU considered the request unjustified.

V.S. Riasnoi, a fifty-two-year-old lieutenant general who had been
dismissed and deprived of his general's rank and a pension with benefits "based on facts discrediting the high rank of general," received
a more categorical refusal to a similar request in August 1956. Riasnoi's
résumé in many ways resembles that of Dolgikh, and, incidentally, those
of many other MVD leaders. Riasnoi had a high-school education and

no professional training. A Komsomol worker at sixteen, his career in the Party and soviets began at the age of eighteen. After serving as first secretary of the Lemeshkinskii raikom, Stalingrad Oblast, he was sent to work in the NKVD (beginning with the GUGB apparatus) in 1937 by order of the Central Committee of the Communist Party. Riasnoi made a felicitous entrance into the Soviet repressive system and began a steady rise up the career ladder. Head of the NKVD administration of the city of Gorkii, minister of internal affairs of the Ukrainian SSR, deputy minister of internal affairs of the USSR, deputy minister of state security, head of the MVD Administration of Moscow Oblast—these are only the highlights of Riasnoi's career as a Chekist. In addition, he was a deputy to the Supreme Soviet of the USSR, was decorated with government medals, and so on. His dismissal from the MVD as "politically unreliable" came as the result of a review of his activities during 1937–38.

During that period, the newly appointed investigator demonstrated unusual abilities for forgery, entrapment, and falsification of cases under investigation. On his conscience lies the death of the plenipotentiary of the USSR in Saudi Arabia K.I. Khakimov, from whom he had requested a favor during an investigation—a translation of a text from Turkish for the leadership. In court this translation of a clearly bourgeois nationalistic text was treated as an original composition. Riasnoi falsified the case of A.S. Sultan-Zade, a former member of the executive committee of the Comintern; that of V.I. Zeimal, an official in the Central Committee of the Communist Party apparatus, and a number of others.

During the postwar years, Riasnoi actively fought against "nationalist bands" in Ukraine and conducted mass arrests of Latvians and Lithuanians "for associating with the bandits." Since such activities during those years were not yet considered to be a crime, the lieutenant general was eager to take credit for them.

There is no need to suggest that Riasnoi understood that what he had done was wrong and regretted it. Just like Dokgikh, he was most concerned with his reduced pension of 950 rubles, his lost benefits, and the attempt by the MIA to confiscate his surplus living space in the center of Moscow. Riasnoi hoped that the Party that had nurtured him for thirty-six years and for which he had not spared his own life would help him, but he was mistaken. The Central Committee of the CPSU concluded, "For careerist reasons, Riasnoi falsified cases under investigation and rapidly advanced in his career." "Careerist reasons" are the key words in the biography of many hundreds of leaders of the MIA.

Great is the number of criminals clothed in official uniforms, but thousands of times greater is the number of their victims.

The totalitarian regime involved a multitude of people in its crimes. It is not always possible, however, to draw a clear dividing line between executioners and victims. Soviet society and the Gulag are much more tightly interwoven than may appear at first glance. The Gulag staffers, in spite of their unique position in Soviet society, still lived according to its norms; even as they went about their illegal and arbitrary activities, they were liable at any moment to find themselves under the millstones of the repressive system. The camp personnel were not an isolated group of people. They lived in society, brought up children, and spent time with their loved ones and those close to them, transmitting to their families and society as a whole the subculture of violence that had taken shape in the world of the camps. At the same time, the Gulag staffers felt more acutely and perhaps earlier than other segments of the population something that was later to become the norm of Soviet life—a split personality, the need to combine within themselves at one and the same time a Communist and a camp morality.

Over a million Soviet citizens worked in the Gulag during the years of its existence. The camp service bestowed a degree of social significance and standing upon people who, due to their own backward nature, poor educational level, and extremely low moral qualities, would not have had a chance at success in any other field of activity. Their social status completely depended on the strength of the existing regime, and it was for this reason that the people working in the Gulag served as one of the strongest pillars of support for the totalitarian system.

Sergei Nikiforovich Kruglov,
who headed the USSR
Ministry of Internal Affairs
from 1946 to 1956.

Vasilii Stepanovich Riasnoi,
who served in leadership
positions in the NKVD (MVD)
system beginning in 1937;
discredited and
dismissed in 1956.

Ivan Ilich Dolgikh, who began as a junior GPU agent and became minister of internal affairs of the Kazakh SSR; head of the Gulag from 1951 to 1954; discredited and dismissed from the MVD in 1956.

Alexander Nikolaevich Komarovskii, head of the Chief Administration for Industrial Construction of the USSR Ministry of Internal Affairs beginning in 1944; managed all the major camp construction projects.

A 1946 photograph of Vasilii Vasilevich Chernyshev (1896–1952), who began his career in the Cheka troops in 1920. From 1937 to 1952, he was deputy people's commissar (minister) of internal affairs of the USSR, combining this position with that of Gulag chief between 1939 and 1941.

Members of the Supreme Court of the USSR selected at the second session of the Supreme Soviet of the USSR in August 1938. Below left: Chairman of the Supreme Court I.T. Goliakov. Below right: military lawyer V.V. Ulrikh. Above left: military lawyer I.G. Nikitchenko. Above right: A.I. Solodilov.

Conclusion

What Was the Gulag?

Concentration camps have been called the plague of the twentieth century. They were the supreme manifestation of totalitarianism and the origin of the phenomenon of "administrative mass murder." According to the French scholar Jacques Rossi, who spent nearly a quarter of a century in the barracks of Siberian camps, "Of all the concentration camp systems of this century, including Hitler's, the Soviet Gulag was not only the most durable, with a life span of seventy-three years, but also the most precise embodiment of the state that created it. It was not a mere slip of the tongue to say that a freed zek had been transferred from the 'small' zone to the 'large' one."[1]

What was this "small zone," populated by millions of people of all ages and nationalities, which world history was to know as the "Gulag"?

The country of colonies and camps owes its birth to the Bolshevik regime, which institutionalized violence as a universal means of attaining its goals. The policy of extrajudicial repressions dissociated a person's life and liberty from his specific actions and intentions. Quite often people were doomed to suffering and death simply because their origins, profession, political convictions, or social or family ties placed them in a special category that had been identified by the Bolshevik leaders as "enemies of the people," "class enemies," "Rightists," "suspicious," "members of the wrong families," and so forth. Legal notions of "guilt" and "innocence" lost their primary meanings. The overwhelming majority of so-called political prisoners had committed no actual illegal acts and consequently could not be considered criminals. They were innocent victims of class struggle, lawlessness, tyranny, and terror.

The threat of "sending the guilty to forced labor in the mines"[2] was made by Bolshevik leaders, Lenin in particular, before the establishment of the first forced-labor camps. By instituting compulsory labor in places of deprivation of liberty, the Soviet authorities hoped to solve two different problems: to use heavy physical labor as a means of punishment of convicts and to make the system of concentration camps economically self-supporting.

F.E. Dzerzhinskii provided the theoretical justification for the use of forced labor. One of the principles in his punitive policy reads, "The republic cannot be merciful toward criminals and cannot waste resources on them; they must cover the costs associated with their care with their own labor; they must be used to settle undeveloped areas in Pechora, in Obdorsk,* and elsewhere."[3] Defining the priority tasks of the OGPU, Dzerzhinskii wrote in 1923 to his deputy I.S. Unshlikht, "We will have to work to organize forced labor (penal servitude) at camps for colonizing undeveloped areas that will be run with iron discipline. We have sufficient locations and space."[4]

During the 1920s, it was quite difficult to realize the plans of "Iron Felix," who had called concentration camps a "school of labor." Economic and political problems (massive unemployment and the lack of large-scale industrial projects, the serious intraparty struggle, and the ongoing debates over how to build socialism) prevented the country's leadership from organizing prison labor on a national scale and limited the scope of the repressions.

The economic crisis of the last third of the 1920s led to a sharp deterioration of the country's social and economic situation. In its search for a solution to the crisis, the Communist Party actively began to create the multifaceted image of an enemy, a "wrecker," "kulak," and "saboteur." Stalin's bloodthirsty thesis "On the Intensification of the Class Struggle on the Path to Socialism" served as the ideological justification for repressions against the "enemies of Soviet power" and, in essence, stimulated them. The relatively liberal political regime of the NEP years quickly turned into totalitarianism, whose most important attribute during its entire existence was the concentration camps. The Soviet camp system took shape during the period of forced industrialization and violent collectivization, which can convincingly be called the godparents of the Gulag.

On July 11, 1929, the Sovnarkom of the USSR adopted a special resolution on using prison labor. The government instructed the OGPU to expand the existing camps and organize new ones in Siberia, in the North, in the Far East, in Central Asia, and in other remote regions of the Soviet Union with the goal of "colonizing these regions and ex-

---

*This was the name, until 1933, of the city of Salekhard in the Arctic Circle.

Table 5

Total Number of Prisoners in Places of Deprivation of Liberty

Date	Number of prisoners		
On January 1	In camps and colonies	In prisons	Total
1930	95,064 in camps alone	179,000 in colonies and prisons of the RSFSR	About 400,000 in the USSR as a whole
1935	792,317	240,259	1,032,576
1939	1,698,776	352,508	2,051,284
1941	1,935,148	470,693	2,405,841
1945	1,460,676	275,510	1,736,186
1949	2,356,685	231,047	2,587,732
1953	2,472,247	152,614	2,624,861
1956	781,630	159,250	940,880

Source: Compiled from *Sistema ispravitel'no-trudovykh lagerei v SSSR. 1923–1960: Spravochnik* (Moscow, 1998), 18, 27, 33, 43, 58, 537, 539; V.N. Zemskov, "GULAG (istoriko-sotsiologicheskii aspekt)," *Sotsiologicheskie issledovaniia,* 1991, no. 6: 11; GA RF, f. 9414, op. 1, d. 1155, l. 2.; TsKhSD, f. 89, per. 16, dok. 1, l. 6, 7.

ploiting their natural resources with the use of prisoners' labor."[5] The camps created in the years that followed, with their inexhaustible resources of mobile and practically cost-free labor, had, already by the beginning of the 1930s, become an important factor in the development of the Soviet economy. The "labor fund" of the Gulag gradually increased (see Table 5), allowing the camp economy to take on large-scale economic projects.

The maximum concentration of prisoners in places of deprivation of liberty occurred in the summer of 1950, when there were over 2,800,000 people in camps, colonies, and prisons. This is due to the fact that, in each of the three previous years, between 1 million and 1.5 million newly convicted prisoners arrived in the Gulag; in the beginning of the 1950s, the annual number of people entering places of deprivation of liberty decreased to between 600,000 and 700,000. It is extremely difficult to determine the precise overall number of people who passed through the hell that was the camps. The documents that have been preserved contain a large volume of statistical data, but due to the differences in record-keeping practices at different periods, many data cannot be compared. Often the documents contain incomplete information, and the numerous reference summaries compiled by the Gulag apparatus are not free of error.[6] It also should be kept in mind that some of the documents are kept in the administrative archives of the Ministry of Internal Affairs and the Federal Security Service, and it remains difficult to gain access to them. In the author's opinion, which is based on an analysis of data on the number of prisoners convicted by judicial and extrajudicial organs, the overall number of victims of the Gulag between the end of the 1920s and the middle of the 1950s was no less than 20 million people. About one-third of them were political prisoners convicted of so-called counterrevolutionary crimes. The number of criminal recidivists was no greater than 10 to 15 percent on average, and the remaining prisoners of the Gulag were simply known, for obvious reasons, as "drudges" [*rabotiagi*].

It was not only prisoners who were subjected to concentration camps and forced labor in the Soviet totalitarian state. Millions of other people lived and worked in the country of Gulag whose place of residence was exile, various forms of special settlements, identification and screening camps, labor armies, camps for prisoners of war and internees, educational labor colonies for juveniles, and others. With a few exceptions, these structures were not officially part of the Chief Administration of Camps, but their inhabitants most certainly can be considered prisoners and victims of the Gulag.

The territory of the "small zone" essentially coincided with the territory of the Soviet Union. There were Gulag facilities in every oblast of the RSFSR and in all the union republics. Furthermore, as N.P. Dudorov, minister of internal affairs, noted in 1956, "The location of corrective-labor camps, their organizational structure, and the size of the camp compounds where the prisoners were kept were largely determined by economic considerations related to production needs."[7] This meant that the camp structures were created where and when there arose a need for a large amount of unpaid labor. When the demand for unskilled forced labor went down, a camp ceased to exist. This is why the author decided not to attempt a cartography of the Gulag. To date Russian historians have discovered and described 476 camps that existed at different times on the territory of the USSR.[8] It is well known that practically every one of them had several branches, many of which were quite large. In addition to the large number of camps, there were no less than 2,000 colonies. It would be virtually impossible to reflect the entire mass of Gulag facilities on a map that would also account for the various times of their existence.

Now a few words about the Gulag economy. At the beginning of the war, it included twenty branches of industry. The largest of these, based on the specific volume of their production, were the mining, timber, and fuel industries. Another extremely important economic activity of the Gulag was capital construction. Forced labor was used on practically all of the large-scale construction projects of the Stalin years.

During the postwar period, the role of the camp economy grew even more. The atomic project and a number of strategic military goals significantly expanded the areas where forced labor was used. In 1949, the MVD system accounted for over 10 percent of the country's gross industrial production. Nevertheless, within two years the camp-industrial complex was going through a serious crisis. It is not at all surprising that the camp system was to undergo a complete reorganization immediately after the death of Stalin.

The intensive economic activity of the Ministry of Internal Affairs, based on exploiting various forms of forced labor, might give rise to a false impression of the efficiency of the camp economy. Of course there were productive enterprises in the MVD system, but they were more the exception than the rule. On the whole, the camp economy was unprofitable. The level of labor productivity in the facilities and construction sites of the MVD was on average 50 percent lower than in branches that hired free workers. The cost of production in camps was substantially higher than that in local facilities, and the quality of the products manufactured by prisoners remained extremely low. Involuntary labor, in spite of its unpaid nature, cost the state dearly. Maintaining the camps and colonies was not covered by income from prisoners' labor, which meant that the Gulag received large annual subsidies from the state budget.

The camp economy was predatory and wasteful. Practically all economic projects undertaken by the MVD were financed based on actual expenditures; often the people managing them had no cost projections or any technical plan for the project. All they had was a plan that had come from the highest levels with a mandate to complete it whatever the cost. Under these conditions, many managers throughout the system recorded inflated numbers in order to demonstrate the completion of the plan and to earn awards. This practice of distorting the numbers was practiced at all stages of the production process, and it naturally led to a rise in the cost of the final product.

The economic expansion of the MVD had a ruinous effect on the country and corrupted the producers. The Gulag destroyed human resources on a huge scale and laid waste to the natural environment. The beginning of the ecological crisis in the USSR is associated with the economic activity of the Gulag.

Of course, the organizers of camp production were aware of the flaws in the system, but they were unable to change it. The accessibility and mobility of forced labor made it an attractive option. The huge masses of prisoners and exiles were a convenient and accessible means for organizing all sorts of production activities and construction projects within a short period of time anywhere, including beyond the Arctic Circle. Prisoners could be forced to work in conditions that the literature has come to call "inhuman," without causing any concerns about conserving human resources or providing social benefits. The "cheap" labor of the Gulag slaves allowed Soviet decision makers to avoid the large material expenditures of paying wages to workers.

It is also important to keep in mind that the entire activity of the Gulag took place in an atmosphere of strictest secrecy. Very often this enabled officials with vested interests to cover up theft, bad management, and waste. On the whole the camp economy, in spite of its innate defects, fit organically into the extensive directive-based economy of the Soviet state.

Directly or indirectly, the camp world drew into its orbit tens of millions of Soviet citizens. This number included the ones who did the arresting, the interrogating, the guarding, the transporting, and so on, that is, the personnel of the Gulag. On the whole these were semiliterate, socially undeveloped people with a low moral level. As a rule they were uneducated and unskilled, but thanks to the specific nature of service in the camps, they managed to acquire social status and to rise in their careers. The central principle of life for this category of citizens was violence in all its forms, which made them a reliable social support for the totalitarian regime.

Finally, as many documents make clear, Stalin personally controlled the functioning of the camps at all times. All of the internal affairs and state security organs' projects and proposals for strengthening repression that came under Stalin's consideration began with the words "In accordance with your instructions . . ."

Afterword

What moves a historian to study the past? A thirst for knowledge? Professional interest? Or a desire to convey to contemporaries the experience of previous generations? While working on this monograph about the Gulag, the author was constantly aware of the words of the American philosopher G. Santayana: "Those who do not remember the past are condemned to repeat it." It is terrible even to think of the possibility of reliving the Gulag, and so we must ensure that its memory, bitter and tragic as it is, will live on for many long years to come. And in order to recall the past, we must first of all come to know it.

Postwar Europe made concentration camps one of the most important areas to study in the quest to understand the ideology and history of fascism. During that period, the sources and nature of totalitarianism were seriously studied not only by scholars and politicians but also by millions of ordinary Europeans who had direct personal experience of the Nazi dictatorship. The philosopher Karl Jaspers, one of the spiritual leaders of postwar Germany, analyzing the problems that would face humanity in the future, believed that the camp system threatened the very roots of human nature. "This reality of concentration camps," wrote the German thinker, "this circular movement of torturers and tortures, this loss of humanity threatens human survival in the future. Confronted with the reality of the concentration camps, we are unable to speak. This is a greater danger than the atom bomb, since it represents a threat to the human soul."[1] When he addressed his fellow countrymen in the 1940s and 1950s on the radio, in articles, and in books, Jaspers continually reminded them of the camps in their recent past: this did take place, it was possible, and this possibility remains; only knowledge will prevent its recurrence. There is no doubt that the scholar's warnings are relevant for our country as well.

The author is keenly aware that this book is only an initial step on the journey toward a more complete knowledge and understanding of the Gulag and its effects. Without such knowledge, it is difficult to imagine the possibility of a healthy, worthwhile future.

Notes

Introduction. Courts and Convicts in Tsarist Russia

1. A.N. Iarmysh, *Sudebnye organy tsarskoi Rossii v period imperializma* (1900–1917) (Kiev, 1990), 34.

2. E.N. Tarnovskii, "Statisticheskie svedeniia o litsakh, obviniaemykh v prestupleniiakh gosudarstvennykh," *Zhurnal Ministerstva iustitsii*, no. 4 (1906): 55.

3. Ibid., 53.

4. E.N. Tarnovskii, "Statisticheskie svedeniia ob osuzhdennykh za gosudarstvennye prestupleniia v 1905–1912 gg.," *Zhurnal Ministerstva iustitsii*, no. 10 (1915): 43.

5. Ibid., 44–45.

6. S.S. Ostroumov, *Ocherki po istorii ugolovnoi statistiki dorevoliutsionnoi Rossii* (Moscow, 1961), 276.

7. Ibid., 271.

8. O.O. Gruzenberg, "Statistika sovershennykh prestuplenii, vlekushchikh smertnuiu kazn' i posledovavshikh smertnykh prigovorov," *Trudy Iuridicheskogo obshchestva pri imperatorskom S-Peterburgskom universitete*, vol. 4: *Prilozhenie* (St. Petersburg, 1912): 51.

9. M.N. Gernet, *Smertnaia kazn'* (1913), 95–96.

10. Gruzenberg, 57.

11. P.I. Liublinskii, *Mezhdunarodnye s"ezdy po voprosam ugolovnogo prava za 10 let (1905–1915)* (Prague, 1915), 294.

12. Ibid., 295.

13. E. Kulisher, "Kak ispolniaetsia smertnaia kazn' i ot kakoi vlasti zavisit ustanovlenie poriadka ispolneniia?" *Trudy Iuridicheskogo obshchestva pri imperatorskom S-Peterburgskom universitete*, vol. 4: *Prilozhenie* (St. Petersburg, 1912), 90.

14. P. Liublinskii, "Otnoshenie k smertnoi kazni obshchestvennogo mneniia," *Trudy Iuridicheskogo obshchestva pri imperatorskom S-Peterburgskom universitete*, vol. 4: *Prilozhenie* (St. Petersburg, 1912), 101.

15. Ibid.

16. M.M. Isaev, "Predstoiashchee preobrazovanie katorgi," *Trudy Iuridicheskogo obshchestva pri imperatorskom S-Peterburgskom universitete*, vol. 4 (St. Petersburg, 1912), 61–62.

17. Ibid., 66.

18. Ibid., 68.

19. Ibid., 64.

20. M.G. Detkov, *Ispolnenie nakazaniia v dorevoliutsionnoi Rossii* (Moscow, 1990), 57.

21. Isaev, 83.

22. M.G. Detkov, *Soderzhanie penitentsiarnoi politiki Rossiiskogo gosudarstva i ee*

realizatsiia v sisteme ispolneniia ugolovnogo nakazaniia v vide lisheniia svobody v period 1917–1930 godov (Moscow, 1992), 5.

23. Ibid., 11–12.

24. Ibid., 8.

25. Ibid., 11.

Chapter 1. Repression and Punishment

1. V.I. Lenin, *Voennaia perepiska (1917–1920 gg.)* (Moscow, 1957), 61.

2. *Sobranie uzakonenii i rasporiazhenii rabochego i krest'ianskogo pravitel'stva RSFSR* (hereafter: SU RSFSR), no. 65 (1918): 710.

3. SU RSFSR, no. 20 (1919): 235.

4. E.M. Giliarov and A.B. Mikhailichenko, *Stanovlenie i razvitie ITU Sovetskogo gosudarstva (1917–1925 gg.)* (Domodedovo, 1990), 54; M.G. Detkov, *Soderzhanie penitentsiarnoi politiki Rossiiskogo gosudarstva i ee realizatsiia v sisteme ispolneniia ugolovnogo nakazaniia v vide lisheniia svobody v period 1917–1930 godov* (Moscow, 1992), 56.

5. Giliarov and Mikhailichenko, *Stanovlenie Soderzhanie*, 54.

6. Detkov, 56–57.

7. *Sistema ispravitel'no-trudovykh lagerei v SSSR, 1923–1960: Spravochnik* (Moscow, 1998), 12.

8. SU RSFSR, no. 23–24 (1921): 141.

9. Giliarov and Mikhailichenko, *Stanovlenie*, 53; Detkov, *Soderzhanie*, 54.

10. Detkov, *Soderzhanie*, 64.

11. *Sbornik normativnykh aktov po sovetskomu ispravitel'no-trudovomu pravu* (Moscow, 1959), 105.

12. Detkov, *Soderzhanie*, 65.

13. Ibid., 63.

14. *Sbornik normativnykh aktov*, 106–7.

15. Detkov, *Soderzhanie*, 63.

16. See *Penitentsiarnoe delo v 1923 g.: Otchet Glavnogo upravleniia mest zakliucheniia Respubliki XI s" ezdu Sovetov* (Moscow, 1924), 12.

17. Detkov, *Soderzhanie*, 100.

18. *Sbornik normativnykh aktov*, 137.

19. See *Penitentsiarnoe delo v 1923 g.*, 3.

20. Giliarov and Mikhailichenko, *Stanovlenie*, 30.

21. SU RSFSR, no. 51 (1922): 646.

22. SU RSFSR, no. 65 (1922): 844.

23. "O vnesudebnykh organakh," *Izvestiia TsK KPSS*, no. 10 (1989): 81.

24. *Sobranie zakonov i rasporiazhenii raboche-krest'ianskogo pravitel'stva SSSR* (hereafter: SZ SSSR), no. 38 (1925): 287.

25. *Stenograficheskii otchet Pervoi Leningradskoi oblastnoi konferentsii VKP(b)* (Moscow–Leningrad, 1927), 28.

26. *Piatnadtsatyi s"ezd VKP(b): Stenograficheskii otchet*, vol. 1 (Moscow, 1961), 291.

27. *XVI Moskovskaia gubernskaia konferentsiia VKP(b): Stenograficheskii otchet* (Moscow, 1928), 338.

28. Dnevnik Borisa Kozeleva: 1927–1930 gg. Manuscript from the personal archive of K.B. Kozeleva, B.G. Kozelev's daughter.

29. Ibid.

30. *Sbornik normativnykh aktov*, 202–7.

31. SZ SSSR, no. 72 (1929): 686.

32. SZ SSSR, no. 22 (1930): 248.

33. SU RSFSR, no. 4 (1931): 38.

34. SU RSFSR, no. 48 (1933): 208.

35. L. Beladi and T. Kraus, *Stalin* (Moscow, 1989), 169–70.

36. SZ SSSR, no. 36 (1934): 283.

37. *Tsentr khraneniia sovremennoi dokumentatsii* (hereafter: TsKhSD), f. 89, per. 18, dok. 33, l. 1.

38. See *Na boevom postu*, December 27, 1989; *Slovo*, no. 7 (1990): 26 (published with an error), et al.

39. *Gosudarstvennyi Arkhiv Rossiiskoi Federatsii* (hereafter GA RF), f. 9401, op. 2, d. 64, 65, 66, 67, 68 (our calculations).

40. TsKhSD, f. 89, per. 18, dok. 2, l. 1.

41. Ibid.

42. GA RF, f. 9401, op. 2, d. 64, l. 53; d. 98, l. 297; d. 95, l. 284.

43. SZ SSSR, no. 11 (1935): 84.

44. "O vnesudebnykh organakh," *Izvestiia TsK KPSS*, no. 10 (1989): 81–82.

45. M.P. Shreider, *NKVD iznutri: Zapiski chekista* (Moscow, 1995), 70.

46. See ibid., 71.

47. See ibid., 42.

48. See *Materialy k zhizneopisaniiu Blagochinnogo g. Kasimova Riazanskoi eparkhii Protoiereia Anatoliia Avdeevicha Pravdoliubova (1862–1937 gg.): Sbornik dokumentov* (manuscript). Prepared for publication by Father Sergii Pravdoliubov.

49. Ibid.

50. A.I. Solzhenitsyn, "Nobelevskaia lektsiia," *Pogruzhenie v triasinu* (Moscow, 1991), 698.

51. TsKhSD, f. 89, per. 48, dok. 1, l. 1.

52. Ibid., dok. 3, l. 1.

53. Ibid., dok. 9, l. 1.

54. Ibid., dok. 17, l. 1.

55. *Tsentral'nyi arkhiv obshchestvennykh dvizhenii g. Moskvy* (hereafter: TsAODM), f. 3352, op. 3, d. 268, l. 152.

56. M.G. Detkov, *Soderzhanie karatel'noi politiki Sovetskogo gosudarstva i ee realizatsiia pri ispolnenii ugolovnogo nakazaniia v vide lisheniia svobody v tridtsatye-piatidesiatye gody* (Domodedovo, 1992), 26.

57. TsKhSD, f. 89. per. 18. dok. 12, l. 7.

58. Ibid., dok. 9, l. 1.

59. Ibid., l. 2.

60. V.N. Zemskov, "GULAG (istoriko-sotsiologicheskii aspekt)," *Sotsiologicheskie issledovaniia*, no. 6 (1991): 20.

61. *Sistema ispravitel'no-trudovykh lagerei v SSSR*, 48, 539.

62. Zemskov, 13.

63. TsKhSD, f. 89, per. 18. dok. 5, l. 4.

64. See ibid., per. 55, dok. 27, l. 1–9.

65. Ibid., l. 3.

66. Ibid., l. 7.

67. Ibid., per. 40, dok. 1, l. 1–6.

68. TsAODM, f. 3352, op. 3, d. 575, l. 19.

69. P. Negretov, *Vse dorogi vedut na Vorkutu* (Benson, Vermont, 1985), 6.

70. "Otriad osobogo naznacheniia No. 41," *Nezavisimaia gazeta*, January 23, 1992: 5.

71. Ibid.

72. "GULAG v gody voiny," *Istoricheskii arkhiv*, no. 3 (1994): 76.

73. TsAODM, f. 3352, op. 3, d. 575, l. 75, 77.

74. A.I. Solzhenitsyn, *Arkhipelag GULAG*, vol. 1 (Moscow, 1990), 95.

75. *Vedomosti Verkhovnogo Soveta SSSR*, no. 19 (1947).

76. GA RF, f. 9401, op. 2, d. 199, l. 447.

77. *SSSR i kholodnaia voina* (Moscow, 1995), 155.

78. "Iz prigovorov raionnykh narsudov o privlechenii k ugolovnoi otvetstvennosti kolkhoznikov po ukazu 1947 g.," *Sovetskie arkhivy*, no. 3 (1990): 58.

79. Ibid., 58–59.

80. Ibid., 59.

81. *Vedomosti Verkhovnogo Soveta SSSR*, no. 19 (1943); *Vedomosti Verkhovnogo Soveta SSSR*, no. 20 (1947).

82. *Vedomosti Verkhovnogo Soveta SSSR*, no. 20 (1947).

83. *SSSR i kholodnaia voina*, 155.

84. GA RF, f. 9401, op. 2, d. 199, l. 197–a.

85. Ibid., l. 197–V.

86. TsKhSD, f. 89, per. 55, dok. 28, l. 16.

87. GA RF, f. 9401, op. 2, d. 199, l. 197–g.

88. Ibid., l. 197–d.

89. TsKhSD, f. 4, op. 9, d. 428, l. 100–101. These special camps were created between 1948 and 1952.

90. TsKhSD, f. 89, per. 60, dok. 11, l. 3.

91. *Vedomosti Verkhovnogo Soveta SSSR*, no. 3 (1950).

92. See V.N. Zemskov, "Politicheskie repressii v SSSR (1917–1990)," *Rossiia–XXI*, no. 1–2 (1994): 110.

93. TsKhSD, f. 89, per. 16, dok. 1, l. 7.

94. Ibid., per. 55, dok. 28, l. 16.

95. Ibid., per. 16, dok. 1, l. 6.

96. Ibid., l. 4, 5, 7, 11, 21.

97. Ibid., per. 18, dok. 36, l. 1–4.

98. A copy of a personal letter by F.P. Krasavin, who was rehabilitated by a commission of the Supreme Soviet of the USSR, was intercepted and ended up in the archive of the Central Committee of the CPSU.

Chapter 2. The Camp Economy

1. See SU RSFSR, no. 35 (1918): 468; no. 54 (1918): 605, and others.

2. SU RSFSR, no. 19 (1918): 284.

3. E.M. Giliarov and A.V. Mikhailichenko, *Stanovlenie i razvitie ITU Sovetskogo gosudarstva (1917–1925)* (Domodedovo, 1990), 60.

4. Ibid., 67.

5. See *Sovetskie arkhivy*, no. 4 (1991): 71–75.

6. Ibid., 75.

7. *Vedomosti Verkhovnogo Soveta SSSR*, no. 13 (1956): 279.

8. V.N. Zemskov, "Spetsposelentsy (1930–1959)," *Naselenie Rossii v 1920–1950–e gody: Chislennost'poteri, migratsii* (Moscow, 1994), 146.

9. TsKhSD, f. 89, per. 16, dok. 1, l. 7.

10. See *Vozvrashchenie pamiati* (Novosibirsk, 1991), 99–100.

11. See I. Chukhin, *Kanaloarmeitsy* (Petrozavodsk, 1990); *GULAG v Karelii, 1930–1941: Sbornik dokumentov i materialov* (Petrozavodsk, 1992), and others.

12. See *GULAG v Karelii*, 58, 63.

13. Ibid., 19.

14. See Chukhin, 30–31; *GULAG v Karelii*, 84.
15. TsAODM, f. 3352, op. 3. d. 175, t. 1, l. 125.
16. A. Iu. Gorcheva, "Budni 'velikikh stroek,'" *Literaturnaia Rossiia*, March 29, 1991: 27.
17. P. Negretov, *Vse dorogi vedut na Vorkutu* (Benson, Vermont, 1985), 5.
18. TsAODM, f. 3352, op. 3, d. 176, t. 2, l. 36, 47.
19. *GULAG v Karelii*, 183–84.
20. A.Iu. Gorcheva, "Glavlit: stanovlenie sovetskoi total'noi tsenzury," *Vestnik Moskovskogo universiteta*, ser. 10, no. 2 (1993): 37.
21. TsAODM, f. 3352, op. 3, d. 176, t. 2, l. 28.
22. Ibid., d. 355, l. 125.
23. Ibid., d. 175, t. 1, l. 33, 34.
24. Ibid., d. 268, l. 121; d. 355, l. 53–54.
25. Ibid., d. 268, l. 124; d. 355, l. 53.
26. Ibid., d. 176, t. 2, l. 58, d. 355, l. 56, 145.
27. Ibid., d. 355, l. 145.
28. GA RF, f. 9401, op. 2, d. 68, l. 111; d. 92, l. 242.
29. TsAODM, f. 3352, op. 3, d. 268, l. 123; d. 393, l. 49–66.
30. Ibid., d. 355, l. 53.
31. Ibid., l. 37–8.
32. M. Kolpakov, "Odnoi sud'boi s narodom," *Sovetskaia Rossiia*, October 25, 1987: 4.
33. TsAODM, f. 3352, op. 3, d. 175, t. 1, l. 32; d. 355, l. 43.
34. Ibid., d. 268, l. 121; d. 355, l. 39.
35. Ibid., d. 355, l. 42.
36. Ibid., d. 393, l. 10–11.
37. *GULAG v Karelii*, 89–90.
38. Ibid., p. 163.
39. *TsAODM*, f. 3352, op. 3, d. 111, t. 2, l. 44–45.
40. Ibid., d. 175, t. 1, l. 25, 31, 33, 35.
41. Ibid., l. 61, 63, 64, 96, 144, 151, 171.
42. Ibid., d. 176. t. 2. l. 9, 11, 19, 20, 23, 33, 34, 52.
43. Ibid., d. 243, l. 22, 31, 37, 87, 101, 131.
44. Ibid., d. 268, l. 122.
45. Ibid., d. 355, l. 41, 47, 59.
46. Ibid., d. 393, l. 15, 18, 39, 59.
47. See "GULAG v gody voiny," *Istoricheskii arkhiv*, no. 3 (1994): 60–86.
48. L. Razgon, *Nepridumannoe* (Moscow, 1989), 174.
49. V.N. Zemskov, "GULAG. Istoriko-sotsiologicheskii aspekt," *Sotsiologicheskie issledovaniia*, no. 6 (1991): 21.
50. TsKhSD, f. 89, per. 40, dok. 5, l. 2. Contemporary researchers, having analyzed the total losses not accounted for previously, have determined the number of Soviet citizens who died in fascist captivity to be 3,712,624. See A.A. Sheviakov, "Repatriatsiia sovetskogo mirnogo naseleniia i voennoplennykh, okazavshikhsia v okkupatsionnykh zonakh gosudarstv antigitlerovskoi koalitsii," *Naselenie Rossii v 1920–1950–e gody*, 212.
51. *Istoricheskii arkhiv*, no. 3 (1994): 62.
52. Ibid., 64.
53. *Istoriia SSSR s drevneishikh vremen do nashikh dnei*, vol. 11 (Moscow, 1980), 112.
54. TsAODM, f. 3352, op. 3, d. 990, l. 45.
55. GA RF, f. 9401, op. 2, d. 202, l. 267.

56. TsAODM, f. 3352, op. 3, d. 1136, l. 101.

57. Ibid., d. 1631, l. 98.

58. GA RF, f. 9401, op. 2, d. 234, l. 148, 153; d. 199, l. 392.

59. Ibid., d. 202, l. 267.

60. TsAODM, f. 2264, op. 1. d. 93–a, l. 157–8.

61. Ibid., d. 44, l. 10–11.

62. A. Antonov-Ovseenko, "Put' naverkh," *Beriia: Konets kar'ery* (Moscow, 1991), 103.

63. GA RF, f. 9401, op. 2, d. 199, l. 391, d. 234, l. 148.

64. Ibid., d. 171, l. 295.

65. Ibid., l. 288–90.

66. Ibid., d. 202, l. 152.

67. Ibid., d. 234, l. 18.

68. A. Sent-Ekziuperi, *Planeta liudei* (Moscow, 1977), 116–17.

69. O. Adamova-Sliozberg, "Put'," *Dodnes' tiagoteet*, no. 1 (Moscow, 1989), 70.

70. See R. Konkvest, *Bol'shoi terror*, vol. 2 (Riga, 1991), 119.

71. TsKhSD, f. 89, per. 16, d. 1, l. 22.

72. *Rodina*, no. 4 (1990): 42.

73. TsKhSD, f. 89, per. 16, d. 1, l. 33, 38, 39, 41.

74. GA RF, f. 9401, op. 2, d. 199, l. 130, 396; d. 234, l. 150.

75. Ibid., d. 202, l. 258.

76. TsAODM, f. 2264, op. 1, d. 93–a, l. 195.

77. Ibid., d. 38, l. 66, d. 65, l. 31; GA RF, f. 9401, op. 2, d. 199, l. 395.

78. TsAODM, f. 3352, op. 3, d. 1472, l. 40, 115.

79. GA RF, f. 9401, op. 2, d. 199, l. 396.

80. "Razbudivshie dzhina," *Moskovskie novosti*, no. 41 (1989): 8.

81. F. Chuev, *Sto sorok besed s Molotovym: Iz dnevnika F. Chueva* (Moscow, 1991), 458–59.

82. GA RF, f. 9401, op. 2, d. 200, l. 83–4.

83. Ibid., d. 137, l. 18–19.

84. Ibid., 366–67.

85. Ibid., 240.

86. Ibid., 244.

87. See Zh. Medvedev, "Atomnyi GULAG," *Poisk*, no. 33–34 (1994): 6.

88. GA RF, f. 9401, op. 2, d. 199, l. 70.

89. TsAODM, f. 3352, op. 3, d. 1302, l. 155.

90. Ibid., l. 146.

91. Ibid., l. 17.

92. Ibid., d. 575, l. 103.

93. Ibid., d. 990, l. 134.

94. Ibid., d. 1472, l. 81.

95. TsAODM, f. 3352, op. 3, d. 1302, l. 131.

96. See Konkvest, vol. 2, 114.

97. TsAODM, f. 3352, op. 3, d. 1472, l. 111.

98. Ibid., d. 1302. l. 104.

99. Ibid., d. 1472, l. 133.

100. Ibid., d. 1631, l. 87.

101. Ibid., d. 1472, l. 109.

102. Ibid., d. 1631, l. 89–90.

103. Ibid., l. 96.

104. V.F. Nekrasov, "Final," *Beriia: Konets kar'ery* (Moscow, 1991), 404.

105. From B. Starkov, "Sto dnei 'lubianskogo marshala,'" *Istochnik*, no. 4 (1993): 89.

106. A. Sakharov, *Mir, progress, prava cheloveka* (Leningrad, 1990), 78.

Chapter 3. Gulag Personnel

1. L. Razgon, *Nepridumannoe* (Moscow, 1989), 153.
2. Ibid., 218.
3. "F.E. Dzerzhinskii o revoliutsionnoi zakonnosti," *Istoricheskii arkhiv*, no. 1 (1958): 5–6.
4. "Pravda dlia sluzhebnogo pol'zovaniia," *Neizvestnaia Rossiia. XX vek*, vol. 1 (Moscow, 1992), 5–6.
5. Ibid., 43–46.
6. TsAODM, f. 3352, op. 3, d. 96, t. 2, l. 15–15 ob.
7. Ibid., d. 132, l. 1.
8. Ibid., d 96. t. 2. l. 13.
9. Ibid., d. 132, l. 4.
10. Ibid., l. 12, 13.
11. Ibid., l. 10–11.
12. Ibid., d. 243, l. 14, 15.
13. Ibid., d. 132, l. 7, 24.
14. Ibid., d. 20–23.
15. Ibid., l. 25–26.
16. Ibid., l. 117.
17. See M.P. Shreider, *NKVD iznutri: Zapiski chekista* (Moscow, 1995), 22–23. I.M. Ostrovskii was arrested in 1937 and later shot.
18. TsAODM, f. 3352, op. 3, d. 92, l. 89–91.
19. Ibid., d. 96, t. 2, l. 73.
20. Ibid., 37.
21. Ibid., 70.
22. Ibid., d. 268, l. 155.
23. Ibid., l. 158–9.
24. Ibid., l. 32.
25. A. Antonov-Ovseenko, "Put' naverkh," *Beriia: Konets kar'ery* (Moscow, 1991), 105.
26. TsAODM, f. 3352, op. 3, d. 268, l. 10, 14–16.
27. F. Chuev, *Sto sorok besed s Molotovym: Iz dnevnika F. Chueva* (Moscow, 1991), 274.
28. TsAODM, f. 3352, op. 3, d. 268, l. 16.
29. *Istoriia SSSR s drevneishikh vremen do nashikh dnei*, vol. 9 (Moscow, 1971), 322.
30. V.B. Zhiromskaia, *"Kadry reshaiut vse!" Formirovanie administrativno-komandnoi sistemy: 20–30–e gody* (Moscow, 1992), 213.
31. *Penitentsiarnoe delo v 1923 g.: Otchet Glavnogo upravleniia mest zakliucheniia Respubliki XI s"ezdu Sovetov* (Moscow, 1924), 16.
32. Ibid., 6, 8, 15.
33. TsAODM, f. 3352, op. 3, d. 111, t. 2, l. 8.
34. Ibid., d. 176, t. 2, l. 12.
35. See Shreider, *NKVD iznutri*, 60–62.
36. TsAODM, f. 3352, op. 3, d. 109, l. 1–4; d. 111, t. 2, l. 40.
37. Ibid., d. 243, l. 144.
38. *Istoricheskii arkhiv*, no. 3 (1994): 60.
39. See Shreider, *NKVD iznutri*, 48.

40. TsAODM, f. 3352, op. 3, d. 243, l. 138, 140.
41. Ibid., d. 111, t. 2, l. 18, 39, 86.
42. Ibid., d. 175. t. 1. l. 21, 31, 56, 63, 155.
43. Ibid., d. 243. l. 109, 117–18.
44. Ibid., l. 36.
45. Ibid., l. 141.
46. F.F. Kudriavtsev, *Primechaniia k ankete: Rasskazy* (Moscow, 1990), 330.
47. TsAODM, f. 3352, op. 3, d. 355, l. 59, 63.
48. Ibid., d. 176, t. 2, l. 58; d. 243, l. 107, 108.
49. Ibid., d. 393, l. 19.
50. Ibid., d. 243, l. 107.
51. *GULAG v Karelii: Sbornik dokumentov i materialov. 1930–1941* (Petrozavodsk, 1992), 11.
52. Ibid., 27.
53. Ibid., 66.
54. TsAODM, f. 3352, op. 3, d. 111. t. 2, l. 7.
55. Ibid., l. 5.
56. Kudriavtsev, *Primechaniia k ankete*, 331.
57. *GULAG v Karelii*, 186.
58. TsAODM, f. 3352, op. 3, d. 268, l. 156.
59. Ibid., d. 111, t. 2, l. 9.
60. Razgon, *Nepridumannoe*, 218–19.
61. TsAODM, f. 3352, op. 3, d. 393, l. 57, 58.
62. "GULAG v gody voiny," *Istoricheskii arkhiv*, no. 3 (1994): 62.
63. Ibid., 63.
64. Ibid., 73.
65. Ibid., 74.
66. Ibid., 85.
67. TsAODM, f. 3352, op. 3, d. 575, l. 134.
68. Ibid., l. 75, 77.
69. TsKhSD, f. 89, per. 18, d. 13, l. 1.
70. Ibid., d. 15, l. 1.
71. Kristofer Endriu and Oleg Gordievskii, *KGB: Istoriia vneshnepoliticheskikh operatsii ot Lenina do Gorbacheva* (London, 1992), 358.
72. Ibid., 359.
73. Ibid.
74. TsAODM, f. 2264, op. 1, d. 77, l. 21, 28, 29.
75. Ibid., d. 48, l. 91.
76. Ibid., d. 77, l. 28.
77. Ibid., d. 93a, l. 197.
78. TsAODM, f. 2264, op. 1, d. 77, l. 28.
79. Ibid., d. 44, l. 7.
80. GA RF, f. 9401, op. 2, d. 199, l. 393.
81. TsAODM, f. 2264, op. 1, d. 44, l. 66.
82. Ibid., l. 4, 9.
83. Ibid., f. 203, op. 1, d. 116, l. 10.
84. Ibid., f. 2264, op. 1, d. 93a, l. 149.
85. Ibid., d. 28, l. 14–15.
86. Ibid., d. 44, l. 9.
87. Ibid., l. 12.
88. Ibid., d. 20, l. 21.

89. Ibid., d. 28, l. 3.
90. Ibid., f. 203, op. 1, d. 359, l. 16–18.
91. TsKhSD, f. 89, per. 16, d. 1, l. 19.
92. See I.N. Kiselev, "Estestvennoe dvizhenie naseleniia v 1930–kh godakh," *Naselenie Rossii v 1920–1950–e gody: Chislennost' poteri, migratsii* (Moscow, 1994), 61–62.
93. TsAODM, f. 2264, op. 1, d. 20, l. 24–25.
94. See ibid., d. 60, l. 123; d. 72, l. 91.
95. Ibid., d. 44, l. 30; f. 203, op. 1, d. 116, l. 43.
96. Ibid., f. 2264, op. 1, d. 60, l. 10, 65.
97. Ibid., f. 3352, op. 3, d. 1136, l. 178.
98. Ibid., d. 1472, l. 133.
99. Ibid., d. 1302, l. 18.
100. *Ozerlag: Kak eto bylo* (Irkutsk, 1992), 9.
101. Ibid., f. 2264, op. 1, d. 63, l. 10; d. 72, l. 98.
102. Ibid., d. 38, l. 20; d. 44, l. 93.
103. Ibid., f. 3352, op. 3, d. 990, l. 80.
104. Ibid., f. 2264, op. 1, d. 44, l. 99.
105. GA RF, f. 9401, op. 2, d. 199, l. 396.
106. TsAODM, f. 2264, op. 5, d. 376, l. 16.
107. TsKhSD, f. 4, op. 9, d. 421, l. 2.
108. See "Dokladnaia zapiska ob organizatsii sovkhoza na Galke," *Vozvrashchenie pamiati* (Novosibirsk, 1991), 100–102.

Conclusion. What Was the Gulag?

1. Zh. Rossi, "Real'nyi sotsializm," *Volia: Zhurnal uznikov totalitarnykh sistem*, no. 2–3 (1994): 178.
2. See, for example, the Sovnarkom resolution of January 1, 1918, and Lenin's telegram sent to V.A. Antonov-Ovseenko in Kharkov in January 1918, in the book *V.I. Lenin: Voennaia perepiska (1917–1920)* (Moscow, 1957), 20–21.
3. "F.E. Dzerzhinskii o revoliutsionnoi zakonnosti," *Istoricheskii arkhiv*, no. 1 (1958): 19.
4. Ibid., 21.
5. *Ekonomika GULAGa i ee rol' v razvitii strany. 30–e gody: Sbornik dokumentov*, no. 1 (Moscow, 1998), 24.
6. Detailed information on the numbers of prisoners is given in the documents of the Accounting and Distribution Department (Uchetno-raspredelitel'nyi otdel) of the GULAG (GA RF, f. 9414, op. 1). The abundance of difficult to analyze statistical material forces researchers to use secondary sources—summaries and reference reports compiled by department officials during later periods (for example, d. 5 of this *fond* contains "A Report on the Number of Prisoners in NKVD Camps (between 1/1/34 and 1/1/39)," compiled in 1939. As a rule, such summaries contain a large number of errors.
7. TsKhSD, f. 89, per. 16, dok. 1, l. 12.
8. See *Sistema ispravitel'no-trudovykh lagerei v SSSR.*

Afterword

1. K. Iaspers, *Smysl i naznachenie istorii* (Moscow, 1994), 161.

Index of Personal Names

Abakumov, Viktor Semenovich, 53, 141–42, 157ʹ
Adamova-Sliozberg, O., 104
Agafonov, M.I., 169
Agarkov, 31
Akimov, F.F., 42
Alexander II, 4
Alshits, D.N., 79
Andreev, 33
Antonov, D.A., 41
Antonov-Ovseenko, A., xxiii, 100, 136
Aremaev, 119
Atakishiev, 180

Bacon, Edwin, xiii
Bacon, Francis, 148
Bartini, R.L., 113
Beloborodov, A.G., 16
Beria, L.P., 26–27, 31, 36, 42, 46, 93, 95, 124, 134–36, 138, 142, 156, 158, 178–79, *(photo)*
Berling, Zygmunt, 158
Berman, Matvei Davidovich, 77, 143
Blagonravov, G.I., 71
Bochkov, M.I., 42
Bokii, G.I., 131
Bokuchava, Sh.I., 178
Borovitinov, M., 6
Brandner, Ferdinand, 115
Brezhnev, L.I., 67
Bronikovskii, S.S., 40–41
Bulatov, D.A., 31–32
Bulatova, A.I., 32
Burdakov, S.N., 119, 168
Busse, Ernst, 115
Bystrov, 180

Chernyshev, Vasilii Vasilevich, 142, 144–45, *(photo)*
Chizhikov, 177
Christian, Manfred, 115
Chubar, V.Ia., 32
Chuev, F., 112

Chuev, V., 29–30
Cohen, Stephen, xix
Conquest, Robert, xix

Daniliuk, 160
Detkov, M., xxiii
Dinariev, 30
Dmitriev, 31
Dobrovolskii, N.A., 121, 123
Dolgikh, I.I., 73–74, 121–22, 176, 177, 179, 181–82, *(photo)*
Dubovik, A.D., 132
Dudorov, N.P., 66–67, 105, 163, 188
Dugin, A., xxiii
Dzerzhinskii, F.E., 70–71, 128, 136, 186

Fedotov, P.V., 42
Feldman, M.F., 71
Filaretov, G.V. 144
Frenkel, N.A., 77–78
Furman, V., 63

Gagarinov, M.P., 45–46
Galon, 152
Gamzatov, Rasul, 58
Gasiukov, 176
Gavrilova, 161
Gernet, M.N., 6
Ginzburg, E., xxiii
Gladkov, 180
Glushko, V.P., 112
Goliakov, I.T., *(photo)*
Golovin, I.N., 111
Gomułka, Władisław, 158
Gorbachev, M., 170
Gorbachev, M.E., 149
Gorkii, M., 79
Gorshenin, K.P., 179
Gorskaia, Nadezhda (pseud.), 60
Grigorian, 180
Gruzenberg, O.O., 5–6
Gurevich, E., 63

Heilandt, Paul, 115
Himmler, H., 100
Hitler, A., 185

Iagoda, G.G., 27, *(photo)*
Iakir, P., 33, 142
Ianov, M.A., 159
Ioffe, S.B., 131
Ioskevich, V.I., 34
Isaev, N., 160
Ivanov, N.A., 177
Ivanov, N.I., 60–61

Jaspers, Karl, 191
Jung, Gerhardt, 115

Kaganovich, L.M., 27, 81
Kalinin, M.I., *(photo)*
Kanevskii, 171
Karmanov, G.K., 123
Kazaev, Kamil, *(photo)*
Kazakov, V.F., 50
Kazakova, M.F., 50
Kerenskii, A.F., 10
Khakimov, K.I., 183
Khlevniuk, O., xix
Khovanov, A.M., 47
Khrushchev, N.S., 25, 57, *(photo)*
Kobulov, B.Z., 32, 42
Kogan, L., 79
Kogan, L.I., 143
Kolesnikov, 131
Komarov, A.R., 64
Komarovskii, A.N., 110, 122–123, *(photo)*
Kork, A., 142
Korolenko, V.G., 6
Korolev, S.P., 112
Korotchenkov, 33
Kosior, S.V., 27, 32
Kozelev. B.G., 22
Kozyrev, V.M., 177–178
Krasavin, F.P. (Felix), 68
Krasikov, P.A., 18
Kruglov, S.N., 25, 34, 53, 86, 98, 115–16, 122–23, 148, 165, *(photo)*
Krupin, V.F., 30
Kucheriavyi, 31
Kudriavtsev, A.A., 30
Kudriavtsev, F.F., 147, 152, 179
Kulisher, E., 7
Kurchatov, I.V., 111
Kurpas, K.S., 182
Kuzmin, S.I., xxii
Kuznetsov, 136

Lane, Arthur Bliss, 158
Lattimore, Owen, 121
Lenin, V. I., iv, 12, 59, 69, 185
Leopold, D.S., 182
Levonets, G., 99, 150
Litkens, 65
Litvinov, 138
Litvishkov, 31
Liublinskii, P., 7
Liutanov, D.N., 175
Lovchev, 176
Lukoianov, L.D., 173
Lysenko, Trofim, 120

Malenkov, G.M., 95, 142, 150, 169–70, *(photo)*
Mamakaev, M., 57–58,
Marchenko, 31
Marchenko, M.A., 51
Markeev, M.I., 178
Maslieva, T.M., 50–51
Merlukov, V.N., 42
Miasishchev, V.M., 112
Mikoyan, A.I., 22 (*(photo)*
Milshtein, S.R., 178
Minskii, 171
Mints, A.L., 112
Miromanov, 110
Molotov, V.M., 24, 26–27, 38, 112, 138 *(photos)*
Morozov, 177

Nasedkin, V.G., 86, 93, 95
Negretov, Pavel, 44, 79
Neizvestnyi, Ernst, *(photo)*
Nikitchenko, I.G., *(photo)*
Nikolskii, 152
Nizhneamurlag, 121
Nordlander, David J., xvi
Novikov, 181

Obruchnikov, B.P., 97, 181
Orev, A.I., 41
Orlov, G.M., 85
Ostrovskii, I.M., 132–33

Pavlov, V.N., 104–5
Petliakov, V.M., 112
Piatakov, G.L., 70–72
Pliner, I.I., 82, 140, 143, 152, 154
Podoprigora, 160
Podvoiskii, Nikolai, 141
Pogodin, N., 79
Popkov, 60

Popkov, I.G., 178
Popov, A.S., 41
Pravdoliubov, A.A., 29–30
Propashkina, E.G., 50–51
Radkiewicz, Stanisław, 158
Razgon, Lev, 93, 127, 154
Riasnoi, V.S., 182–83
Riasnoi, Vasilii Stepanovich, (photo)
Rogov, V.P., 178
Romanychev, 31
Rossi, J., xxiii, 185
Ruchkin, 180
Rudenko, R.A., 25
Rybanov, 124
Rykov, A.I., 21
Ryzhikov, 32

Saint-Exupery, 104
Sakharov, A.D., 125
Salyn, E.P., 28
Santayana, G., 191
Schmidt, P.P., 7
Selkov, 45
Semenov, 181
Sergienko, 180
Serov, I.A., 39, 63, 67, 158
Shalamov, V., xxiii
Shamarin, A.V., 178
Shamil, 58
Shklovskii, V., 79
Shpindel, 161
Shreider, M.P., 27, 141
Shulakov, 177
Shulgina, Mariia, 52
Shumakov, I.V., 62
Shumskii, 31
Slobodianiuk, I.A., 41
Slutskii, A.A., 131
Slutskii, B., 63
Sokolovskii, 158
Sokolskii, P.P., 177
Solodilov, A.I., (photo)
Solzhenitsyn, A.I., xxi-xxiii, 32, 49,
    174
Sretenskii, S.S., 177
Stakhanov, Alexei G., 78
Stalin, xiv, 22, 24–27, 32–33, 35–38,
    52–53, 56, 57, 59, 61, 62, 65, 68,
    78, 81, 95, 105–6, 110, 120, 124,
    126, 130, 132, 138, 149, 165, 179,
    186, 189–90, (photos)

Stechkin, B.S., 112
Sukhodolskii, V.N., 63, 65, 159
Sultan-Zade, A.S., 183
Sviridov, A.S., 171–72

Tarnovskii, E.N., 3
Tereshkov, 176
Timofeev, 123
Timofeev, M.M., 88
Timoshenkov, 171
Tomita, 41
Tomskii, M., 19–20
Trotsky, Leon, 21, 131
Tsarev, Vladimir Afanasevich, iii
Tuberovskii, A.M., 31
Tukhachevskii, M., 33, 142
Tupolev, A.N., 112–114

Uborevich, 33
Ufliand, Nina, 63
Ukhanov, 168
Ulianov, 171
Ulrikh, V.V. (photo)
Unshlikht, I.S., 186

Varskoi, E., 47
Vavilov, A.P., 47
Veinshtok, Ia.M., 133
Vladimirova, E.L., 54, 66, 102–3,
    117
Volkov, F. P., 30
Volkov, Oleg, xxii-xxiii
Voroshilov, K.E. (photo)
Vradii, I.I., 178, 180
Vyshinskii, Andrei Ianuarevich,
    (photo) 26–27

Wallace, Henry, 121

Zaveniagin, A.P., 85

Zeimal, V.I., 183
Zemskov, V., xix, xxiii
Zhelonkin, I.A., 177
Zhizhilenko, A.A., 10
Zima, V.F., 49
Zinoviev, G.E., 21
Zorin, 31
Zubkova, Elena, xvi
Zverev, 60

Index of Camp Names

Abiaz Camp, 106
Andronev Camp, 13
Angarlag, 121
Arkhangelsk plant, 85

Bacchante Camp, 117
Bakovskii Corrective-Labor Camp, 119
Belbaltlag, 76. *See also* White Sea–Baltic
  Complex
Bukachachlag, 83
Bukhband, 151
Butyrki (Butyrskaia Prison), *(photo)*

Dalstroi Butugychag Camp, 103 *(photo)*

Far Eastern complex, 87

Gusino Lake, 83

Ikshansk Colony for Juveniles, *(photo)*
Irkutsk Province prisons, 8
Ivanov Camp, 13
Ivdelsk Camp, 175

Karagandinsk State Farm Camp (Karlag),
  84, 120
Karelo-Murmansk camps, 72
Kargopolskii Camp, 52, 79, 89
Karlag, 89, 92
Kholmogory Camp, 19
Kizellag, 121
Kizelovsk Camp, 176
Krasnoiarsk Camp, 176
Kriukovskaiia colony, 100

Lokchimlag, 91
Luchlag, 54

Moscow Camp No. 19, 171

Nemnyrsk Corrective-Labor Camp,
  175
Nerchinsk region prisons, 8
Nizhneamurlag, 121
Norilsk camps, 59–60, 89, 95
Norilsk Nickel Complex, 85
Norrillag, 121
North Urals Camp, 172
Northeast camps, 43
Northern Kuzbass Corrective-Labor
  Camp, 169, 177
Novopeskovskii Camp, 13
Nyroblag, 121
Nyrobsk Camp, 176, 178

Omsk Colony #1, 45,
Ozernyi Camp, 170–171

Pertominsk Camp, 19
Peschanyi Camp, 66
Peschlag, 54
Poliansk Camp, 178

Raichikhlag, 83, 90

Segezhsk plant, 85, 89
Selenginsk Camp, 177
Sevurallag, 93, 121
Siberian administration, 72
SIBLAG, 72–75, 89, 92
SIBULON, 72
Solikamsk plant, 85
Solovetsko-Kem Camp (SKITL), 72
Solovki Island Complex, 17, 19–20, 72,
  77, 150
Spasskii branch Camp, 54
Steplag, 54
Stepnoi special camp, 54
Svirskoe administration, 72

Taishetlag, 91
Temnikovskoe administration, 72
Tobolsk hard-labor prison, 20

Ukhtinsk complex, 83–84, 87, 89
Ukhtizhemlag, 121
Ukhto-Izhemskii Camp, 83
Ukhtpechlag, 83, 90
USIKMITL, 72
USLAG, 72, 76
Usollag, 91
Ust-Vymsk Camp (Ustvymlag), 121, 177

Verkhne-Uralsk prison, 20
Viatlag (Viatsk Camp), 61,
    121
Volgostroi, 85, 89, 91
Vorkuta camps, 43–45, 79–80, 83,
    105
Vorkutinsk Camp, 83
Vorkutlag, 121

White Sea-Baltic complex (BBK;
    Belbaltlag), 76–78, 87–88, 147,
    153–154

Galina Mikhailovna Ivanova is a 1978 graduate of Moscow University. She received her Candidate's degree in 1988 in the field of Soviet history, and currently is a senior research scholar at the Russian Academy of Sciences Institute of Russian History. Her current research concerns the evolution of the Gulag system. Apart from this book, she has authored numerous articles on the subject, which have been published in Russia and Germany.

Series editor **Donald J. Raleigh** is Pardue Professor of History at the University of North Carolina, Chapel Hill. He is the author of *Revolution on the Volga: 1917 in Saratov* and other studies, several of which have been published in Russia. His current project is a monograph on the Russian Civil War entitled "Experiencing Civil War: Politics, Society, and Revolutionary Culture in Saratov, 1918–1922." Professor Raleigh translated and edited E.N. Burdzhalov's *Russia's Second Revolution: The February 1917 Uprising in Petrograd* and edited Oleg V. Khlevniuk's *In Stalin's Shadow: The Career of "Sergo" Ordzhonikidze.* He is also the editor of two anthologies: *Soviet Historians and Perestroika: The First Phase* and *The Emperors and Empresses of Russia: Rediscovering the Romanovs.*

Translator **Carol Flath** is Associate Professor of the Practice of Slavics at Duke University, a conference interpreter of Russian, and a translator of Russian and Japanese. Her translation of *The Phoenix Tree and Other Stories,* by Kizaki Satoko, won the Japan-U.S. Friendship Commission Prize for the Best Translation of Japanese Literature in 1988. She is the author of several scholarly articles on nineteenth-century Russian literature. Her current research interests include Chekhov and Dostoevsky, Russian prose fiction, language pedagogy, and problems of translation.

DATE DUE